ROMANCING THE MAYA

ROMANCING THE MAYA

MEXICAN ANTIQUITY
IN THE
AMERICAN IMAGINATION
1820–1915

R. TRIPP EVANS

UNIVERSITY OF TEXAS PRESS
AUSTIN

Requests for permission to reproduce material from this work
should be sent to Permissions, University of Texas Press,
P.O. Box 7819, Austin, TX 78713–7819.

(∞) The paper used in this book meets the minimum
requirements of ANSI/NISO Z39.48–1992 (R1997)
(Permanence of Paper).

LIBRARY OF CONGRESS
CATALOGING-IN-PUBLICATION DATA

Evans, R. Tripp, 1968–
Romancing the Maya : Mexican antiquity in the American
imagination, 1820–1915 / R. Tripp Evans.
p. cm.
Includes bibliographical references and index.
ISBN: 0292722214
1. Mayas—Antiquities. 2. Mayas—Transatlantic influences.
3. Mayas—Middle Eastern influences. 4. Mayas in popular
culture. 5. Archaeological expeditions—Mexico—History.
6. Maya architecture—Mexico. 7. Architecture—Mexico—
Attribution. 8. Stephens, John Lloyd, 1805–1852.
9. Catherwood, Frederick. 10. Smith, Joseph, 1805–1844.
11. Charnay, Désiré, 1828–1915. 12. Le Plongeon, Augustus,
1826–1908. 13. Le Plongeon, Alice D. (Alice Dixon),
1851–1910. 14. Cultural property—Mexico. 15. Mexico—
Antiquities. I. Title.
F1435.E88 2004
972.8105—dc22   2003025085

FOR LIZ

AND 133 MANSFIELD STREET

CONTENTS

ACKNOWLEDGMENTS, *XI*

INTRODUCTION
1

1 / THE SECOND DISCOVERY OF AMERICA
10

2 / INCIDENTS OF TRANSCRIPTION:
'AMERICAN' ANTIQUITY IN THE WORK
OF STEPHENS AND CATHERWOOD
44

3 / JOSEPH SMITH AND THE ARCHAEOLOGY OF REVELATION
88

4 / THE TOLTEC LENS OF DÉSIRÉ CHARNAY
103

5 / BORDERING ON THE MAGNIFICENT:
AUGUSTUS AND ALICE LE PLONGEON
IN THE KINGDOM OF MÓO
126

EPILOGUE, *153*

NOTES, *163*

BIBLIOGRAPHY, *183*

INDEX, *191*

LIST OF ILLUSTRATIONS

1.1   Human sacrifice at the great temple of the Aztecs, *12*

1.2   Aztec ceremonial precinct, *15*

1.3   Inner sanctuary, great temple of Tenochtitlan, *15*

1.4   José Antonio Calderón, Temple of the Sun relief; Frederick Catherwood, Temple of the Sun relief, *16*

1.5   Antonio Bernasconi, Temple of the Inscriptions and Temple of the Cross, Palenque, *17*

1.6   Ricardo Almendáriz, Palace tower at Palenque, *18*

1.7   Tower at Palace Group, Palenque, *19*

1.8   Ricardo Almendáriz, plan of Palace tower at Palenque, *21*

1.9   Plan of Palace tower, Palenque, *21*

1.10   José Luciano Castañeda, pyramid with planar sides, *24*

1.11   Castañeda, head fragment from Tula (Temple of the Warriors), *24*

1.12   Castañeda, El Palacio, Mitla; interior, El Palacio, Mitla, *25*

1.13   Castañeda, section of Palace at Palenque, *27*

1.14   Castañeda, head fragment found near Tepeyacan, *28*

1.15   Castañeda, figurine found near San Pablo del Monte, *28*

1.16   Castañeda, tumulus near Monte Alban, *30*

1.17   Castañeda, tumulus near Monte Alban, *31*

1.18   Castañeda, Temple of the Sun, Palenque; Temple of the Sun, Palenque, *33*

1.19 Jean-Frédéric Waldeck, Temple of the Magician figure, Uxmal, *38*

1.20 Waldeck, figure from Palenque, *39*

1.21 Waldeck, "elephant" glyph taken from Palenque; photo of Chac deity at the Nunnery complex, Chichen Itza, *40*

1.22 Waldeck, elevation of *Le Pyramide de Kingsborough,* Uxmal, *41*

1.23 Waldeck, plan of *Le Pyramide de Kingsborough,* Uxmal, *41*

1.24 Étienne-Louis Boullée, *Cénotaphe dans le genre égyptien, 42*

2.1   American Antiquarian Society Seal, *47*

2.2   Frederick Catherwood, *View of Mt. Aetna from Tauramania, 50*

2.3   Catherwood, *Colossi of Memnon (Amen-Hotep III)—Thebes, 51*

2.4   Catherwood, Stele F at Copan; twentieth-century photograph of Stele F at Copan, *52*

2.5   Catherwood, ruined church in Honduras, *59*

2.6   Catherwood, Temple of the Inscriptions, Palenque, *60*

2.7   Catherwood, Temple of the Inscriptions (reconstruction), Palenque, *61*

2.8   Catherwood, tablet from the Temple of the Inscriptions, Palenque, *64*

2.9   Catherwood, arch at Kabah, *65*

2.10 Piranesi, *Arch of Constantine, 65*

2.11 Catherwood, wooden beam from Kabah, *74*

2.12 Catherwood, *Broken Idol at Copan* (Stele C), *77*

2.13 Catherwood, engraving of Stele C, *77*

2.14 Catherwood, Stele F at Copan, *78*

2.15 Catherwood, engraving of Stele F at Copan, *79*

2.16 Catherwood, House of the Governor, Uxmal, *81*

2.17 Catherwood, Pyramid of the Magician, Uxmal, *82*

2.18 Catherwood, panoramic view of Kabah, *84*

2.19 Barnum's "Aztec Children", *86*

4.1   Charnay, Iglesia, Chichen Itza; Catherwood, Iglesia, Chichen Itza, *108*

4.2   Charnay, eastern facade of Nunnery complex, Uxmal; Catherwood, eastern facade of Nunnery complex, Uxmal, *109*

4.3   Charnay, "Toltec King", *117*

4.4   Molded clay heads, Teotihuacan, *118*

4.5   Aztec "idols" at the Museo Nacional in Mexico City, *120*

4.6   Temple of the Sun, Palenque; Japanese Temple, *123*

5.1   Le Plongeon's chacmool figure, Chichen Itza (labeled "Prince Coh"), *132*

5.2   Le Plongeon posed with chacmool, Chichen Itza, *133*

5.3   "Prince Coh," detail from the Temple of the Jaguars mural, Chichen Itza, *137*

5.4   Queen Móo's Talisman, *138*

5.5   Alice Le Plongeon wearing Queen Móo's Talisman, *138*

5.6   North wing, House of the Governor at Uxmal, *142*

5.7   Le Plongeon's composite photograph/reconstruction drawing, Platform of Venus, Chichen Itza, *143*

5.8   Sophie Schliemann wearing King Priam's Treasure, circa 1872, *146*

5.9   Sophie Schliemann at the Tomb of Clytemnestra, Mycenae, 1876, *147*

5.10   Alice Le Plongeon at the House of the Governor, Uxmal, *147*

5.11   Drawings derived from the Iowa and Alaska "inscriptions", *150*

6.1   Thompson's plaster reconstruction of the Arch of Labná, Chicago World's Columbian Exposition of 1893, *154*

6.2   Plaster fragments of the Governor's Palace and Nunnery, Uxmal; Chicago World's Columbian Exposition of 1893, *154*

6.3   Alfred P. Maudslay, eastern wing of the Nunnery, Chichen Itza, *157*

6.4   Plan, fairgrounds of World's Columbian Exposition, Chicago, *159*

ACKNOWLEDGMENTS

When I entered Professor Mary Miller's Aztec Art seminar in my first year of graduate school, I was like someone—as she later put it herself—who had landed on the moon. Unfamiliar with pre-Columbian art of any period, I had chosen the course as a counterpoint to my chosen field in American architecture of the nineteenth century. Before the close of the semester my academic interests had taken a sharp turn south of the border, ultimately resulting in the work before you.

I thank Professor Miller for the many thought-provoking seminars I took with her at Yale, for her superb and creative scholarship, and for opening my eyes to the stories of men and women who, like me, initially encountered the pre-Columbian past with more enthusiasm than experience. I would also like to thank Professors Edward Cooke and Esther da Costa Meyer, whose seminars helped me understand material culture and architectural history in ways that will always inform my work. It was Professor da Costa Meyer, in particular, who taught me that any art historical question worth answering is first and foremost a *human* question. I, and my own students, owe her a great debt for that lesson.

Without the support of my fellow graduate students at Yale, and of my colleagues at Wheaton College, I could not have produced this book. My special thanks go to Kim Smith, Michael Lobel, Romita Ray, Nancy Marshall, David Barquist, and Jessica Smith of Yale's History of Art Department; to Sophie Carter, visiting fellow at Yale's Center for British Art; and to Marina Moskowitz, Cathy Gudis, Elspeth Brown, Martin Berger, and Jeff Hardwick of Yale's American Studies Department. I'm extraordinarily lucky to share a field with them, and even more fortunate to count them as friends. At Wheaton, I am grateful to all of my colleagues for their continued support—especially Paula Krebs, for her academic tough-love and (sadly futile) bowling tips; Christin Ronolder, for her hard work in preparing the images for this text; and Gail Sahar, for her invaluable friendship, tremendous cooking, and admirable sense of perspective.

I have been extremely fortunate in the institutional support I've received while writing this book. First and foremost, I am grateful to the Albers Foundation at Yale, who funded the entirety of my travel in Mexico, Honduras, and Guatemala. In addition, I would like to thank the Paul Mellon Foundation and the Henry S. McNeil Foundation for their generous financial support; the staff of the Beinecke Library at Yale, and of the Bancroft Library at the University of California, Berkeley, for helping me locate so many useful sources; and Wheaton's Provost Susanne Woods, whose institution of the fully paid junior sabbatical allowed me the necessary time and funding to complete my final manuscript. Provost Woods not only supports the research interests of the Wheaton faculty but also demonstrates a genuine interest in and engagement with our work—she is a Renaissance woman, indeed.

To have written this book without the extraordinary friendship and encouragement of Joe Flessa and Beth Loffreda is inconceivable. Mary Miller may have introduced me to the Maya, but it was through Joe that I fell in love with Mexico. I stand in amazement of his Olympic-level skills as host, jungle chauffeur, storyteller, and procurer of smoky, blue drinks in Mexico City. Without Beth this book would have remained permanently in disk form, and I in a fetal position. I am forever grateful for her manuscript midwifery, her promotion of pseudoscience/authentic pleasure, and the beautiful example of her own writing. With apologies to the anonymous *Los Girasoles* poet, I can think of no other friends with whom I'd rather glance at the Inferno.

Lastly, I would like to thank my parents for their never-failing love, support, and abiding faith that, despite all early evidence to the contrary, I might one day spend more time in the classroom than in the principal's office. Whatever skills I possess as a teacher and scholar are inherited from a father who taught me the importance of honesty, fairness, and commitment and from a mother whose tremendous creativity, wit, and ability to weave dazzling stories from the most unlikely material—the mark of a true historian—are profoundly missed by all who knew her.

ROMANCING THE MAYA

INTRODUCTION

O N   S E P T E M B E R   8 ,   2 0 0 0 , the *New York Times* ran a page-one story announcing an important archaeological discovery at Cancuen, in Guatemala. Entitled "Splendid Maya Palace Is Found Hidden in Jungle," the article begins:

> In a remote jungle of Guatemala, among the remains of a little-known ancient city with a name meaning Place of the Serpents, archaeologists have uncovered one of the largest and most splendid palaces of Maya kings ever discovered . . .[1]

In both language and tone the article's author, John Wilford, evokes the powerful combination of mystery and exoticism that American readers have associated with pre-Columbian archaeology since its modern inception in the nineteenth century. The passage could well be mistaken, in fact, for one of John Lloyd Stephens' archaeological narratives of the 1840s.

The remainder of the *Times* article, however, markedly departs from nine-teenth-century models — demonstrating the profound changes that have trans-formed Mesoamerican archaeology since Stephens' day. The *Times* reader learns, for instance, that the structure at Cancuen dates from the eighth century; that it is believed to be the royal seat of a king named as "Tah-ak-Chaan"; that his reign lasted from 740 to 790 A.D.; and furthermore, that glyphic records indicate a mar-riage between a princess from this site and a prince from Dos Pilas.² Had Stephens or any other nineteenth-century archaeologist found the site at Can-cuen, rather than Arthur Demarest in the year 2000, the discovery would have re-tained its romantic appeal while yielding none of this crucial historical informa-tion. In fact, the site may not even have been designated as "Maya" at all but rather credited to the ancient Israelites or to refugees from Atlantis.³

For nineteenth-century archaeologists working in Latin America, the absence of any certifiable, historical information about the ancient Maya explains how they were able to mythologize the Mesoamerican past; in effect, no scholar could conclusively challenge even the most bizarre theory about the ruins' age or au-thorship. *Why* these explorers invented or distorted archaeological information, however—and why American explorers showed a particular susceptibility to this practice—is the subject of this book.

Prior to the expulsion of Spain from Latin America in the 1820s, the very exis-tence of most pre-Columbian sites was generally unknown. Their rediscovery fol-lowing Spain's departure initiated a period of exploration that the New World had not seen since the sixteenth century, undertaken at a time when ancient geogra-phy, biblical history, and even the source of human origins itself were all being se-riously questioned. The ruins of Mexico and Central America in this era were, for a variety of different intents and purposes, a historical tabula rasa.

In their attempts to explain the existence of this lost civilization, previously unknown or only partially known in the West, scholars eagerly sought its descen-dants. Determining that this rediscovered culture had left no legitimate modern heirs, amateur archaeologists, travel writers, and self-proclaimed prophets from America claimed the United States' next-of-kin status to the ancient city-builders. Those who made no such direct link nonetheless considered the United States as the most appropriate custodian for this antiquity, insisting that politi-cally unstable and "culturally inferior" Latin American nations were inappropri-ate guardians of such a valuable legacy. Cultural claim-staking in the region was not only possible but also inevitable in this period, given Latin America's porous borders, dependence upon foreign investment, and ever-changing leadership. During Mexico's difficult first century of independence, history became its greatest export and the United States, itself a young republic, the most eager consumer of this past.

Paralleling their colonization of the New World, European explorers initiated the reclamation of Mexican antiquities. In chapter 1, I examine the earliest European images of ancient Mesoamerican architecture, concentrating upon the late colonial works of Antonio del Río, José Luciano Castañeda, and Jean-Frédéric Waldeck. Appearing for the first time during the decades following Mexican independence, these works were modeled upon the eighteenth-century French *Encyclopédie*, pairing technical illustrations with systematic scholarly commentary.

The formal orthodoxy of these publications contrasted sharply with the fantastic cultural treatises offered by their authors. As each grappled with the question of America's cultural origins, he inevitably enlisted "scientific" illustrations to support highly conjectural cultural-migration theories. Artists either represented Mesoamerican antiquities in isolated illustrations or within fictional Arcadian landscapes, while their accompanying texts suggested the ruins' analogous—or actual—relationship to ancient Greco-Roman architecture. In American hands, both the formal presentation and the cultural projections of such works would substantially change.

Between 1839 and 1843, American writer and amateur archaeologist John Lloyd Stephens and British architect Frederick Catherwood collaborated on four volumes devoted to ancient Maya architecture, the most complete record of pre-Columbian sites that had ever been produced. Whereas previous European works had been produced in expensive limited editions, Stephens and Catherwood published their *Incidents of Travel* series cheaply and in enormous quantity, reaching an unprecedented readership in the United States. Catherwood's illustrations of Maya ruins departed from earlier models by providing accurate, if romantic, engravings of the buildings in situ, while Stephens' documentation and commentary parted company with the bizarre origin theories proposed by the first generation of European scholars.

For much of the nineteenth century, the United States founded its domestic and foreign policies upon the paired principles of manifest destiny—the presumption of Americans' territorial "divine right"—and the Monroe Doctrine, which barred future European colonization in the Americas. Stephens, whose role as a U.S. diplomat is discussed in greater detail in chapter 2, managed to combine both of these policies in his archaeological investigations. Not only did he attempt the wholesale purchase of ancient Maya sites by authority of the U.S. government, but he also actively sought to exclude Europeans from attempting similar actions. These operations represented more than mere territorial acquisition, for it was Stephens' plan to physically remove the sites' structures to New York City, reerecting them within a proposed national museum of American antiquities. Within this institution, Stephens hoped to unite the material culture of living Native Americans with his "reclaimed" Mesoamerican antiquities. Gathered under one roof, the exhibits would have presented a seamless narrative of the American past that was, in reality, neither truly "American" nor "past."

In chapter 3, I examine the work of Stephens' contemporary Joseph Smith, founder of the Church of Jesus Christ of Latter-day Saints, who shared Stephens' desire to adopt the archaeological past of Latin America. Publishing his revelations as the Book of Mormon in 1830, Smith claimed that the Americas had been settled in ancient times by wandering members of the House of Israel. As proof of this assertion, Smith and other Mormon church leaders eagerly embraced Stephens' newly rediscovered ruins—which, they proposed, represented the remains of an apocalyptic battle between warring factions of the church's Israelite ancestors.[4] Like Stephens, Smith sought to collapse North American and Mesoamerican antiquities within the same framework, yet his reasons for doing so were spiritual rather than overtly nationalistic or territorial. Seeking the reestablishment of God's chosen people on the North American continent, Smith believed that these ruins provided the historical foundation for his new Zion.

With the advent of field photography in the later nineteenth century, visually faithful documentation of the ruins developed in tandem with increasingly subjective theories of their cultural origin. Of the two principal photographers from this period, Désiré Charnay and Augustus Le Plongeon, Charnay was considered by his contemporaries to be the greater scholar and technician—even if Le Plongeon's discoveries ultimately proved to be more valuable. In chapter 4, I examine Charnay's guiding belief that Mesoamerica derived from the Toltec civilization, a group he distantly linked to the presumed Aryan ancestors of northern Europe. By insisting upon the unity of all ancient North American cultures and suggesting their ethnic distinction from contemporary Latin American indigenous groups, he confirmed the primacy of the United States in the region's archaeology.

The career of Le Plongeon and his wife, Alice Dixon Le Plongeon, who were Charnay's field competitors in the 1870s and 1880s, was characterized by early

successes and ultimate discrediting. Basing his theories upon the dubious scholarship of diffusion theorist Charles-Étienne Brasseur de Bourbourg, Le Plongeon
made a variety of important finds yet published doctored photographs of
Mesoamerican sites that "proved," among other things, their astoundingly remote
origins as well as their role in the foundation of Freemasonry. Le Plongeon argued not only that world culture had originated from the American continent but
also that he and his wife were, themselves, the reincarnated monarchs of this so-
called former Kingdom of Móo.

In the epilogue, I consider the culmination of nineteenth-century America's
perceptions of ancient America, and the ultimate transformation of Mesoamerican archaeology into a professional field. A comparison of the anthropological/
archaeological exhibits at the 1893 World's Columbian Exposition in Chicago and
at the 1915 Panama-California Exposition in San Diego reveals a paradigmatic
shift in the public presentation of Maya architecture. At Chicago the installment
of life-size Maya temples, cast in plaster, evoked a sense of virtual reality for fairgoers; arranged in a Stonehenge-like configuration, these structures were land-
scaped with clinging vegetation and were artificially aged to simulate their decay,
re-creating the romantic settings of Catherwood's engravings. At San Diego, by
contrast, exhibitors presented fairgoers with fully reconstructed, yet miniatur-
ized, models of Mesoamerican architecture in the fair's California Building.
Whereas the San Diego fair still emphasized the physicality of the ancient structures, the aesthetic shift from 1893 to 1915 demonstrated that the American concept of Maya architecture itself had changed. Evolving from a romantic emblem
of "America's" lost architectural past, this antiquity was now perceived as a distinctly regional and foreign tradition—and one that belonged to the domain of
professional, institutionally supported archaeologists.

The period preceding the San Diego fair also marked a new beginning for
Mexico and for pre-Columbian studies in a general sense. Following years of revolution and the eventual establishment of a united republic, Mexico had firmly
delineated its political borders by 1915, sharply reducing its susceptibility to territorial or cultural claims from the north. Second, with the successful correlation of
the Christian and Maya calendars by J. T. Goodman in 1905, the ancient Maya too
came into their own. From this point forward, archaeologists were compelled to
consider the ancient Maya a historical group acting within a quantifiable
chronology and—most importantly—to recognize them as the ancestors of the
living Maya. With the advent of this newfound cultural independence, American

claims on the Mesoamerican past, and the heyday of the amateur explorer, ultimately came to an end.

Although the chapters of this book are arranged chronologically, they are not intended to illustrate a linear narrative. Chapter 1 establishes the circumstances under which the Mexican past was rediscovered, and it attempts to explain why this legacy proved useful in the hands of American writers and audiences. Chapters 2 through 5 split this narrative into four separate treatments, the last three roughly contemporary with one another, in order to explore the same period from different vantage points. The picture they present is a cumulative rather than a progressive one.

Changes in methodology from one chapter to the next are intentional. Stephens' and Catherwood's illustrated texts require close visual readings, for example, whereas the Book of Mormon does not; in Charnay's work the role of patronage comes under careful scrutiny, whereas in the Le Plongeons' story this element is less important. Though each of these chapters could stand alone, together they illustrate the multilayered nature of American responses to Mexican antiquity. In my epilogue I depart from the character-driven nature of the five preceding chapters, attempting to provide a bird's-eye view of the late nineteenth and early twentieth centuries. The phenomena I explore here, primarily the changing roles that Mexican antiquities played at world's fairs, represent the culmination of this period but invite development as studies in their own right.

My reasons for undertaking this project stem from the fact that although several authors have treated pre-Columbian historiography in a general fashion, few have critically examined the cultural agendas of these nineteenth-century explorer-artists. Of the general surveys, Robert Brunhouse's *In Search of the Maya* (1973) and Claude Baudez' *Lost Cities of the Maya* (1992) are two of the best examples. Both works provide engaging narratives of the period's history, yet fail to contextualize early archaeologists' work within the larger framework of nineteenth-century nationalism. Furthermore, their inclusion of such a wide range of archaeologists in this period—regardless of nationality or professional status—spreads these otherwise valuable treatments somewhat thinly.

In addition to the few broadly focused surveys devoted to this period, several authors have produced excellent biographies of the American explorers from this era, including Victor Van Hagan's *Maya Explorer: John Lloyd Stephens and the Lost Cities of Mexico and Central America* (1947), Keith Davis' *Désiré Charnay: Expedi-*

tionary Photographer (1981), and Lawrence Desmond and Phyllis Messenger's *A Dream of Maya: Augustus and Alice Le Plongeon in Nineteenth-Century Yucatan* (1988). These biographies were extraordinarily helpful to me, both in terms of tracking down useful sources and in understanding the larger context of these explorers' careers, yet the authors do not situate their subjects' work within the larger historical and nationalistic questions of this period.

In still another category, there are several treatments of pre-Columbian historiography that subordinate the period I examine to more esoteric issues of Maya scholarship. Two examples include Michael Coe's *Breaking the Maya Code* (1992), a study of the developments that led to Maya glyph decipherment, and Barbara Braun's *Pre-Columbian Art and the Post-Columbian World* (1993), an examination of the role that pre-Columbian art has played in the work of twentieth-century artists. Lastly, although Marjorie Ingle's *The Mayan Revival Style* (1984) examines certain late nineteenth-century perceptions of the Maya, her material represents the culmination, rather than the beginning, of the attitudes I examine in this project. Ultimately I believe that the present book combines the best of all of these approaches, providing as complete a picture of the period as possible, within a thematically unified framework, while using a relatively limited number of case studies.

Regarding the title of this book, I would like to say a word about the terms "Mexican" and "American," because each can be interpreted in several different ways. My use of the term "Mexican" reflects the fact that the majority of the sites I discuss lie within the current national boundaries of Mexico. Other important sites I examine do not. Copan and Quirigua, for example, are found in Honduras; Tikal, in Guatemala. Even the area of Yucatan, now contained within Mexican borders, maintained a hostile, quasi-independent status from Mexico for much of the nineteenth century (similarly, most but not all of the sites in this study were produced by the ancient Maya).

I justify using the umbrella term "Mexican" for this work because of the fluid nature of Latin American nationhood in this period. In the wake of Spain's departure from the region, it was not known to Mexicans or to foreigners whether the present-day nations of Central America would remain independent from Mexico or would eventually become absorbed by it. For foreign travelers in this region, consequently, the terms "Mexico" and "Mexican" encompassed a far greater territory than the area currently contained within the country's borders (obviously so, of course, when one considers the Mexican lands annexed by the United States following the Mexican-American War).[5] I hope that readers will allow for the word's historical elasticity, while understanding that in the text itself I generally use the terms "Mexico" and "Mexican" only in their specific, national contexts.

Equally problematic, perhaps even more so, are the labels "America" and "American." In chapter 2, I address the slippery history of these terms but feel it necessary to first explain my own use of them. In my title and throughout this book I use "American" and "America" as synonyms for the United States, although these terms could be applied to other nations within North America. I do this for two reasons. First, as a purely mechanical consideration, I do this because the term "United States" resists transformation into adjectival form. Second, I use the word as I do because most of the explorers from this period did so as well—even when they, too, were aware of its ambiguous meanings (and often, in fact, because they wished to exploit this ambiguity). My own usage springs from the wish for clarity and should not be interpreted as an example of chauvinism.

Concerning the historical parameters of my project, the dates 1820–1915 roughly correspond to the period between Mexican independence and revolution—two events that neatly bracket the first era of archaeological investigation in this region. This bracketing does not imply, however, that no important discoveries preceded Latin American independence or that nineteenth-century explorers in the region were the first to link archaeology and national mythmaking (the Aztecs themselves had transported Toltec artifacts to their capital as evidence of their mythologized descent from this group). It was only the *publication* of the ruins, however—a phenomenon that clearly postdates independence—that allowed their consumption and transformation by and for American audiences.

As for the end date of my project, one could argue that postrevolutionary Mexico witnessed the amplification of archaeological research by American explorers, rather than its diminution. Although this is true, it is important to note the disappearance of the *amateur* American archaeologist from this period forward; by 1915 at the latest, figures like Stephens, Charnay, or Le Plongeon had been replaced in the field by professional archaeologists working for institutions like the Smithsonian or university-affiliated museums.[6] These professional archaeologists were not immune to institutionally sanctioned looting, it is true, yet their work was arguably more scientific in both structure and in tone.[7]

For twentieth-century Americans, the allure of pre-Columbian Mexico increasingly lay in its foreign qualities, rather than in its potential to bolster the United States' cultural pedigree. This shift was the result of both Mexico's increased self-confidence as a nation and the United States' waning interests in territorial or historical annexation in Latin America. The United States' continued romanticization of Mexico, then, became a form of exoticism rather than misguided identification. Most importantly, of course, two dramatic developments in Maya archaeology since 1915 — pinpoint archaeological dating and increasingly accurate glyph decipherment — led to the American recognition of indigenous authorship and local precedence at these sites.

Certain nineteenth-century attitudes toward the ancient Mesoamerican past, however, continue to persist — especially where local governments remain politically unstable, and when the scientific value of a site requires an aggressive claim against potential looting. In an uncanny evocation of the nineteenth-century's sometimes militaristic approach to Latin American archaeology, the *Times* article concerning the site at Cancuen explains:

> The region is free of civil war now, Dr. Demarest said, but the government of Guatemala has little presence there, and it is still a virtually lawless place. Dr. Demarest said the expedition has mobilized and trained the people of the nearest village, El Zapote, to stand guard over the new-found palace.[8]

1

THE SECOND DISCOVERY OF AMERICA

It must be recognized that, for the second time,
America is a new world.

—HENRI BARADÈRE, *Antiquités Mexicaines* (1834)

FOLLOWING MEXICO'S independence from Spain in 1821, the sudden accessibility of its colonial archives and archaeological sites fueled dramatic foreign interest in the nation's pre-Hispanic past. More publications devoted to Mexican antiquities appeared within the nation's first two decades of independence, in fact, than had been produced during the past three centuries of Spanish rule. The enthusiasm generated by these publications, however — mostly reprints of formerly unobtainable colonial surveys — often compromised their authors' search for archaeological truth.

Fusing decades-old archaeological surveys with contemporary commentaries, European publishers in the 1820s and 1830s served an eager yet restricted constituency of wealthy, foreign antiquarians — most of whom valued quantity of information over its accuracy. Given their particular fervor for archaeological acquisition within this period, British and French antiquarians proved to be the most enthusiastic consumers of these works. Their interest in Mesoamerican archaeology remained constant throughout the nineteenth century, sometimes supporting but often colliding with the aims of North American explorers.

The primary question facing nineteenth-century scholars of the Mesoamerican past concerned the monuments' ethnic and historical authorship. Both preceding and following Mexico's independence from Spain, European writers failed to recognize an ethnic connection between Latin America's indigenous population and the ancient city-builders. Furthermore, nearly all denied the possibility of independent cultural development in the region, allowing no exception to the genealogical framework of the Christian Bible, which explained humanity's descent from Adam and, following the Great Flood, from Noah.[1]

Attempting to reconcile the coexistence of pre-Columbian civilization with the ancient cultures of the Old World, authors either implicitly or explicitly linked the two, discrediting ethnic continuity in Latin America as well as accounts of parallel creation. Proposing various theories of trans-Atlantic migration, early writers on Mexican antiquities supported the commonality of man's descent from the Old World — an insistence that justified Mexico's cultural colonization in the wake of Spain's departure.

To fully understand the excitement generated by this publishing renaissance, one must consider the disjointed nature of preindependence scholarship. Although colonial authorities had sponsored several important investigations of preconquest culture in the sixteenth century, no archaeological surveys had been undertaken in New Spain until the last decades of Spanish rule.[2] By this period, however, political unrest and royal xenophobia had consigned the results of these investigations to an intentional obscurity. Until the 1820s, the only generally available information concerning pre-Columbian architecture derived from vague literary descriptions left by the conquistadors or from the rare accounts written by foreign travelers in New Spain.

The incomplete nature of these early colonial sources stems from several factors. First, because they regarded preconquest shrines as impediments to political and religious conversion, colonial government and church officials had destroyed these "pagan" temples, assigned them to benign neglect, or incorporated them within new structures. By the mid-seventeenth century, for example, all traces of the Aztec capital Tenochtitlan — including its colossal pyramid-temple — had disappeared beneath the colonial development of what is now Mexico City. Second, the Spanish were largely ignorant of the nature and extent of precontact Maya culture. Not only had classic Maya civilization collapsed centuries before

1.1. HUMAN SACRIFICE AT THE GREAT TEMPLE OF THE AZTECS (Théodore De Bry, *Grands Voyages*, vol. 9: 1601).

European arrival on the continent, but its cities had also mostly flourished in areas far removed from later colonial settlements. Ultimately, Spain's inability to understand the origins, style, or function of these ancient monuments reflects the more general limitations of its worldview.

Within a century of the Spanish establishment of New Spain, René Descartes had postulated that "it is a frequent habit, when we discover resemblances between two things, to attribute to both equally, even on points in which they are in reality different, that which we have recognized to be true of only one of them."[3] Though Descartes' remark pertains to problems of scientific classification, it illuminates the idiosyncratic nature of the earliest accounts of pre-Columbian architecture. To provide cultural legibility for their European audiences, early eyewitnesses translated the radically foreign architecture of this region into more easily understood idioms.

In his second letter to King Charles V, for example, Hernando Cortés likened the streets of the Tenochtitlan to those of Madrid and its principal temple to the Cathedral of Seville.[4] The account of one of Cortés' captains, Bernal Díaz del

Castillo, proved equally myopic, describing the Aztec sacred precinct as "a great enclosure of courts . . . larger than the plaza of Salamanca."⁵ Passages such as these, the only firsthand Western accounts of a living pre-Columbian culture, formed the basis for much of the future confusion regarding the accurate portrayal of the vanished works.

One of the earliest European images of pre-Hispanic architecture, Théodore De Bry's engraving of the Aztecs' Templo Mayor — an enormous, stepped pyramid dismantled by the Spanish in the sixteenth century — demonstrates the initial European reliance upon faulty or incomplete literary sources. An artist from Liège who had never traveled to New Spain, De Bry illustrated the writings of the Jesuit historian José de Acosta in the ninth volume of the artist's *Grands Voyages* series (1601).⁶ De Bry's representation of the great pyramid of Tenochtitlan (fig. 1.1) faithfully illustrates Acosta's text, although the Jesuit's misinformation and the artist's imagination combined to create an image that bore no relation to historical reality.

In describing a scene of human sacrifice atop the Aztec pyramid, Acosta relates:

[A]ll their prisoners were led up to the Mexican Temple where the "Mountain of the Round Skulls" is. . . . Shortly afterwards, a priest descended from the highest square mountain, wearing his ceremonial robe and holding a statue of their god in one hand . . . after which a prisoner was taken to the top of this mountain where the sacrifice took place. . . . The body was rolled down the steps.⁷

De Bry's accompanying image reflects Acosta's erroneous conflation of the main temple with another Aztec structure, the tzompantli, or skull rack, and translates Acosta's "square mountain" into a classical, colonnaded cube peopled by figures in Greco-Roman attire. By means of this classical lens, De Bry initiated the Westernization of the pre-Hispanic past for European audiences.

Tracing the trajectory of this strategy, one arrives at the fantastic images of pre-Hispanic architecture found in such works as *Le Voyage de Thomas Gage* (1720), a travel account written by an English Jesuit. The illustrator of Gage's text presents the same temple illustrated in De Bry's work, as well as its inner sanctuary and cult image, yet in these renderings the building and its surrounding wall are transformed into a European baroque idiom (figs. 1.2 and 1.3). The Aztec temple precinct appears as an eighteenth-century French courtyard, complete with rusticated gateways and mansard roofs, surrounding a baroque pyramid topped with domed tempiettos. In the artist's illustration of the temple's primary cult figure, visually derived from Díaz' accounts of the Aztec war god Huitzilopochtli ("a half-man/half-beast figure covered in jewels, a mantle, and caked in blood"),[8] he references the compositions of two well-known classical Greek cult images: Phidias' Athena Parthenos, the cult statue that originally stood inside the Parthenon, and the same sculptor's seated image of Zeus from the Temple of Zeus at Olympia.

Images such as these indicate that, by the eighteenth century, the visual memory of the authentic pre-Columbian past had been replaced by a more recognizable system of Western signs. Although the speculative nature of such illustrations has justified their dismissal by modern archaeologists, it is their very inaccuracy that constitutes their current value as cultural documents.

Significantly, Gage's audience considered his account an adventure tale of a forbidding and mysterious region. The Dutch publisher of the 1720 edition, Paul Marret, celebrates Gage as a kind of cultural blockade-runner, asserting, "[Gage] was not content simply to enter the Sanctuary of the Spaniards, but he discovered the mysteries that they had hidden from us with great care. . . . He has broken the silence of two centuries."[9] Marret's assurance of public interest in the ruins demonstrates the negative success of Spain's xenophobia, for the monuments' enforced obscurity only increased their value as sensational material. In light of such publications, Spain increasingly regarded pre-Hispanic antiquity as a valuable commodity to be safeguarded from foreign curiosity seekers.

Whereas Marret's audience knew little of the Mesoamerican past, Spanish administrators, church officials, and indigenous groups in New Spain had always been aware of a range of ancient works. In Friar Diego de Landa's sixteenth-century account of Yucatan, for example, he refers to the ruined Maya cities of Uxmal and Chichen Itza, as well as to the contemporary knowledge and destruction of other Maya sites.[10] In Central Mexico, at sites such as Cholula, ancient structures were often preserved as the foundations for Catholic churches; although the monuments' authorship may have been forgotten, they remained as visible emblems of the preconquest past. In a similar fashion, government and church officials often preserved architectural fragments, sculpture, and other preconquest artifacts by incorporating them into the walls of their homes and churches.[11]

The group most familiar with these ancient ruins was of course the indigenous population of New Spain. Although disease and warfare had greatly reduced their numbers in the colonial period, the Maya of Yucatan, Chiapas, and Guatemala, as well as the Nahua-speaking peoples of central Mexico, remained connected to

1.2. AZTEC CEREMONIAL PRECINCT (Thomas Gage, *Le Voyage de Thomas Gage:* 1720).

1.3. INNER SANCTUARY, GREAT TEMPLE OF TENOCHTITLAN (Thomas Gage, *Le Voyage de Thomas Gage:* 1720).

1.4. *Above:* JOSÉ ANTONIO CALDERÓN,
TEMPLE OF THE SUN RELIEF (Juan Muñoz,
*Expediente sobre el descubrimiento de una gran
ciudad en la provincia de Chiapa: 1786).*
   Below: FREDERICK CATHERWOOD'S EN-
GRAVING OF THE TEMPLE OF THE SUN RELIEF,
1841 (John Lloyd Stephens, *Incidents of Travel in
Central America, Chiapas, and Yucatan,* vol. 2: 1841).

their traditional lands — often living near "undiscovered" or abandoned ancient settlements. According to accounts from the sixteenth through the nineteenth centuries, the groups even appear to have maintained the former religious function of certain preconquest sites, despite strict bans on such practices.[12]

It was from the reports of local Maya that the most famous of the nineteenth-century rediscoveries was made, the ruins of Palenque in the state of Chiapas. Indios' stories of an abandoned settlement of "stone houses" in the jungle had piqued the interest of the local curate Antonio de Solís, who arrived at the village of Santo Domingo de Palenque in 1764; although Solís died before executing a full-scale investigation, a local priest named Ramón Ordóñez adopted the project, mounting an expedition to the site in 1773.[13] Ordóñez' group submitted its report to Joseph Estachería, president of the Royal Audiencia de Guatemala, whose subsequent investigations came to the attention of the royal historiographer of the Spanish American colonies, Juan Bautista Muñoz. Through Muñoz, Estachería's reports ultimately captured the imagination of the Crown itself.

Although this haphazard trail of administrative reports led from colonial to royal circles, support for these investigations proceeded in the opposite direction. The late eighteenth century had witnessed a profound shift in the Spanish Crown's attitude toward its American possessions, manifested in part by the lifting of the "pagan" stigma that had previously excluded the pre-Hispanic past from serious inquiry. Following the War of the Spanish Succession, the newly established Bourbon monarchy had displayed a keen interest in its overseas empire.

Because this interest primarily concerned the generation of greater colonial revenue, Carlos III actively encouraged his viceroys to explore the mineralogy, geology, and geography of New Spain.[14] The exploration of pre-Columbian ruins formed a natural corollary to such investigations, for it promised the possibility of riches while lending the Bourbons' patronage an Enlightenment cachet.

Under Carlos III's direction, Estachería commissioned Jose Antonio Calderón to undertake the first visual record of Palenque in 1784. In his report, Calderón claimed to have surveyed several hundred buildings, yet he wrongly described their placement along European-style streets and produced only four rather primitive drawings of the site, including the sculptural reliefs of Palenque's Cross Group temples (fig. 1.4).[15] Included in Muñoz' *Expediente sobre el descubrimiento de una gran ciudad en la provincia de Chiapa* two years later, the work of this untrained local official failed to convey the technical skill and naturalism of the actual reliefs, their glyphic content, or their architectural contexts.

In the following year Estachería sent Antonio Bernasconi, an official from Guatemala City, to produce a more complete set of images for the royal archives. Though Bernasconi had trained as an architect, his education proved as great a stumbling block as Calderón's ignorance. In his depiction of the Temple of the In-

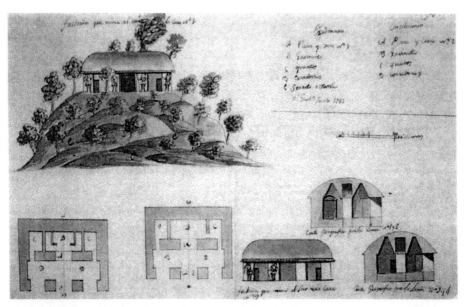

1.5. ANTONIO BERNASCONI, TEMPLE OF THE INSCRIPTIONS AND TEMPLE OF THE CROSS, PALENQUE
(Juan Muñoz, *Expediente sobre el descubrimiento de una gran ciudad en la provincia de Chiapa: 1786*).

1.6. RICARDO ALMENDÁRIZ, PALACE TOWER AT PALENQUE (Antonio Del Río, *Description of the Ruins of an Ancient City:* 1822).

scriptions and the Temple of the Cross (fig. 1.5), which had also appeared in Muñoz' work, the relative accuracy of his plans and sections sharply contrasts with his omission of key elements such as the buildings' roof combs (although omitting the roof comb of the Temple of the Inscriptions is more understandable, for it has suffered far more damage than that of the Temple of the Cross).[16] Intended to bear the ideological weight of the temple, these crowning structures originally acted as armatures for inscriptions and religious sculpture. The inscrutability of the roof combs' function, however, apparently rendered them meaningless for Bernasconi's investigation.

Estachería's dissatisfaction with both Calderón's and Bernasconi's work grew not only from their failure to produce accurate visual records but also from their inability to resolve his prescribed set of inquiries. The men were charged with determining the age and former population of the city, the ethnic origin of its builders, and the reasons for its downfall, as well as the use, style, and construc-

1.7. TOWER AT PALACE GROUP, PALENQUE (author's photo).

tion method of all of the site's extant structures.[17] Unaware of the Herculean scale of these demands, Estachería mounted a third investigation in 1786 to be led by Captain Antonio Del Río and an accompanying artist named Ricardo Almendáriz.[18] By pairing an investigator-writer with a subordinate artist figure, Estachería established the archetype for subsequent British and French archaeological explorations in the region — an arrangement that often led to an uneasy alliance between text and image.

Del Río's report represented less than a month's work at the site (May–June 1787), included only a scant number of architectural drawings, and raised more questions than it answered, yet it remains the first modern attempt to decode an ancient Mesoamerican site. Encapsulated within this short document are many of the idiosyncrasies that would reappear in later studies, chief among them the conflation of ancient Mexican and Greco-Roman civilizations.

After ransacking Palenque for hidden treasures, such that "there remained neither a window nor a doorway blocked up; a partition that was not thrown down, nor a room, corridor, court, tower, nor subterranean passage in which excavations were not effected,"[19] Del Río attempted to focus on the larger questions with which Estachería had charged him. In a passage that set the tone for his entire report, Del Río postulates:

> It might be inferred that this people had had some analogy to, and intercourse with the Romans. . . . I do not take upon myself to assert that these conquerors did actually land in this country; but, there is reasonable ground for hazarding a conjecture that some inhabitants of that polished nation did visit these regions; and that, from such intercourse, the natives might have imbibed, during their stay, an idea of the arts, as a reward for their hospitality.[20]

Del Río peppers his report with classical terminology, describing the "pillars" and "architraves" of the buildings as well as the "Grecian heads" that adorned them.[21] In one passage, Del Río refers to the writings of Padre Jacito Garrido, a seventeenth-century friar who believed that North America had been discovered by the ancient Greeks.[22] Not only does Del Río fail to question the theory, but he also laments that the priest did not provide a specific date for the Greeks' arrival on these shores. Finally, in writing about the sculptures of the Cross Group temples, Del Río notes that "we seem to view the idolatry of the Phoenicians, the Greeks, and the Romans most strongly portrayed."[23]

Although the images accompanying Del Río's text are often inaccurate, they hardly reflect the fantastic nature of his commentary. Of the twenty-five plates prepared by Almendáriz, only fourteen images were eventually published;[24] of these, twelve depict stucco reliefs, while the remaining two illustrate a plan and elevation of the tower belonging to the so-called Palace structure. By comparing Almendáriz' tower elevation with the modern reconstruction of the building (figs. 1.6 and 1.7), one can easily distinguish the artist's license in representing the structure.

Not only is the tower erroneously depicted as an independent structure, but it also features open, inset doorways and decidedly non-Maya elliptical archways. Similarly, Almendáriz' plan of the Palace complex bears little resemblance to the building's actual configuration (figs. 1.8 and 1.9). Drastically simplifying the structure into a grid of four rectangular courtyards, he reduced the building's acute angles, rhomboid spaces, and warren-like passageways to a conventional European diagram of right-angled symmetry. Representing a site that must have

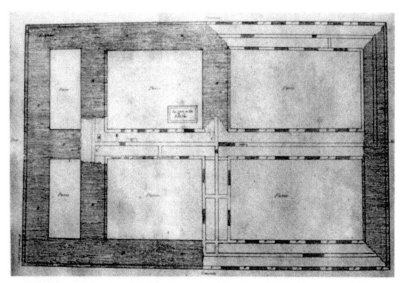

1.8. RICARDO ALMENDÁRIZ, PLAN OF PALACE TOWER AT PALENQUE (Antonio Del Río, *Description of the Ruins of an Ancient City:* 1822).

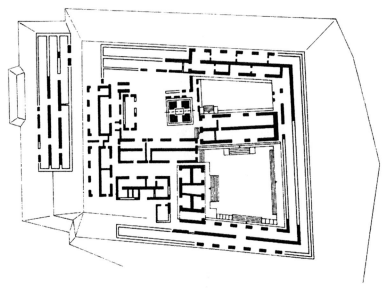

1.9. PLAN OF PALACE TOWER, PALENQUE (Henri Stierlin).

been wildly overgrown and, to Almendáriz' eyes, entirely foreign, these images are not only inaccurate but also disappointingly banal.

The disjunction between text and image in the Del Río report is peculiar, for its textual links to classical precedent are both imaginative and intentionally provocative. The report's conflation of Mesoamerican and classical architecture, a phenomenon more understandable in the work of earlier artists such as De Bry, took on a new authority in the context of this eyewitness report. For later explorers John Lloyd Stephens and Frederick Catherwood, Del Río's writings would suggest, if not the actual possibility of Roman-Mesoamerican contact, then at least the confirmation that such works constituted legitimate equivalents to classical culture.

As the Del Río report gathered dust in the royal archives of Guatemala, the German naturalist Alexander von Humboldt began the serial publication of his exhaustive thirty-volume opus on the Americas, *Views of the Cordilleras and Monuments of the Indigenous Peoples of America* (1810–1813). Granted the rare privilege of an unrestricted travel visa by Carlos IV, von Humboldt and his colleague Aimée Bonpland spent 1803–1804 in New Spain assembling material for von Humboldt's encyclopedic work on the geography, natural resources, and ancient art of Spain's New World possessions. Von Humboldt's work constituted a virtual second discovery of the New World, yet his images of pre-Hispanic art and architecture primarily consisted of works and monuments already known to Spanish officials.

The sole volume devoted to Mexican antiquities in the *Views of the Cordilleras* series, von Humboldt's *Picturesque Atlas*, illustrates the Central Mexican sites of Cholula, Xochicalco, and Mitla. Because this volume principally treats Aztec codices and monumental sculpture, these three sites appear to have represented a subordinate interest for the naturalist.[25] Accompanying the illustrations of the monuments are brief descriptions, which, though not entirely accurate, never approach the conjecture of Del Río's writings. Von Humboldt incorrectly ascribes Cholula, for example, to the Toltec civilization[26] and illustrates the upper register of Mitla's frieze as if the element constituted the entire façade of the building. Ultimately von Humboldt's interest in the sites is confined to the etymology of their names, their geographical setting, and the nature of their building materials.

Within a year of von Humboldt's departure from New Spain the Spanish Crown commissioned its last and most extensive survey of known pre-

Columbian monuments, a series of three expeditions led by Captain Guillermo
Dupaix in the years 1805–1807. Dupaix's appointment no doubt derived from his
reputation as an aficionado of pre-Hispanic architecture; as early as 1804, according to von Humboldt, the captain had planned to publish a private report on the
ancient Veracruz site of El Tajín.[27] Dupaix's scholarship was matched by the skills
of his accompanying artist, José Luciano Castañeda, a professor of drawing and
architecture in Mexico City. Though his style rigidly adhered to European academic standards, Castañeda recorded the unusual structures he encountered
with an accuracy that surpassed the efforts of earlier artists. The body of work he
produced, nearly 150 drawings in all, constituted the most extensive visual record
of pre-Hispanic monuments yet assembled.

Royal support for Dupaix's expeditions stemmed from the same motives that
had allowed von Humboldt such freedom of movement within New Spain. Under
the aegis of Enlightenment investigation, Carlos IV hoped to know more about his
colony's resources, both natural and historical. The formula for Dupaix's reports to
the Crown loosely derived from the paragon of Enlightenment investigation, Denis
Diderot's *Encyclopédie* (1751–1772); as with the French model, Dupaix's report
linked technical illustrations with individual scholarly commentaries. In the case
of Dupaix's colonial project, however, this form of "scientific" presentation often
belied his inability to grasp the meaning of the works he investigated.

Because Dupaix's expedition combined military and artistic agendas, it bears
closer comparison to Napoleon's infamous Egyptian expedition of 1798. In both
cases, the ambitious scientific and artistic goals of the missions were ultimately
intended to amplify the conquering nation's cultural hegemony. The size of
Napoleon's Egyptian expedition dwarfed Dupaix's more modest undertaking, yet
the latter also faced a far greater intellectual challenge. As Dupaix's publisher later
cautioned: "let us remember . . . that when [Napoleon's] celebrated expedition
took place, Egypt was already known. . . . Here, to the contrary, everything is as
new as it is marvelous."[28]

Unlike his contemporaries, who largely ascribed pre-Hispanic ruins to trans-
Atlantic contact, Dupaix felt that these monuments represented a culture previously unknown in the Western world. Attempting to answer the question "from
whom did the ancient Mexicans receive their first notions of the arts?"[29] Dupaix
ultimately concludes that ancient Mexico, though not reaching the "Greek state of
perfection," nonetheless "produced works . . . endowed with their own genius,
their own force of imagination, and that progressed over the course of the cen-

1.10. *Above:* JOSÉ LUCIANO CASTAÑEDA, PYRAMID WITH PLANAR SIDES
(Edward King, *Antiquities of Mexico,* 2d expedition, plate 16: 1831.)

1.11. *Above right:* CASTAÑEDA, HEAD FRAGMENT FROM TULA (Temple
of the Warriors) (Henri Baradère, *Antiquités Mexicaines,* 1st expedition, plate 13: 1844).

turies," all of which was achieved "without the help of foreigners." [30] Dupaix's re-
marks stop short of crediting the indigenous populations of Mexico with city-
building ancestors, asserting that the monuments were built by a long-vanished
race; his insistence upon an independent development of the arts in the Americas, however, served as a principal stepping-stone for the work of later North
American explorers. [31]

Whereas Dupaix generally restricted his commentaries to observable evidence,
Castañeda's illustrations occasionally yielded ground to trans-Atlantic contact theory. Whether this disjunction represents a separate artistic agenda, the uncon-
scious recasting of an unfamiliar culture, or the work of later engravers is unclear.
The fact remains, however, that the contemporary belief in a Mexican-Egyptian
correspondence, springing from these cultures' shared phenomena of glyphic inscriptions and pyramids, left an indelible stamp upon his work. In describing the
typical stepped Mexican pyramid, Dupaix had carefully distinguished it from planar-sided Egyptian models, adding that "among all the works in pyramidal form
that I've observed, and that belong to ancient times, not one [in Mexico] ends in a

1.12. *Above:* CASTAÑEDA, EL PALACIO, MITLA (Edward King, *Antiquities of Mexico,* 2d expedition, plate 29: 1831).
Below: INTERIOR, EL PALACIO, MITLA (author's photo).

point."[32] Nevertheless, Castañeda illustrated several planar-sided structures apparently built in the Egyptian manner (fig. 1.10), as well as figural sculpture featuring Egyptianized eye profiles and pharaonic headdresses (fig. 1.11).

In other cases, Castañeda's drawings demonstrate a reliance upon Greco-Roman references. At the site of Mitla, for example, Castañeda depicts the Palace structure's short, drumlike supports as tall, tapering columns with perceptible classical entasis (fig. 1.12). The resulting image takes its cue from eighteenth-century romantic treatments of Greco-Roman ruins, as does Dupaix's accompanying text, which eulogizes: "the prospect of these ancient fragments, from a certain distance, produces a great effect; they offer a striking image of this venerable antiquity, and of the ravages that time inexorably exercises upon the fragile works of man."[33] In this pairing of text and image, the distinctly foreign quality of the ruins is softened by more familiar rhetoric about the ephemeral nature of civilization. Implicit is the parallel between the courses of ancient American and Greco-Roman cultures.

In their presentation of Palenque, the team adopted a similar approach, modifying the proportions and details of buildings to suggest more recognizably European forms. By adding an additional story to Palenque's tower, for example, Castañeda suggests its termination in an obelisk (fig. 1.13), an Egyptian form used in the West since Roman times. The artist's depictions of other monuments at Palenque feature a uniform system of moldings and regularized plans, visual conceits that disguised the structures' wide divergence in style and date, as well as their characteristic departure from right-angled Western symmetry. "They made rectangles of various sizes," Dupaix erroneously explains, ". . . [and] had a certain predilection for the straight line, which is most fitting for works of architecture."[34] Although Dupaix and Castañeda never explicitly conflate Mesoamerica with the Greco-Roman world, their "adjustments" indicate an insistence upon viewing its remains through a classical filter.

The team's perceptions of classical correspondence extended equally to issues of ethnicity, for Dupaix often contextualized figural sculpture and contemporary indigenous groups within Greco-Roman artistic traditions. In describing the *indios* of Mexico, Dupaix states:

> I have seen Indians, in various parts of the kingdom, particularly in the mountains where the race has kept itself pure and intact, who, for the beauty of their form and proportions, could serve as models in the academies of Europe. I have seen faces

1.13. CASTAÑEDA, SECTION OF PALACE AT PALENQUE; TOWER ON RIGHT (Henri Baradère, *Antiquités Mexicaines*, 3d expedition, plate 13: 1844).

there of such noble character that they would have been appreciated even by the Greeks.[35]

Inexplicably, Dupaix manages to link this ethnically "pure" people to the sophisticated portrait-sculpture of their ancestors, without crediting the former group with any connection to civilized peoples. In his illustration of a sculpted head found near Tepeyacan, for example, Castañeda demonstrates the "nearly Greek" physiognomy that Dupaix ascribes to the Mexicans (fig. 1.14).[36] Recast through Castañeda's eyes, the figure's hairstyle and features bear no relation to known Central Mexican sculptural traditions. Similarly anomalous are the pose and execution of a subsequent discovery, a stone figurine of a woman found near the village of San Pablo del Monte (fig. 1.15). Despite Castañeda's apparent remodeling of the work, Dupaix praises it as a representative example of the regional "type," adding that it bears a "certain resemblance to the Medici Venus"; such works, he insists, "convince us that this era that we regard as barbaric . . . is far from meriting such an opinion."[37]

The oddest example of cross-cultural insistence in Dupaix's report, however, involves a series of ruined mounds that the team encountered near Monte Alban (figs. 1.16 and 1.17). In Dupaix's descriptions of these constructions, which undoubtedly represented the overgrown remains of pyramids, he refers to them as

1.14. CASTAÑEDA, HEAD FRAGMENT FOUND NEAR TEPEYACAN (Henri Baradère, *Antiquités Mexicaines*, 1st expedition, plate 2: 1844).

1.15. CASTAÑEDA, FIGURINE FOUND NEAR SAN PABLO DEL MONTE (Henri Baradère, *Antiquités Mexicaines*, 2d expedition, plate 62: 1844).

tumuli—a Latin term for the rounded, Etruscan burial mounds found at sites in central Italy. Although Dupaix's perception of a formal similarity between the two types is understandable, Castañeda's illustrations unduly amplify the comparison. Rather than illustrating the mounds as they must have appeared — irregular, thick with vegetation, and impenetrable — he presents an imaginary series of reconstructed ruins. Perfectly circular in plan, these half-dozen tumuli range from beehive shapes to hemispheres, with arched entryways, ventilation shafts, and sophisticated interior vaulting. Castañeda's drawings undoubtedly derive from the cruciform tombs of Monte Alban and Mitla, yet his hemispheric elevations and vaulted interiors bear a far stronger resemblance to well-known Etruscan or even ancient Aegean funerary complexes.

Within the context of Castañeda's work, such embellishment of the archaeological record is unusual. An explanation for this departure, however, lies in a passage by Charles Farcy, a contemporary analyst of Castañeda's drawings. While "the United States offers vestiges of tumuli," Farcy insists, ". . . [they] bear no comparison to these admirable monuments in stone and brick."[38] Both Castañeda and Farcy, it appears, wished to distinguish Mesoamerican mounds from their less distinguished North American cousins, the recently rediscovered burial mounds of the Mississippi and Ohio Valley regions. Although the distinction is materially valid, given the masonry understructure of the Mesoamerican mounds, its basis was more likely related to nineteenth-century conceptions of racial hierarchy. Because archaeologists in the United States attributed the country's burial mounds to extant North American ethnic groups, Mesoamerican explorers wished to associate the works they found with a more "civilized" Old World tradition.

Castañeda's and Dupaix's conflation of pyramids and preclassical tumuli may represent an intentional gesture, yet this team also innocently misrepresented structures that they failed to understand. In one case, the pair mistook ruins of a colonial-period bridge near Tlaxcala for an ancient Mesoamerican structure; its brick masonry, baroque finials, and arched waterways all proclaim a European origin, yet Dupaix praised the "majestic sight" of this "ancient bridge, mistreated by the centuries"[39] as if it were the product of ancient Central Mexican builders. In another example, Castañeda mistakenly drew the roof comb of Palenque's Temple of the Sun as a partial second story (fig. 1.18). In the presence of structures he failed to understand, Castañeda, like Bernasconi before him, resorted to their Westernization.

1.16. CASTAÑEDA, TUMULUS NEAR MONTE ALBAN (Henri Baradère, *Antiquités Mexicaines*, 2d expedition, plate 28: 1844).

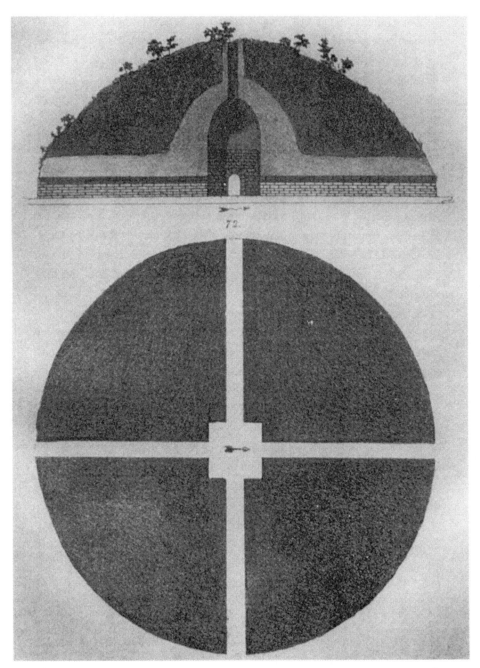

1.17. CASTAÑEDA, TUMULUS NEAR MONTE ALBAN (Edward King, Lord Kingsborough, *Antiquities of Mexico*, 2d expedition, plate 28: 1831).

The sculptural reliefs at Palenque proved the greatest stumbling block of all for these two, as indicated by Dupaix's faulty descriptions of the works' positioning and, in crucial instances, his failure to remark upon them at all. In describing the sculptural panels of the Cross Group temples, for example, Dupaix gives the false impression that the doorjamb and interior sculptures exist within a single plane. Furthermore, in his passage describing the Temple of the Inscriptions, he fails to remark upon the enormous glyph panels that cover its rear walls; such negative evidence suggests that Dupaix either did not personally explore the interior or that he simply ascribed no importance to the glyphs (by later nineteenth-century standards, Dupaix's reluctance to explain the iconography and glyphic texts of Palenque shows an admirable sense of restraint).[40] "How these enigmas oppose our research!" Dupaix laments near the end of his report, adding somewhat prophetically that "we are reduced to the sad resource of conjecture, the last refuge of the antiquarian."[41] For the explorers who succeeded him, this "last refuge" often served as a starting point.

In the period following Dupaix's expedition, the greatest obstacles to archaeological research derived not from the inscrutability of the Mesoamerican past but from the turbulent political events leading to Mexican independence. Spanish control of New Spain, which had begun to disintegrate with the death of Carlos III in 1788, was first significantly challenged by criollo groups who wished to supplant Spanish authority in the colony. In 1809, army captain Ignacio Allende planned a bloodless coup to establish criollo authority, choosing popular leader Miguel Hidalgo as his ally; Hidalgo, however, aimed to destroy the colonial system altogether. Foiling Allende's plan for criollo leadership in 1810, Hidalgo called for popular revolt and the arming of the populace, a battle cry that led to the failed insurgency period.[42]

Over the next ten years, the bloody struggle for the control of New Spain witnessed the rise and fall of a number of viceroys and revolutionary leaders. Though the Crown's authority was briefly reestablished by Viceroy Félix Celleja in 1816,[43] Vicente Guerrero and other revolutionaries remained active until 1820, when Spain's General Agustín de Iturbide finally united with them in the cause for independence. The Spanish Crown, weakened by Napoleon's invasions at home and its failure to command colonial armies abroad, eventually recognized Mexico in September of 1821.

The impact of Mexican independence upon pre-Columbian scholarship was immediate. Within the country's first year of nationhood, British publisher Henry

1.18. *Above:* CASTAÑEDA, TEMPLE OF THE SUN, PALENQUE (Henri Baradère, *Antiquités Mexicaines, 3d expedition,* plate 34: 1844).
    Below: TEMPLE OF THE SUN, PALENQUE, SHOWING ROOF COMB (author's photo).

Berthoud published Del Río's report under the title *Description of the Ruins of an Ancient City Discovered near Palenque*. Although the reprinted document was more than three decades old, it created a considerable stir among London antiquarians, most of whom had never heard of Palenque.[44] The document's journey from the royal archives in Guatemala to Berthoud is a mysterious one, for although he asserted that the report was legitimately "liberated" during the revolution, the papers had in fact been stolen from the newly formed federation government.[45] Unmoved by Mexican demands for the report's return, Berthoud justified this act of scholarly espionage as a strike for intellectual disclosure — explaining in his introduction that "these sheets were rescued from that oblivion to which they had been so long assigned."[46] With Berthoud's publication of this report, open season had been declared on the archives of former New Spain.

Despite Berthoud's claims, the final appearance of Del Río's report bore little resemblance to the original document. Not only were his plates reengraved by Jean-Frédéric de Waldeck, soon to become an explorer in his own right, but the number of images was sharply reduced and the report's content somewhat modified as well.[47] To enlarge the twenty-one-page report for publication, Berthoud added a lengthy introduction and appended a treatise of highly questionable scholarship, entitled "Teatro Critico Americano, or A Critical Investigation and Research into the History of the Americans," written by Dr. Félix Cabrera. With the inclusion of this essay, Berthoud's volume swelled to nearly a hundred pages, reducing Del Río's relatively brief text to the position of prologue.

Cabrera, an Italian living in Guatemala City, had used the writings of Del Río and Fray Ramón Ordóñez, the priest who had initiated the first Palenque investigation in 1773, as the basis for his essay. Proposing a wildly convoluted theory of trans-Atlantic contact, his work cast Del Río's classical speculations in a relatively conservative light. In his conflation of historical, biblical, and Greek mythological timelines, Cabrera alternately asserted that America's first settlers derived from Mount Hebron or Mount Olympus.[48] Even given their unfamiliarity with ancient Mesoamerican history, many of Cabrera's readers perceived when the boundary between fact and fiction had been crossed. As a contemporary reviewer noted, the volume combined "ingenious perceptions . . . mixed with the most problematic assertions."[49]

Soon after the publication of Del Río's expedition, Dupaix's papers met with a similar fate. Extracted from Mexico City's Cabinet of Natural History in an equally mysterious manner, a copy of the manuscript found its way to the collection of Frenchman François Latour-Allard.[50] From this Parisian collection, the document eventually fell into the hands of Englishman Edward King, Lord Kingsborough, who included the reports within his nine-volume work *Antiquities of Mexico*. Appearing between 1830 and 1848, this series published all known materials relating to ancient Mexico, including the Dresden, Mendoza, and Telleriano-Remensis Codices, the Florentine Codex of the sixteenth-century Franciscan friar Bernardino de Sahagún, selections from Humboldt's *Picturesque Atlas*, and a host of essays by King and his intellectual coterie.

The scholarly chapters in King's volumes supported his belief that ancient Mexican civilization had been founded by the lost tribes of Israel. In a two-hundred-page essay in volume 6, entitled "Arguments to Show That the Jews in Early Ages Colonized America," King asserted that the "hooked" noses of the ancient figures depicted at Palenque, for example, indicated their Semitic origin. The author furthermore constructed an elaborate correspondence between Levitical law and Aztec religious practice, drawing a parallel between animal and human sacrifice.[51] In volume 8, King's theories were amplified in an essay by the American scholar James Adair, entitled "On the Descent of the American Indians from the Jews"; proposing that all the "red races" of the Americas had descended from the lost tribes of Israel, Adair united the culture areas of the Americas while still proclaiming their descent from Old World civilization. Amid such mountains of conjectural scholarship, the significance of Dupaix's publication was greatly weakened.

Two years prior to the appearance of King's work, French publisher Henri Baradère had received permission from the Mexican government to print an authorized copy of Dupaix's expeditions. Appearing in 1834 under the title *Antiquités Mexicaines*, Baradère's version remained more textually and pictorially faithful to the original document; like King and Berthoud before him, however, Baradère used the text as a springboard for the reflections of scholars with no firsthand knowledge of the monuments. Included in the massive two-volume work were essays such as Alexandre Lenoir's "Comparisons of the Ancient Monuments of Mexico with Those of Egypt, India, and the Rest of the Ancient World" and American scholar David Bailie Warden's "Research on the Antiquities of North and South America, and on the Primitive Populations of the Two Continents."

These treatises bore little connection to Dupaix's work, yet the inclusion of Warden's essay cast Dupaix's expeditions in a new light. Because Warden perceived a cultural connection between the antiquities of North, Central, and South

America, he used the Dupaix expedition to support his theory of a unified, pan-American antiquity. In introducing Warden's essay, Baradère spoke in celebratory terms of "the reunion, on American soil," of the monuments of ancient Mexico with the earthworks and ancient artifacts of North America — a "reunion" that would shape the writings of subsequent American explorers and eventually the doctrines of the Mormon Church.[52]

Following the appearance of King's and Baradère's works, Jean-Frédéric Maximilien de Waldeck, the artist who had reengraved Almendáriz' plates for Berthoud's *Description of the Ruins of an Ancient City*, decided to publish his own account of the ancient monuments. In describing his work on the Del Río report, Waldeck asserted that "from the moment that I saw the pen-and-ink sketches of that work, I doubted that they were faithful and I nourished the secret desire to see them for myself and draw the originals."[53] Waldeck's wish to see the ruins stemmed not only from the desire to record them more accurately, however, but also from his sense that they represented a final archaeological frontier. Calling upon fellow European adventurers, Waldeck exhorted:

> Today, the Orient holds no more secrets for the European intellectual; the cradle of Antique civilization has been explored in every part; archaeology and history have no more to glean from the vast lands of Moses and Jesus Christ. . . . It is time for Europe to fix its attention upon an unknown world, equally rich in scientific treasures and the memories that accompany them.[54]

Embarking for Mexico in 1825, the Frenchman worked as a hydraulic engineer with an English mining company in Michoacán for three years, followed by six years in Mexico City, where he worked as a portraitist and part-time engraver for the new National Museum.[55] In his final two years in Mexico, Waldeck traveled, sketching and painting archaeological sites in Yucatan. The result of this expedition, published in 1838 as *Voyage pittoresque et archéologique dans la province d'Yucatan*, laid the capstone on the scholarship of this period.

Appearing at the critical moment when European exploration was giving way to more organized North American efforts, Waldeck's work provided the first eyewitness views of the ruins since Mexican independence — yet perpetuated the reckless theorizing that had characterized European publications of the 1820s. His illustrations for *Voyage pittoresque* and the much later *Monuments anciens du Méxique* (1866),[56] though technically impressive, often exaggerate, alter, or completely reinvent the monuments he visited. Such distortions further muddied the waters of archaeological scholarship, while illuminating the increasingly strained position of trans-Atlantic contact theory.

Born in Paris in 1768, Waldeck was the first in a long line of colorful Westerners to explore newly independent Mexico. As circumstances suited, he variously claimed British, French, German, and Austrian citizenship — and periodically altered, augmented, or dropped the aristocratic title of "Baron."[57] His personal acquaintance with figures of the French Enlightenment was probably second- or thirdhand at best, yet he boasted a wide acquaintance among the intelligentsia of pre-and postrevolutionary France and named the painter David as his artistic instructor and mentor (the claim is unsubstantiated by David scholarship, yet Waldeck may have worked in the studio of the lesser-known Joseph Vien).[58]

In 1947, Howard Cline disproved the artist's more extravagant assertions, although Waldeck's acquaintance with Enlightenment texts appears to be well founded. Included among his belongings in Mexico, for example, were the fourteen volumes of Voltaire's *Philosophical Dictionary,* as well as Diderot's twenty-eight-volume *Encyclopédie.*[59] Though he characterized himself as more of an artist than a philosopher, Waldeck apparently aspired to the latter — with mixed results.

Aside from his attachment to Enlightenment literature, the most important circumstance shaping Waldeck's work was his exclusion from Napoleon's Egyptian expedition of 1798. Although Waldeck participated in Napoleon's siege of Toulon in 1794 and later claimed to have accompanied the 1798 expedition, his 1832 letter to Edme François Jomard, one of the leaders of the expedition, indicates his absence from this scientific campaign.[60] Waldeck's lifelong fascination with Egyptian archaeology, combined with his disappointment at missing its greatest moment, ultimately manifested itself in his tendency to "Egyptianize" the monuments he encountered in Yucatan.

Though Waldeck avoided making explicit connections between Egyptian and ancient American cultures in his text, his illustrations speak volumes on the subject. In plate 9 of *Voyage pittoresque,* for example, he recasts a figure from the Pyramid of the Magician at Uxmal in a decidedly Egyptian style (fig. 1.19). Crossed-arm figures are known at Uxmal, albeit at smaller scale, yet Waldeck clearly intends his readers to interpret this model's pose, head covering, and mantle as traditional Egyptian motifs. In a telling passage Waldeck cautions future explorers that he alone knows the secret location of this remarkable work; "to protect my treasure from any kind of looting," he explains, "I buried it in a place to which I alone hold the key."[61] Another of Waldeck's Egyptian figures, found at Palenque, apparently

1.19. JEAN-FRÉDÉRIC WALDECK, TEMPLE OF THE MAGICIAN FIGURE,
UXMAL (Jean-Frédéric Waldeck, *Voyage pittoresque*, plate 11: 1838).

met with a similar fate (fig. 1.20). Featuring a pharaonic headdress and the horns
of the Egyptian deity Hathor, the statue was subsequently hidden by Waldeck "to
prevent speculators from the village from learning about it."[62]

Waldeck's most consistent attempt to insinuate a connection between the Old
and New Worlds, however, was his insistence that elephants had once roamed Yucatan. Citing fossilized evidence of their presence in the area, he authoritatively
states that "all conjecture aside, the elephant *did exist* in Mexico [his italics]."[63]
The fossil record was borne out, he claims, by numerous appearances of elephant

1.20. WALDECK, FIGURE FROM PALENQUE. (Jean-Frédéric
Waldeck and Charles-Étienne Brasseur de Bourbourg, *Monuments
anciens du Méxique*, plate 25: 1866).

heads in the ancient art of Yucatan — notably in the "elephant glyphs" that he illustrates from Palenque (fig. 1.21) and in the decorations of ancient architecture in
northern Yucatan. "The symbolic elephant is depicted on [these buildings] at the
rounded corners," Waldeck explains, "its trunk raised in the air on the east side";[64]
these trunklike extensions, typically found at the corners of all Puuc-style buildings (ca. 800–1000 A.D.), are today recognized as a standardized portrait of the
Maya deity Chac.

By "proving" the elephant's presence in North America, Waldeck invited speculation about the direction of their migration. Although readers of *Voyage pittoresque*—and Waldeck himself—may have believed that the connection ran
from Africa to America, later diffusion theorists employed Waldeck's "elephant
thesis" to assert that world culture had originated in the Americas, most notably
G. Elliot Smith, whose treatise *Elephants and Ethnologists* (1924) resurrected and
amplified Waldeck's theories.

The most striking example of trans-Atlantic confusion in Waldeck's work,
and an image that betrays contemporary French artistic sources, is his rendering
of the so-called Pyramid of the Magician at Uxmal (figs. 1.22 and 1.23). Entitled *Le
Pyramide de Kingsborough,* the image honors Waldeck's patron, Lord Kingsborough, who had met Waldeck in London and had subsidized the artist's mission in
Yucatan. Fittingly, Waldeck employs the rhetoric of religious conversion in his description of the work: "You will see that I baptised, in his name, the most beautiful
building in Itzalane."[65]

In artistic terms, Waldeck's double-page illustration of this pyramid is a hom-
age to the large-scale, fantastic works of the eighteenth-century French architect
Étienne-Louis Boullée. Although Waldeck asserts that "one cannot scale [the

1.21.
Above: WALDECK, "ELEPHANT"
GLYPH TAKEN FROM PALENQUE
(Jean-Frédéric Waldeck and Charles-
Étienne Brasseur de Bourbourg,
Monuments anciens du Méxique,
plates 24 and 26: 1866).
Right: PHOTO OF CHAC DEITY
AT THE NUNNERY COMPLEX,
CHICHEN ITZA (author's photo).

1.22. WALDECK, ELEVATION OF *LE PYRAMIDE DE KINGSBOROUGH*, UXMAL
(Jean-Frédéric Waldeck, *Voyage pittoresque*, plate 10: 1838).

1.23. WALDECK, PLAN OF *LE PYRAMIDE DE KINGSBOROUGH*, UXMAL
(Jean-Frédéric Waldeck, *Voyage pittoresque*, plate 9: 1838).

pyramid] even with the aid of the trees and undergrowth that push up through the gaps in the stones," the structure in Waldeck's image appears immaculately pristine — with the exception of the large cavity he had created at its center (an excavation that yielded, he adds, "no important results").[66] Furthermore, Waldeck elongates the building's upper temple, omits its midlevel sanctuary, and translates the pyramid's distinctive, elliptical form as a planar, crisply four-sided structure.[67]

Although the exact scale of the pyramid remains unclear in Waldeck's elevation, the reflections of passing clouds at its base indicate a grandeur of Wagnerian proportions. The result is uncannily similar to Boullée's imaginary renderings of pyramids "in the Egyptian manner" from the 1780s (fig. 1.24), a series with which Waldeck was undoubtedly familiar. In Boullée's works, idealized Egyptian pyramids function as visionary emblems — their impossible size representing the am-

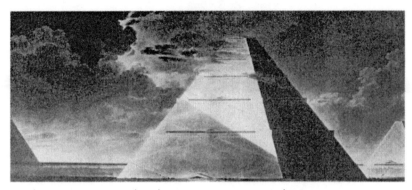

1.24. ÉTIENNE-LOUIS BOULLÉE, *CÉNOTAPHE DANS LE GENRE ÉGYPTIEN* (Bibliotheque
Nationale, Paris).

bitious aspirations of Enlightenment endeavor. Waldeck's *Pyramide de Kingsborough,* by contrast, purports to illustrate a structure existing in reality. By thus re-
alizing the utopian visions of Boullée and surpassing the comparatively pedes-
trian pyramids of the Egyptian campaign, Waldeck neatly compensated for his
exclusion from the pantheon of great Enlightenment artists.

    Though Waldeck makes no definitive statement about trans-Atlantic corre-
spondence in the Americas, asserting only that "the works of Yucatan resemble
those of Egypt,"[68] his book does contain oblique references to an annihilated
group of Mesoamerican culture bearers. Far from asserting indigenous authorship of the ruins, he asserts that the original builders, led by a mysterious figure
named Zamna, were overthrown by their slaves—the ancestors, he says, of the
contemporary Maya.[69] Further confusing the issue, Waldeck proceeds to explain
King's theory that the lost tribes of Israel, supposedly a mixed constituency of
Hebrews and Egyptians, had found their way to American shores. Tracing their
peregrination to Chicomoztoc, the Aztecs' mythological site of origin, he adds
that Palenque's figures belong to "a white race" of "the Arab 'type.'"[70] Though the
ethnic composition of this group remains somewhat ambiguous, Waldeck insists
that the group had originated in Europe and was currently as extinct as the North
American elephant.

    Waldeck supported many of the theories proposed by his contemporaries, yet
the format of his work ultimately departs from that of earlier studies. Despite
earnest attempts to record the monuments in a scientific manner, his text often
gives way to romantic, highly personal soliloquies. In a typical passage, he writes:

    [A]t night, by the light of the moon, . . . these colossal masses, surrounded by a
    solemn silence and half-enveloped shadows, inspire melancholic reveries and trans-

port the thoughts to faraway times when a population with strange customs . . . inhabited the grand city whose debris we now trample with our feet. The memory of heroes from Antique ballads combines with the evocation of a past full of mystery, for it is in this place of lugubrious memory that the bloody drama, consecrated by the poetic tradition, took place.[71]

Although similar passages are found in the work of Dupaix and appear in the later works of Catherwood and Stephens, Waldeck's romanticism differs in its explicit evocation of Old World associations — specifically, the destruction of a civilized group at the hands of barbarians (the "bloody drama" to which he refers is not the Spanish conquest but rather the imagined slave rebellion). Ultimately, Waldeck's hybridization of scientific and romantic strategies proves unsuccessful. As the title of *Voyage pittoresque* suggests, Waldeck's travel narrative is far more concerned with the picturesque, rather than the anthropological or archaeological, legacy of New World civilization.

From the earliest visual accounts of the Mesoamerican past to the recycled and amplified works of the 1830s, this first phase of scholarship demonstrates a consistent faith in Enlightenment methodologies. Emmanuel Kant's charge to his own age, *sapere aude* ("dare to know"),[72] however, proved an impossible task at this stage of Mesoamerican studies. The unhappy marriage of science and conjecture in the works of the 1820s and 1830s not only deprived readers of the authentic pre-Hispanic past but also inspired a general despair that the ruins might never be deciphered. A more complete understanding of the monuments would require not only the jettison of Enlightenment models but also the denial of biblical chronology itself.

The limited audiences and manifold agendas of European publications of this period gave way in the next decade to the best-selling works and clearer nationalist objectives of John Lloyd Stephens and Frederick Catherwood. Adopting a more journalistic approach to their work, these American explorers thrilled readers with firsthand accounts of their discoveries, while providing up-to-date information concerning political and economic developments in Latin America. Most importantly, while Europe had recast Mesoamerica in light of its own antiquities, Americans like Stephens enthusiastically adopted the cause of indigenous authorship — a declaration of cultural independence intended to glorify the United States by historical extension. By midcentury, the explorers from the United States would regard the ancient Mexican past with a xenophobia far exceeding that of Spanish colonial rule.

INCIDENTS OF TRANSCRIPTION

'AMERICAN' ANTIQUITY IN THE WORK

OF STEPHENS AND CATHERWOOD

> We see a line of ancient works, reaching from the south
> side of Lake Ontario to the banks of the Mississippi,
> through the upper parts of Texas, around the Mexican
> Gulf, quite into Mexico: increasing in number, and
> improving in every respect as we have followed them.
>
> —AMERICAN ANTIQUARIAN SOCIETY (1820)

EUROPEAN SCHOLARS assumed that this new period of archaeological investigation would mirror their ancestors' territorial conquests in sixteenth-century America. Within a decade of Mexican independence, however, this second
phase of exploration was overtaken by John Lloyd Stephens, an American travel
writer from New York who sought to exclude Europe from either exploring its
former colonial empires or perpetuating historical links to the area's rich archaeological legacy. Stephens' cultural enforcement of the newly established Monroe
Doctrine, combined with his interpretation of the United States' "manifest destiny" on the North American continent, constituted a double-barreled campaign
to claim the Mesoamerican past as the United States' cultural inheritance.

Between 1839 and 1843, Stephens collaborated with the British artist Frederick
Catherwood to produce two double-volume sets of archaeological travel accounts, entitled *Incidents of Travel in Central America, Chiapas, and Yucatan* (1841)
and *Incidents of Travel in Yucatan* (1843).[1] Departing from the *Encyclopédie-*

derived format of earlier Mesoamerican archaeological surveys, these works consisted of a running text punctuated by finely detailed steel engravings. The writing was conversational in tone, the images startlingly precise, and the production costs kept so low that the works fell within the reach of the middle-class reading public. For the first time since Spain's expulsion from the region, accurate information concerning Mexico's pre-Columbian past was available to Americans in a readable and inexpensive format.

In composing these archaeological travel narratives, Stephens consciously distanced himself from the dubious scholarship that had characterized works of the previous generation. Indeed, for one reviewer of *Incidents of Travel in Central America, Chiapas, and Yucatan,* the work's apparent lack of a theoretical system represented its greatest virtue. In response to scholarly complaints that Stephens "presented no clear method of philosophy," the critic demanded to know "what under the sun has ... Stephens to do with philosophy, or profundity, or deductive reflection, or any other part of the learned lumber with which erudite persons ... bemuddle their own brains and set those of their readers to aching?"[2]

Stephens' avoidance of historical philosophy did not indicate, however, a lack of "deductive reflection" in his work. To the contrary, he geared his project toward dismantling European theories that proposed the monuments' Old World origin and prehistoric date of construction. Through persuasive, object-driven arguments and Catherwood's carefully composed images, Stephens not only proposed an indigenous authorship and more recent date for the ruins but also harnessed these two assumptions to imply the United States' vested interest in the region.

Despite the increased scholarly interest in ancient Mesoamerica, the works of von Humboldt, Del Río, Dupaix, and Waldeck had remained relatively unknown to North Americans in the 1820s and 1830s. Berthoud's 1822 repackaging of the Del Río expedition, for example, had failed to find a general audience even in London, while the enormous cost of Humboldt's, King's, Baradère's, and Waldeck's works effectively prohibited their purchase by more than a handful of wealthy European antiquarians.[3] Produced in multivolume editions with hand-colored lithographs, the works often commanded prices of several hundred dollars per volume—resulting not only in their limited circulation but also in some cases the financial ruin of their publishers (the enormous production costs of the nine-volume *Antiquities of Mexico,* for example, had landed King in debtor's prison). As late as 1840 the *North American Review* asserted that "only one copy [of Baradère's work] ... has reached this country," noting three years later that only three or four copies of Waldeck's "costly and rare" *Voyage pittoresque* had found their way across the Atlantic.[4] By the time of Stephens and Catherwood's first trip to Central America in 1839, then, the subject of Mesoamerican archaeology effectively remained, in the words of the *North American Review* critic, "a sealed book" to the United States' reading public.

Despite their ignorance of ancient Mesoamerica, North American antiquarians in the early 1800s had developed a keen interest in the remains discovered within the United States' newly defined borders. Following the Louisiana Purchase of 1803, settlers pouring into the Ohio and Mississippi River Valleys had discovered the earthworks, fortifications, and burial mounds of the region's ancient inhabitants. These earthworks, collectively referred to as products of the Moundbuilder cultures, belonged to a variety of different ethnic groups and had been constructed in various forms across several centuries. A rich new source for archaeological investigation, these discoveries led in turn to the 1812 founding of the American Antiquarian Society in Worcester, Massachusetts. Unlike earlier, more broadly focused antiquarian groups in the United States, such as Philadelphia's American Philosophical Society, the Worcester association restricted its investigations to the United States, claiming three distinct areas of inquiry: the ancient mounds and earthworks of the western territories, artifacts related to contemporary native North Americans, and the remains of early colonial settlements.

Like the United States itself, the American Antiquarian Society soon outgrew its originally prescribed territory. By the time of Isaac Goodwin's address to his fellow society members in 1820, the group's mission had expanded "to preserve ... every thing illustrative of the ancient history of this *continent* [my italics]," a pursuit that was essentially "founded in individual patriotism."[5] Goodwin's speech indicates not only that North Americans' local archaeological interests had overstepped the country's political boundaries but also that the study of the continent's ancient past implied a national duty.

The chauvinistic tone of the American Antiquarian Society's mission highlights the United States' sense of cultural rootlessness in this period. In the same year as Goodwin's address, an American writer mourned that "the country ... possesses no architectural ruins, no statues, sculptures, and inscriptions, like those of the Old World," describing North America as "destitute ... of monuments of art, and of former grandeur."[6] Given the enormous advances that had taken

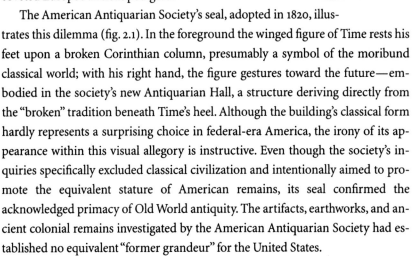

2.1. AMERICAN ANTIQUARIAN SOCIETY SEAL (*Annals of the American Antiquarian Society* 1: 1813–1854).

place in Old World archaeology over the preceding century—including the rediscovery of Pompeii and Herculaneum and, more recently, the massive Egyptian campaign led by Napoleon—North Americans were keenly aware of their region's archaeological inferiority. Despite their professed desire for cultural independence, Americans coveted Europe's ancient pedigree.

The American Antiquarian Society's seal, adopted in 1820, illustrates this dilemma (fig. 2.1). In the foreground the winged figure of Time rests his feet upon a broken Corinthian column, presumably a symbol of the moribund classical world; with his right hand, the figure gestures toward the future—embodied in the society's new Antiquarian Hall, a structure deriving directly from the "broken" tradition beneath Time's heel. Although the building's classical form hardly represents a surprising choice in federal-era America, the irony of its appearance within this visual allegory is instructive. Even though the society's inquiries specifically excluded classical civilization and intentionally aimed to promote the equivalent stature of American remains, its seal confirmed the acknowledged primacy of Old World antiquity. The artifacts, earthworks, and ancient colonial remains investigated by the American Antiquarian Society had established no equivalent "former grandeur" for the United States.

North Americans initially failed to include the ancient monuments of Mexico, Yucatan, and Central America within their national mythology, but the criollos of New Spain had successfully demonstrated that the Mesoamerican past could be harnessed to serve nationalist ends. In the twilight of Spanish rule, criollo scholars had seized upon the antiquities of Mesoamerica as a point of cultural distinction from their Spanish countrymen. Perceiving themselves as Mexicans rather than Spaniards, the criollos rejected Spain's vilification of preconquest civilizations, embracing a (misplaced) identification with native populations.[7]

In championing the region's indigenous past, the criollo agenda substituted a soil-based identification for the culture to which the group was ethnically or historically related. With the birth of Mexican nationhood, however, the criollos' newly elevated status obviated their need to emphasize cultural distinction from Spain. As these leaders of post-independence society distanced themselves from indigenous groups, past and present, antiquarians in the United States adopted their model of geographical identification, erroneously linking the ancient remains of its western territories with those of Mexico.

In tracing the path of the ancient earthworks found in the western valleys of the United States, the American Antiquarian Society concluded:

> We see a line of ancient works, reaching from the south side of Lake Ontario to the banks of the Mississippi, through the upper parts of Texas, around the Mexican Gulf, quite into Mexico: increasing in number, and improving in every respect as we have followed them; and showing the increased numbers and improved condition of their authors, as they migrated toward the country where they finally settled.[8]

By conflating the remains of the North American Moundbuilder cultures with those monuments found south of the U.S. border, the society extended its territorial as well as its typological range of inquiry. Moreover, by insisting upon a north-to-south migration route, they confirmed the Mesoamerican works' genesis within U.S. borders. In Mexico, this passage declares, "our works are continued." Although the society's conclusions remained impressionistic in this period, its argument would take a far more persuasive cast in the subsequent work of Stephens and Catherwood.

The pair's first journey to Latin America spanned just over nine months, lasting from October 3, 1839, to July 31, 1840. Sailing from New York, the writer and the artist began their journey in British Honduras (present-day Belize), followed by an exhaustive tour of the former Central American Federation, including the countries of Guatemala, Honduras, Nicaragua, El Salvador, and Costa Rica. From this region, the two headed northward to Chiapas and Yucatan, territories that had recently achieved quasi-independence from Mexico.[9] Over the course of this journey, the two visited and surveyed the four ancient cities of Copan, Quirigua, Palenque, and Uxmal; although none of these sites constituted new discoveries, Stephens and Catherwood's investigations there represented, in the words of Michael Coe, "a quantum jump from anything that had been heretofore published on the antiquities of the New World."[10]

Stephens' biographer Victor Van Hagen and other twentieth-century historians have often characterized Stephens' work as a heroic effort to correct the inaccuracies of earlier explorers' accounts, yet his primary motive for undertaking this first journey was more financial than scientific. It is true that his interest in the ruins had sprung from his introduction to the works of von Humboldt, Del Río, Dupaix, and Waldeck, yet in 1839 Stephens hardly considered himself an archaeologist.[11] By this date, Stephens' only qualification as an explorer rested upon his two previous travel accounts, *Incidents of Travel in Egypt, Arabia Petraea, and the Holy Land* (1837) and *Incidents of Travel in Greece, Turkey, Russia, and Poland* (1838). Written as tourist guides, these popular works aimed "to give a narrative of everyday incidents that occur to a traveler," rather than to provide archaeological or historical information. In his introduction to the first work, in fact, Stephens specifically declares a lack of interest in these areas, explaining that "[the author] has presented things as they struck his mind, without perplexing himself with any deep speculations . . . nor has he gone into detail in regard to ruins."[12] Choosing Latin America for his next travel project, Stephens and his New York publishers Harper and Brothers envisioned a similar format, while hoping that the area's mysterious past would yield even greater sales.

Although the promise of profit provided Stephens' primary motivation for undertaking the trip, his journey officially fell under the aegis of the U.S. government itself. Upon the 1839 death of William Leggett, the former U.S. representative to the Central American Federation, Stephens had successfully applied to President Martin Van Buren, a distant acquaintance and fellow New Yorker, for the post (a favor Stephens returned by dedicating his first volume to the president).

During Leggett's tenure the sixteen-year-old Central American Federation had dissolved into civil war, and by the time of Stephens' appointment Guatemala, Costa Rica, and Nicaragua had banded together against the remnants of the federal government maintained by El Salvador, the splinter republic of Quetzaltenango, and federally occupied Honduras.[13] In naming Stephens as special confidential agent to Central America, Secretary of State John Forsyth charged him with finding the region's primary seat of power, establishing its formal diplomatic relationship with the United States, and, most important, securing the ratification of a trade agreement with this new government. Stephens failed to fulfill even one of Forsyth's requirements, yet his position as a U.S. diplomat profoundly shaped the character of his work in the region.

While Stephens' diplomatic appointment provided him with unparalleled access to the closely guarded borders of Central America, it was his newly formed partnership with Catherwood that proved most important to his ultimate success. The artist's credentials were impressive; having served a five-year architectural apprenticeship in London, Catherwood had completed his studies at the Royal Academy, studying under such illustrious figures as John Soane, Henry Fuseli, John Martin, and J. M. W. Turner.[14] Following his formal education,

Catherwood had marketed his drafting and painting skills as a traveling illustrator, specializing in the depiction of archaeological ruins. Between 1821 and 1835, his itinerary had paralleled that of Stephens, including sites in Egypt, Greece, Italy, and the Near East.

Two works from this period demonstrate the development of Catherwood's style as an illustrator. In an 1823 watercolor entitled *View of Mt. Aetna from Tauramania* (fig. 2.2), one can clearly detect the lessons he had learned under the Romantic masters of the Royal Academy. In his bold use of chiaroscuro, his mournful presentation of the backlit ruins, his facility for landscape composition, and his inclusion of "colorful" local inhabitants, Catherwood hints at the dramatic, evocative style that would characterize his later work in Latin America. In another work from this period, a pencil drawing of the Colossus of Memnon at Thebes (fig. 2.3), Catherwood demonstrates his equal facility for painstakingly produced, archaeologically faithful line illustration. The hyperclarity of the image seems nearly photographic, yet his careful illustration of the monument's hieroglyphs conveys information that only an artist's eye could transcribe. Catherwood's work for Stephens ultimately combined the approaches of these two im-

2.2. FREDERICK CATHERWOOD, *VIEW OF MT. AETNA FROM TAURAMANIA* (1823; Hoppin Collection, New York).

2.3. CATHERWOOD, *COLOSSI OF MEMNON (AMEN-HOTEP III) — THEBES* (British Museum).

ages, creating works of unparalleled accuracy that owed a large debt to the Romantic tradition.

Catherwood's early career paralleled Stephens' not only in terms of its itinerary but also in the entrepreneurial cast it eventually assumed. Joining Robert Burford in 1835 as a partner in his Leicester Square Panorama, Catherwood provided the drawings to construct a ten-thousand-square-foot mural of Jerusalem, a 360-degree view of the city that quickly became the enterprise's greatest attraction.[15] It

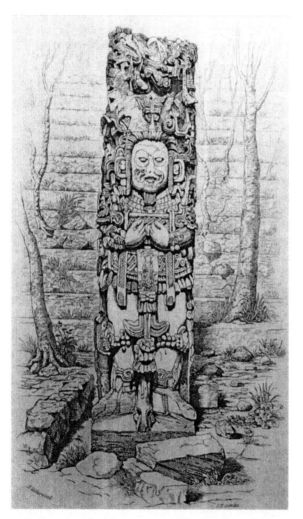

2.4. *Left:* CATHERWOOD, STELE F AT COPAN (John Lloyd Stephens, *Incidents of Travel in Central America, Chiapas, and Yucatan,* vol. 1: 1841). *Right:* EARLY TWENTIETH-CENTURY PHOTOGRAPH OF STELE F, COPAN (J.-P. Courau).

was here, in fact, that Stephens and Catherwood met in 1835. Attending one of Catherwood's lectures at the panorama that year, Stephens soon established a professional acquaintance with the artist and created a formal partnership with him three years later. By that time Catherwood had moved to New York City, established an architectural office on Wall Street, and inaugurated the Catherwood Panorama on Broadway. Eventually Catherwood's Panorama, the first of its kind in New York, represented a greater source of income than his architectural practice did.[16] In agreeing to accompany Stephens on his Central American journey in 1839, Catherwood hoped to acquire material for a new panorama attraction; neither he nor Stephens, at this stage, realized how radically the journey would alter the trajectory of their careers.

In their first encounter with an ancient Mesoamerican city, the site of Copan in present-day Honduras, Stephens and Catherwood established the future tenor of all their subsequent explorations. Although the site had been rediscovered five years previously by Captain Juan Galindo, Stephens insisted that he and Catherwood were "entering abruptly upon new ground."[17] Finding the site completely overgrown, the pair were nonetheless electrified by the city's remarkable state of preservation.

Initially, Catherwood's sense of awe reduced him to despair. Stephens relates that, in his first attempt to draw one of the site's many carved stelae, Catherwood found "the designs so intricate and complicated, the subjects so entirely new," that his preliminary drawings "failed to satisfy himself or even me . . . the 'idol' seemed to defy his art."[18] Catherwood eventually overcame his difficulties, using a camera lucida to project the sculpture's image directly onto lined graph paper, where its scale and the complexity of its carving could be captured more easily. Although European artists had been using the camera lucida for centuries, Catherwood was the first to employ this technique in illustrating Mesoamerican ruins (and even continued to use this tool on his second journey to Yucatan, when he and Stephens had also brought a daguerreotype camera with them). A comparison of Catherwood's final engraving with a modern photograph of the same monument, Stele F at Copan, demonstrates his ultimate success (fig. 2.4). Not only does Catherwood convey the depth and complexity of the original work, but he also faithfully records the stele's exact state of preservation. Stephens' accompanying descriptions and measurements of the stele, ruined pyramids, and extensive terraces at Copan demonstrate his equally painstaking, faithfully rendered style of observation.

Copan not only marked the beginning of Stephens and Catherwood's re-markably accurate archaeological treatments, but it was also here that Stephens initiated the nationalist agenda of his work. Within twenty-four hours of his ar-rival at the site, Stephens announced a bold plan:

> All day I had been brooding over the title-deeds of Don José Maria, and suggested to Mr. Catherwood "an operation." (Hide your heads, ye speculators in up-town lots!) To buy Copan! remove the monuments of a by-gone people from the deso-late region in which they were buried, set them up in "the great commercial empo-rium" [New York City], and found an institution to be the nucleus of a great na-tional museum of American antiquities![19]

Over the course of the next week, Stephens' negotiations with Don José Maria reached a crescendo in which Stephens, despairing at the man's reluctance to sell, resorted to his own authority as a U.S. diplomat. "For a finale," Stephens relates, "I opened my trunk and put on a diplomatic coat with a profusion of large eagle buttons. . . . Don José Maria could not withstand the buttons on my coat."[20] In tri-umph, Stephens boasted that "the reader is perhaps curious to know how old cities sell in Central America. Like other articles of trade, they are regulated by the quantity in market, and at that time were dull of sale. I paid fifty dollars for Copan."[21]

The transaction Stephens describes involved more than his desire for exotic real estate. First, in announcing his plan to form a national museum of American antiquities, Stephens implied ambitions of a far greater magnitude than his initial goal to write a travel journal. Second, Stephens negotiated the purchase by claim-ing to represent the U.S. government itself; though his diplomatic display was a sham, his act nonetheless assumed the tone of a governmental intervention. Third, by characterizing the site as the product of a "by-gone people" in a "deso-late region," Stephens divorced the site from any connection to viable local cul-ture. Finally, by casually referring to this ancient Mesoamerican site as an "article of trade," Stephens provided a chilling forecast of his subsequent operations in the region. That Stephens' action escaped State Department censure, even after this passage had become widely read, indicates at least a sin of omission on the part of the United States (despite Stephens' utter failure as a diplomat, he was of-fered the position of U.S. consul to Mexico five years later).

In his visits to Quirigua, Palenque, and Uxmal, Stephens similarly attempted the purchase of each site. At Quirigua, as at Uxmal, his first consideration after ex-ploring the area concerned the site's availability for removal. "Besides their entire newness and immense interest as an unexplored field of antiquarian research," he related, "the monuments were but a mile from the river, the ground was level to the bank, and the river was navigable; the city might be transported bodily and set up in New-York."[22] Despite protracted negotiations with the heirs to the property, the Payes brothers, Stephens proved unable to arrive at an agreeable price. Here, the ruins were hardly "dull of sale."

Undaunted, Stephens attempted the purchase of Palenque, enlisting the aid of Charles Russell, the U.S. consul to Mexico at Laguna, as a proxy. For Stephens to purchase real estate connected with the village of Palenque, he was faced with either marrying a Palencana (a prospect he rejected only after reviewing a lineup of possible spouses) or arranging the purchase through someone married to a national. Russell, whose Castilian-born wife held Mexican citizenship, qualified as proxy—yet the consul would offer only financial support to Stephens' ultimately failed transaction.[23] At Uxmal, Stephens made another unsuccessful offer to the site's owner but, cutting his losses, was able to remove some of the site's more interesting works without offering compensation. In speaking of a sculpted door lintel at Uxmal, for example, Stephens related that he "immediately determined to secure this mystical beam" without its owner's knowledge. Increasingly, Stephens' foiled attempts to purchase sites and objects led to this kind of outright theft.[24]

Stephens' compulsion to own the sites he explored not only indicated personal ambition but also reflected the United States' dramatic territorial expansions of the early nineteenth century. From Stephens' vantage point, the most important of these had been the annexation of Spanish Florida through the Adams-Onis Treaty of 1819. The relatively new territory comprised only a fraction of the land acquired in the Louisiana Purchase, yet it represented the United States' first toehold in the formerly jealously guarded territory of Spanish America. The Adams-Onis Treaty had resulted in the first recognition of a border between the United States and the area that would become the Republic of Mexico, yet that boundary remained fluid in the minds of most North Americans. For Stephens, no political considerations barred his acquisition of land that lay just a few hundred sea miles from Florida.

Within four years of the U.S. annexation of Spanish Florida, President James Monroe had established new foreign policy that would directly shape Stephens' assumption of U.S. rights in Mesoamerican archaeology. Primarily a reaction to the Latin American revolutions of the 1820s, the Monroe Doctrine, as it came to be known, proclaimed that "the American continents ... are henceforth not to be considered as subjects for future colonization by any European powers."[25] Invoking the spirit of this policy, Stephens extended its authority to exclude Europeans from purchasing or collecting Mesoamerican sites or artifacts. In contemplating the casting and removal of Copan's monuments, Stephens reasoned:

> The casts of the Parthenon are regarded as precious memorials in the British Museum, and casts of Copan would be the same in New-York. . . . Very soon their existence would become known and their value appreciated, and the friends of science and the arts in Europe would get possession of them. They belonged of *right* [my italics] to us, and . . . I resolved that ours they should be.[26]

In his attempts to acquire the site of Quirigua, where negotiations had collapsed because of French interference, Stephens had had his first encounter with European competition. Upon hearing that Stephens expected to pay "a few thousand dollars" for the site, the French consul general had advised the owners of the property that the French government had paid several hundred thousand dollars for removing the obelisks of Luxor—thereby driving Quirigua's price beyond Stephens' budget.[27] Although the Frenchman expressed no intention of buying the ruins for France, Stephens suspected unfair foreign competition.

Determined to prevent further foreign meddling, Stephens broadly declared his desire that

> England and France, whose formidable competition has already been set up, . . . will respect the rights of nations and discovery, and leave the field of American antiquities to us; that they will not deprive a destitute country of its only chance of contributing to the cause of science, but rather encourage it in the work of bringing together, from remote and almost inaccessible places, and retaining on its own soil, the architectural remains of its aboriginal inhabitants.[28]

As this passage illustrates, Stephens' insistence upon the U.S. right to Mesoamerican antiquities was predicated upon the country's continental contiguity with Latin America. In Stephens' eyes, the English and French were similarly justified in acquiring the antiquities of Old World civilizations; the Europeans' allowance to collect on American soil, however, had been forfeited along with their rights to colonize the area.

Catherwood's images were essential to Stephens' agenda of acquisition. Because of their exacting archaeological accuracy, Stephens insisted that Catherwood's "copies" represented facsimiles rather than mere illustrations. "Except for the stones themselves," he wrote, "the reader cannot have better materials for speculation."[29] The artist's tireless efforts to clear, measure, and "copy" the sites, often undertaken when Stephens' diplomatic duties required his presence elsewhere, constituted anticipatory acts of ownership. Following Catherwood's surveying exercises, offers of cash were never long in materializing.

In addition to his extensive drawing and mapping activities, Catherwood instructed Henry Pawling, an American acquaintance he and Stephens had made in Laguna, to carry out the plaster casting of Palenque's principal monuments.[30] In a rare instance of local protest, three citizens from the village of Palenque eventually halted the project, confiscating the casts already made and demanding compensation for the right to undertake further casting. In writing to Consul Russell, they argued:

> The said moulds are so much like the originals, that at first sight it may be observed that they may be taken, surely, for second originals, and no doubt they may serve to mould after them as many copies as may be wished, and in this manner they may supply the world with these precious things without a six cents' piece expense.[31]

As the authors of the letter fully understood, Catherwood's mission to replicate the ruins mirrored Stephens' attempts to physically acquire the works.

Rather than chastening Stephens, the Palencanos' request for compensation offended his sense of proprietary rights. Citing the citizens' letter in full, Stephens expressed his "hopes that the Government of Mexico will not only release the casts, but . . . will enrich her neighbors of the North with the knowledge of the many other curious remains scattered throughout her country."[32] Stephens' misplaced optimism in this passage logically derived from his carefully constructed portrayal of Latin America, a region, in his mind, so pliable that it would enthusiastically participate in its own cultural dismantling.

Rationalizing his purchase of Mesoamerican monuments, Stephens situated the works within an archaeological continuum that originated inside the borders of the United States. Echoing the conclusions of the American Antiquarian Society, Stephens linked the western mounds of the United States with the monumental remains of Latin America, broadly ascribing the authorship of Copan's ruins to "the people who once occupied the Continent of America"; in this same passage, Stephens spoke of "the opening of forests and the discovery of tumuli or mounds" in Ohio, Mississippi, and Kentucky, claiming that "the same evidences continue in Texas, and in Mexico they assume a still more definite form."[33]

Though scrupulous in maintaining distinctions among Mexico, Central America, and Yucatan in matters of political organization, Stephens promoted an intentional ambiguity in the modifier he used for ancient works he encountered in these regions, universally referring to them as simply "American." In denying the works' geographical specificity, Stephens' label implicitly linked them with the United States; for although eighteenth-century and early nineteenth-century historians had used the term "America" to describe the North American continent generally, including Mexico (in William Robertson's *History of America* [1788], for instance, only two of its ten chapters concern settlements in the area later known as the United States), the term had more recently evolved as a synonym for the United States.

By Stephens' own definition, the residents of Latin America rightfully belonged to the great family of "continental America." In practice, however, Stephens' references to the North American continent were most often linked with phrases such as "*our* country" or "*our* continent [my italics]," confirming for his readers the territorial primacy of the United States. To what continent, then, did the southern populations belong? For Stephens, this was a moot question. Upon visiting a semi-demolished colonial church at the start of his first journey to Latin America, he related that the ruin "gave evidence of a retrograding and expiring people."[34] Subsequently and repeatedly, Stephens intimated that Central Americans stood on the brink of cultural annihilation — from civil war, the collapse of colonial administration, poverty, and disease. Characterizing the Latin Americans as a withering branch of the American family tree, then, Stephens effectively eliminated them from the continent's archaeological inheritance.

In the 1854 edition of *Incidents of Travel in Central America,* Catherwood confirmed Stephens' message of doom by including his image of the previously mentioned church (fig. 2.5). Presenting the structure in a moonlit landscape with a glowering mountain backdrop, Catherwood creates a mournful effect that recalls his image of the Tauramanian ruins (see fig. 2.2). In both works, the artist exploits strong backlighting as a romantic metaphor for cultural expiration; in the Central American image he even anthropomorphizes the desolate structure, transforming its side windows into pairs of unblinking, nocturnal eyes. Completing the scene of historical decay, Catherwood includes three foreground figures dressed in the costume of Spanish conquistadors — an anachronistic element that consigns the entire scene to the past. Catherwood's image not only amplified

2.5. CATHERWOOD, RUINED CHURCH IN HONDURAS (John Lloyd Stephens, *Incidents of Travel in Central America, Chiapas, and Yucatan*, vol. 1: 1841).

Stephens' pessimism but also, as the opening illustration of the 1854 edition, underscored the pair's "salvation" efforts in the region.

Having reduced Latin Americans' ownership of the ruins to a temporary custodianship, Stephens sought to prove their neglect of even this responsibility, citing local disregard for, or ignorance of, the ancient monuments. In describing the city of Copan, he compared the site to a ghost ship set adrift in an ocean of trees, guarded only by the monkeys living in the surrounding forest; pointedly, he indicated that his host, Don Gregorio, had never visited the ruins until Stephens' guided tour of the newly purchased site.[35] Noting similar instances of local unfamiliarity with other sites, Stephens equated the regional absence of "antiquarian feeling" with the "illiterate and ignorant" attitude of the conquistadors, who, "eager in pursuit of gold, were blind to everything else."[36]

Catherwood's striking images of overgrown archaeological sites underscored this theme of neglect. In his illustration of the Temple of the Inscriptions at Palenque (fig. 2.6), for example, his composition highlights the choking grip of the forest that surrounds the structure. While nature is cast as the villain here, the Spaniards and the Mexicans are seen as accessories to this process of destruction; "in that country," Stephens explained in the accompanying text, "[the ruins of Palenque] were not appreciated or understood."[37]

Although Stephens' remark was not entirely unfounded — most Palencanos, in fact, seemed to demonstrate very little interest in the ruins — his attempts to purchase and remove portions of the site can hardly be justified on this basis (the Mexican and Yucatec governments, which alternately held the rights to these cultural properties, had restricted the export of any ancient materials since 1827). By emphasizing the building's dramatic arboreal submergence, Catherwood evoked the mythical image of Sleeping Beauty's thorn-rimmed castle. Cursed and ownerless, it awaits the life-giving touch of Stephens, who is depicted on the point of entering the structure. If the site were under his custodianship, Stephens explained, he "would fit up the palace and re-people the old city"; ultimately he contented himself with Catherwood's speculative reconstruction of the temple (fig. 2.7).[38]

On at least two occasions, at Palenque and at Uxmal, Stephens had voiced this desire to "refit" the site's structures and repopulate their cities. It is unclear what Stephens could have meant by such statements. While it is doubtful that he intended to literally revive these abandoned urban centers, he may have envisioned their "repopulation" by tourists, following the sites' removal to the United States. In an age when wealthy U.S. industrialists purchased European castles and monasteries for reconstruction in the United States, Stephens may have envisioned living in a transported Maya city himself — perhaps along the Hudson,

2.6. CATHERWOOD, TEMPLE OF THE INSCRIPTIONS, PALENQUE (John Lloyd Stephens, *Incidents of Travel in Central America, Chiapas, and Yucatan*, vol. 2: 1841).

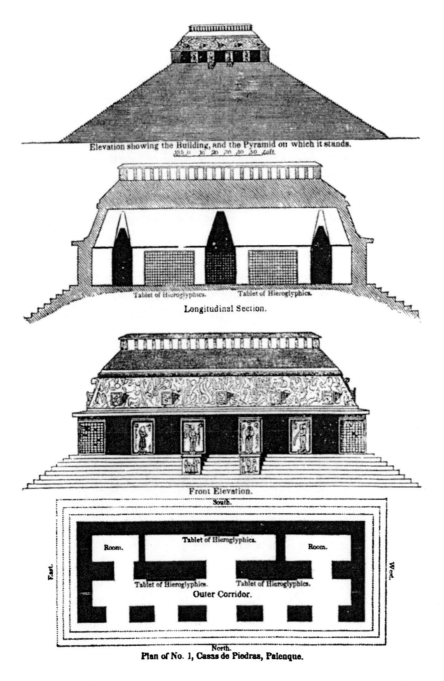

2.7. CATHERWOOD, TEMPLE OF THE INSCRIPTIONS (RECONSTRUCTION), PALENQUE (John Lloyd Stephens, *Incidents of Travel in Central America, Chiapas, and Yucatan*, vol. 2: 1841).

where one of his more spectacular finds, a carved doorjamb from Kabah, eventually formed part of a pre-Columbian garden folly on his friend John Church Cruger's estate.[39]

Stephens' diplomatic search for Central America's seat of government proved as mystifying to him as the character and authorship of the ruins he explored. Repeatedly he spoke of his "fruitless search" and "desperate chase" for a government, whose form — "a glimmering light, shining and disappearing" — constantly eluded him.[40] At the time of Stephens' appointment, the participants in the Central American civil war had polarized into two camps: the federalists, led by Francisco Morazán, and the rebel forces, led by Rafael Carrera. While Stephens met with the federalists at the Guatemalan Assembly, "a scene that carried me back to the dark ages," as well as with Carrera, whom he correctly predicted was "destined to exercise . . . a controlling influence on the affairs of Central America," he found himself unable to commit the U.S. legation to either side.[41] Declaring the government "shattered," "broken up," "in ruins," and "beyond restoration," Stephens officially renounced his appointment in early 1840, returning his official papers to Secretary Forsyth with the terse message: "After diligent search, no government found."[42]

Stephens' "desperate chase" for a government paralleled his equally feverish hunt for ancient Mesoamerican sites; his concluding descriptions of the Central American political situation, in fact, rely heavily upon archaeological language. Whether or not Stephens deliberately constructed this extended metaphor, it nonetheless sheds light on the way he and his readers perceived his dual mission in Central America. Whereas his search for a government proved fruitless, he was successful in locating the ruins; whereas the government was "in ruins" and "beyond restoration," he hoped for the salvation of the area's antiquities. Ultimately, in his conclusion that regional government had ceased to exist, he implicitly declared the archaeological landscape to be politically unaffiliated.[43]

Stephens' circuitous attempts to disinherit Latin America from its ancient past contrast sharply with his more directed campaign to abolish connections between the ancient Old and New Worlds. After his many years of travel in Europe, Egypt, and the Near East, Stephens' firsthand experience with Old World antiquities surpassed that of most of his countrymen—a factor that might have led him, like Del Río, Castañeda, and Waldeck before him, to project the image of classical antiquity onto the Mesoamerican past. Throughout his Latin American travels, however, Stephens' descriptions of the ruins constantly reinforced their individual character; Copan was described as "entirely new," Palenque "perfectly unique," and Uxmal "formed a new order" of architecture.[44]

Stephens' insistence upon the unique character of the ruins reached a crescendo at the close of his second volume, where, in a six-page, point-by-point analysis, he declared the works' cultural independence from Cyclopean, Greek, Roman, Asian, Indian, and Egyptian architecture, ultimately concluding:

> We look elsewhere in vain. They are different from the works of any other known people, of a new order, entirely and absolutely anomalous: they stand alone . . . not derived from the Old World, but originating and growing up here, without models or masters, having a distinct, separate, independent existence; like the plants and fruit of the soil, indigenous.[45]

In the analysis preceding this statement, Stephens founded his arguments exclusively upon observable evidence, wisely avoiding historical debates concerning trans-Atlantic correspondence. In its breadth and visual acuity, Stephens' argument for indigenous authorship represented the most convincing analysis of the ruins to date; not only did it place Mesoamerican scholarship on an independent footing, but it assured his North American readers that their cultural "inheritance" owed no allegiance to Europe. The ruins were as homegrown as "the plants and fruits of the soil" and equally ripe for harvesting.

Stephens' claims for the ruins' cultural independence were tempered, however, by his insistence upon their *equivalence* to the Old World past. Mapping the New World in classical terms, he established a metaphorical, rather than an actual, relationship between the ancient cities of Europe and those of Mesoamerica. He asserted, for example, that Palenque rivaled the majesty of Constantinople; hailed Uxmal as the New World Thebes;[46] and, in another passage, linked Copan with Periclean Athens ("Here, as the sculptor worked," Stephens imagined, "he turned to the theatre of his glory, as the Greek did the Acropolis of Athens, and dreamed of immortal fame").[47] While freeing the monuments from their historical connection to the Old World, Stephens relied upon this metaphorical language to provide a mooring for his readers. Without it, the mystery surrounding the ruins threatened to dim their glory. As Stephens reminded his readers, "but for written records, Egyptian, Grecian, and Roman remains would be as mysterious as the ruins of America"[48] (Stephens also recognized, far ahead of his time, that Maya glyphic inscriptions constituted written historical documents).

The most compelling evidence for the ruins' indigenous authorship was pro-

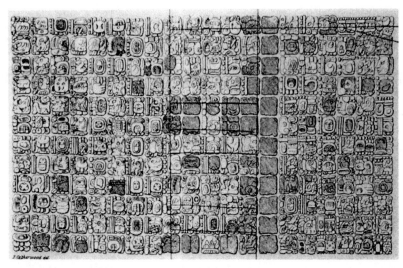

2.8. CATHERWOOD, TABLET FROM THE TEMPLE OF THE INSCRIPTIONS, PALENQUE (John Lloyd Stephens, *Incidents of Travel in Central America, Chiapas, and Yucatan*, vol. 2: 1841).

vided by Catherwood's engravings. Like Stephens, Catherwood never allowed his familiarity with the antiquities of Europe to influence his vision of Mesoamerica. His images, in fact, provide the most accurate visual record of this region prior to the advent of photography. In his illustration of the central glyph panel at Palenque's Temple of the Inscriptions, for example, Catherwood demonstrates his remarkable ability to preserve the character of works whose function and composition he would have found entirely inscrutable (fig. 2.8). Though neither he nor Stephens understood the inscriptions' content, Catherwood nevertheless spent countless hours in the temple, unaided by his camera lucida, transcribing the glyphs by torchlight. Previous explorers, choosing to focus on sculptural and architectural works that held some echo of Old World traditions, had entirely ignored these historically priceless stone tablets.[49]

Like Stephens, Catherwood never directly linked the monuments he encountered with Old World prototypes, yet he often constructed romantic images of the ruins that acted as parallels to the glory of the classical past. His illustration of the arch at Kabah (fig. 2.9), for example, evokes the picturesque classicism of the great Italian printmaker Giovanni Battista Piranesi, whose works Catherwood had studied at the Royal Academy.[50] In comparing the arch at Kabah to Piranesi's rendering of the Arch of Constantine, from the 1748 *Antichità Romane* (fig. 2.10), one can clearly see the lessons Catherwood learned from the Italian master. In

2.9. CATHERWOOD, ARCH AT KABAH (John Lloyd Stephens, *Incidents of Travel in Yucatan,* vol. 1: 1843).

2.10. PIRANESI, *ARCH OF CONSTANTINE* (Giovanni Battista Piranesi, *Antichità Romane*: 1748).

both images the monuments are shown from a low vantage point, looming above the viewer; although Piranesi vastly exaggerates the scale of his subject, he, like Catherwood, faithfully portrays the work's structure and articulation. By positioning the arch at Kabah in a rocky landscape, emphasizing its dilapidation, and highlighting the clinging vegetation that threatened to complete the process of destruction, Catherwood invokes the spirit, if not the heroic scale, of Piranesi's image.

In his accompanying description of this arch, Stephens explicitly connected Catherwood's image to the Roman prototypes so well known in Piranesi's work, intentionally underscoring Catherwood's (and Piranesi's) message of picturesque morbidity. "It is a lonely arch," Stephens explained, "disconnected from every other structure in solitary grandeur. Darkness rests upon its history, but in that desolation and solitude, among the ruins around, it stood like the proud memorial of a Roman triumph."[51] The connection Stephens made here remains, as always, metaphorical. By equating the Mesoamerican and classical pasts, rather than conflating them, he and Catherwood strengthened their case for indigenous authorship while establishing the ruins' equivalent grandeur.

To emphasize the dissonance between past glory and present degradation, both Piranesi and Catherwood often included foreground details that situated the viewer's position within contemporary time. At the foot of the Arch of Constantine, described above, Piranesi illustrates a poorly constructed hut; dwarfed by the looming arch it represents, in architectural terms, the depths to which the Roman Empire eventually fell. In the foreground of the Kabah arch image, for his part, Catherwood includes the figure of a Maya to similar effect. Staring up at the monument, either in mournful reverie or a lack of recognition, the figure served to remind readers that the great city-builders had effectively vanished. In their place stood those whose skills had devolved to the roles of manual laborer and jungle guide.

Although Stephens insisted upon the indigenous authorship of Mesoamerica's ancient cities, he initially considered no direct ethnic connection between contemporary and ancient indigenous populations. Repeatedly he referred to the cities' authors as "a race now lost," and although he provided "conclusive evidence that all the ruined buildings . . . were the work of the same race of people," he cautioned that "who these races were, I do not undertake to say."[52] In one instance at the village of Palenque, Stephens approached a connection between the two groups; remarking upon a local youth's resemblance to the stucco portraits at the ruins, Stephens asserted that "he might have been taken for a lineal descendant of the perished race" but concluded that "the resemblance . . . was perhaps purely accidental."[53]

By the close of his four volumes Stephens eventually acknowledged a link between the ancient and contemporary populations, yet added his reservation that the latter group represented a pale reflection of their ancestral past. Citing similarities between the exhumed bones from an ancient burial site and the skeleton of a contemporary Maya, Stephens announced:

> These crumbling bones declare, as with a voice from the grave, that we cannot go back to any nation of the Old World for the builders of these cities; these are not the works of people who have passed away, and whose history is lost, but of the same great race which, changed, miserable, and degraded, still clings to their ruins.[54]

In a lengthy passage at the end of *Incidents of Travel in Yucatan*, Stephens blamed the "degraded" state of the present indigenous population on the Spanish, whose descendants in Latin America he considered equally corrupt. "In both," Stephens insisted, "all traces of the daring character of their ancestors are entirely gone."[55]

Stephens' eventual connection between ancient and contemporary Maya populations failed to result in his acknowledgment of their proprietary rights in the region. Characterizing the Maya he encountered as weak, intemperate, improvident, profoundly lazy, and ignorant of the rules of private property, he echoed his countrymen's depictions of native North Americans—whose presence also impeded the process of territorial acquisition. In asserting that the ruins' "discovery" by white men trumped indigenous groups' historical connection to the sites, he reflected the spirit that had led to the U.S. Indian Removal Act of 1830. As Lewis Cass had observed in the 1820s, "the Indians are entitled to the employment of all the rights that do not interfere with the obvious designs of Providence."[56]

Stephens' recognition of the contemporary Maya's ancestry grew from his assumption that the ruined cities had been constructed far more recently than formerly believed.[57] Whereas previous explorers had hypothesized a fairly remote antiquity for the sites, establishing their construction in the prehistoric period, Stephens insisted that the cities of Central America, Chiapas, and Yucatan had remained occupied until the time of the Spanish conquest. Declaring the "ancient races" of this region to be contemporaries of the Aztecs, Stephens contradicted written accounts of the conquest. Because nearly all of the Maya sites had been abandoned centuries prior to the Spaniards' arrival, the Europeans had left no records of a living classic Maya city in this region; of all the ancient sites Stephens visited in Yucatan, only one had been inhabited at the time of the Spanish conquest—the fortress-town of Tulum, on the eastern coast of Yucatan. Though this postclassic settlement dates from the same period as the Aztec capital, its modest

scale and awkward construction in no way approach the grandeur of either the
Aztecs' Tenochtitlan or the earlier Maya cities that formed the core of Stephens'
work.

Suspecting colonial historians of willful distortion, Stephens provided his
own evidence for the groups' existence at the time of the conquest. In a convent at
Mérida, for instance, he cited the appearance of a Maya corbelled arch as confirmation of the ancient builders' participation in colonial construction. "There can
be no mistake about the character of this arch," he explained; "it cannot be for a
moment supposed that the Spaniards constructed anything so different from
their known rules of architecture."[58] As further evidence, Stephens pointed to the
absence of deterioration in the carved wooden lintels of Uxmal—a site, he
claimed, that the Maya maintained as a worship center well into the colonial
period.[59]

Stephens' insistence upon the ruins' relatively recent construction is most
clearly demonstrated by his belief in the existence of a still-inhabited "lost city" in
Chiapas. During Stephens and Catherwood's stay at Santa Cruz del Quiché, the
local padre had told them "something that increased our excitement to the highest pitch"; between the Cordilleras mountains and the border of the state of Chiapas, he claimed, lay "a living city, large and populous, occupied by Indians, pre-
cisely in the same state as before the discovery of America."[60] Although he had not
visited the city himself, the padre insisted he had seen "its turrets, white and glit-
tering in the sun" from the summit of the Cordilleras (given the location of the
Padre's sighting, he may well have mistaken the "white turrets" of Tikal's tall pyramids for those of a living city).[61]

Although Stephens expressed a "craving desire to reach the mysterious city,"
he decided to proceed on his appointed journey to Palenque;[62] for the duration of
his travels, however, the vision of this lost city continued to haunt him. Speculat-
ing on the existence of other such cities, he expressed a hope that the ancient
builders' uncorrupted descendants "are still in the land, scattered, perhaps . . . into
wildernesses which have never been penetrated by a white man; living as their fa-
thers did, erecting the same buildings . . . and still carving on tablets of stone in
the same mysterious hieroglyphs."[63]

Had he discovered the padre's lost city, Stephens did not intend to establish
diplomatic relations with its citizens. Outlining a plan of conquest, he proposed
spending two years forming an alliance with the city's neighboring tribes—as
Cortés had done in sixteenth-century Mexico—followed by a military assault on

the town. "Five hundred men could probably march directly to the city," he estimated, adding that "the invasion would be more justifiable than any made by the
Spaniards."[64] In a similarly militaristic tone, he extended this imaginary campaign to include the whole of Yucatan; "I can hardly imagine a higher excitement,"
he said, "than to go through that country with a strong force, time, and means at
command to lay bare the whole region."[65] In both passages Stephens essentially
proposed a reenactment of the Spanish conquest. By seeking cultural treasures,
rather than gold, however, he justified this invasion on scientific grounds.

Stephens' contemporary dating of the ruins sprang from his wish to correct
the historical consequences of the sixteenth-century invasion. Citing the Spanish
conquest as the sole cause for ancient Mesoamerica's demise, he characterized the
colonial period as an anomalous, dormant phase of the region's indigenous culture. "In my opinion," he explained, "teaching might again lift up the Indian,
might impart to him the skill to sculpture stone and carve wood; and if restored
to freedom . . . there might again appear a capacity to originate and construct,
equal to that exhibited in the ruined monuments of his ancestors."[66] For Stephens,
granting the Maya their freedom would not only inspire a renaissance of indigenous craftsmanship, erasing the damage wrought by Spain, but also serve to glorify the enlightened leadership of the United States, the presumed liberator of the
Maya.

Even given his visions of armed conquest, Stephens avoided identifying himself with the unsympathetic character of Cortés; rather, he established himself as
the new Columbus. At the start of *Incidents of Travel in Central America*, Stephens
referred to the "the romance connected with the adventures of Columbus," and
his excitement at "follow[ing] in his track."[67] At the close of his *Incidents of Travel
in Yucatan*, he appropriately ended his narrative before Columbus' grave. "By the
light of a single candle, with heads uncovered," he solemnly wrote, "we stood before the marble slab enclosing the bones of Columbus."[68] In aligning his travels
with the life of Columbus — who, by the 1840s, had been adopted as the ur-figure
of U.S. history — Stephens ensured that his readers would perceive his own archaeological work as a similarly heroic, "victimless" act of discovery. At Copan
and subsequent sites, Stephens claimed to have arrived, like Columbus, on virgin
soil. Whereas Columbus had claimed the New World for territorial expansion,
however, Stephens claimed his discoveries in order to colonize history itself.[69]

In his careful orchestration of its publication, Stephens ensured not only that
Incidents of Travel in Central America would constitute a new benchmark of

American exploration but also that the work would reach as many of his compatriots as possible. Insisting upon an economical octavo format, Stephens avoided the fate of costly European folios like King's and Baradère's; at five dollars a set, Stephens' book fell within the range of most middle-class pocketbooks. Catherwood, for his part, oversaw the production of his illustrations with meticulous care. Providing the engravers with his original watercolors and pencil drawings, he discarded the initial set of wood engravings for their failure to evoke "the true character and expression of the originals," ultimately adopting the finer-detailed medium of steel engraving.[70] Stephens' insistence upon economy and Catherwood's commitment to accuracy combined to astounding success. Appearing on June 25, 1841, more than twenty thousand copies of their two-volume set sold within the first three months of printing.[71]

The unprecedented popularity of *Incidents of Travel in Central America* was equaled by its favorable critical reception. The critic of the *Knickerbocker Magazine,* the first to review the work, exclaimed: "Wonderful! Wonderful! . . . Stephens' volumes will take their stand at once among the foremost achievements of American literature, not only in the estimation of his own country men but in that of the whole enlightened world."[72] Others praised the work for its popular style, the *New York Review* finding Stephens "an uncommonly pleasant writer . . . possessing in an extraordinary degree the power of imparting to his reader the charm of his own disposition."[73]

Ultimately, the work's great success cannot be attributed to its literary merit. By comparison, no other work of American literature, and none of Stephens' previous travel accounts, had ever sold so well. Rather, the power of Stephens and Catherwood's work lay in the way it addressed the contradictory longings of urban, white America of the 1840s—a demographic that romanticized the daring of the pioneer while yearning for the security of historical roots. To this readership, Stephens represented both Daniel Boone and cultural redeemer; as the *Knickerbocker Magazine* critic boasted, "what discoveries of the present century can compare with those laid bare by Stephens?"[74]

The success of Stephens and Catherwood's first volumes determined the two men to undertake a second journey to Mexico in 1841, resulting in the double-volume work *Incidents of Travel in Yucatan* (1843). Although this series echoed the narrative format and nationalist agenda of *Incidents of Travel in Central America,* it featured several important departures from the pair's earlier work. Whereas their first journey had represented a fairly extensive itinerary, the 1841 trip was

entirely conducted within northern Yucatan. Stephens compensated for this territorial circumscription, however, by vastly increasing the number of ruins he and
Catherwood surveyed. Visiting more than forty different sites in less than a year,
Stephens boasted that, following his reinvestigation of Uxmal, "we hade 'done up'
a city a day."[75] This dramatic increase in pace was paralleled by Stephens' greater
sense of urgency on this trip; believing that every ruin tottered on the brink of
destruction, Stephens sharply escalated his campaign of acquisition—hoping,
still, to establish a national museum of American antiquities in New York City.

While Stephens' earlier predictions of Central America's demise seemed no
cause for regret, his belief in the *ruins'* imminent doom proved a continual source
of pain to him. "Time and the elements are hastening them to utter destruction,"
he mourned in the preface to the second series; "within a few generations, great
edifices, their facades covered with sculptural ornaments, already cracked and
yawning, must fall, and become mere shapeless mounds."[76] At nearly every site he
visited on this journey, Stephens repeated the same verdict. Not only did the
monuments seem to be disappearing before his eyes, but their fate appeared to be
preordained. After investigating the structure now known as El Mirador at Sayil,
he asserted that "in a few years it must fall . . . human power cannot save it."[77]

In language as well as spirit, Stephen's dire predictions closely paralleled those
of his countryman George Catlin, whose forecast of the native North Americans'
demise fueled his own travel account, *Letters and Notes on the Manners, Customs,
and Conditions of the North American Indians* (1841).[78] Published in the same year
as *Incidents of Travel in Central America,* Catlin's project also mirrored Stephens'
format. Combining a running narrative with his own engravings, he catalogued
his eight years of travel in the western territories—an area equally unfamiliar to
most of his readers as Yucatan was to Stephens'. As both writer and artist, Catlin's
mission comprised "the production of a literal and graphic delineation . . . of a
race of people who are rapidly passing away from the face of the earth."[79] Like
Stephens, he perceived his subject's extinction as a regrettable yet inevitable
process.

The truth of each man's predictions was, in some measure, borne out. Within
five years of Catlin's visit to the Mandan peoples, for example, the tribe was entirely destroyed by smallpox. Similarly, many of the ruins Stephens visited did, in
fact, crumble into "shapeless mounds"—evidenced by the eventual dilapidation
of the Kabah arch that Catherwood had illustrated in 1841. Catlin's and Stephens'
forecasts of complete destruction, however, proved premature; neither the native

North Americans nor the ruins of Mesoamerica suffered the cataclysmic fate
these men envisioned. By exaggerating their sense of urgency, as sincere as it
might have been, the explorers justified their campaigns of acquisition while
masking their own participation in the destructive process.[80]

Because Catlin's recording work obviated the need to save native groups
themselves, it sometimes led, indirectly, to their actual demise; by comparison,
Stephens' hand in the destruction of Mesoamerican antiquities is even clearer.
Though Stephens is often hailed as the first systematic Mesoamerican archaeologist, his excavation techniques at times involved the irreversible dismantling of
entire structures. Discovering a subterranean passage in a ruined pyramid near
the Cave of Maxcanú in Yucatan, for example, Stephens determined "not to leave
the spot till I had pulled down the whole mound and discovered its secrets."[81]
Prying delicate carvings and paintings from other structures, Stephens either destroyed the objects' context or, in some cases, the works themselves. In a structure
near Kabah, Stephens found painted handprints on the wall "so fresh, with seams
and creases so distinct, that I made several attempts with the machete to get one
off entire," only to watch the plaster wall crumble before his eyes.[82] Most damag-
ing of all, however, were Stephens' exhortations that one of his countrymen, "beginning where we left off . . . will push his investigations much farther."[83] In these
and other instances it was Stephens himself, rather than time and the elements,
hastening the works to their destruction.

Stephens and Catlin shared more than a common rhetoric. In establishing a
national museum of American antiquities, the project Stephens had first envisioned after his arrival at Copan, he had planned to "draw to it Catlin's Indian
Gallery, and every other memorial of the aboriginal races, whose history within
our own borders has already become almost a romance and a fable."[84] Catlin's Indian Gallery, established in 1837, comprised hundreds of the artist's original
paintings as well as his collections of Native American artifacts. Initially a neigh-
bor of the Catherwood Panorama on Broadway, the gallery had grown so popular
that Catlin had taken it on an international tour in 1839. By incorporating Catlin's
gallery within his own project, Stephens hoped not only to gain the artist's ticket-
buying public but also to institutionalize the connection between the indigenous
cultures of the United States and Mesoamerica. Together, the exhibits would have
formed a unified "memorial" to the nation's noble past.

Although the activity of collecting has often been categorized as a means to
construct difference, Stephens' museum project would have reversed this model—

subsuming ethnic and regional distinctions in the interest of a national culture-myth. Susan Stewart has proposed that "in the New World ... antiquarianism centered on the discovery of a radical cultural other, the Native American, whose narrative could not easily be made continuous with either the remote past or the present as constructed by non-Native historians."[85] In the case of Stephens' museum, however, the founder's sole aim was to achieve a continuous—albeit artificial—narrative, in which conflated indigenous groups would serve as the first cultural strata of U.S. cultural history. To construct this narrative, it was imperative that Catlin and Stephens destroy their subjects' original contexts. Whereas Catlin declared the native North Americans' extinction in order to make them "live again upon the canvas," Stephens consigned Mesoamerican antiquity to a similar fate in order to present his writings and collections as its proxy.[86] Disconnecting the works from their source, Catlin and Stephens became their sole custodians—and the museum, their sole context.

Until Stephens could construct his museum, he planned temporarily to display his collections at Catherwood's Panorama. The venue particularly suited Stephens' taste for mixing scholarship and entertainment, echoing his fantastic scheme to remove Uxmal to the banks of the Mississippi and, surrounding it with a high fence, to charge an admission fee.[87] Throughout his second journey, Stephens had shipped all of his collections to the panorama for storage, including carved wooden lintels, architectural fragments, ceramic vessels, and various sculpted decorations. Before the objects could be unpacked, however, disaster struck. On the night of July 31, 1842, hardly a month after Stephens and Catherwood's return, one of the panorama's gaslights ignited the building, destroying all of its contents—including many of Catherwood's original drawings and plans from the second journey. According to the next day's *New York Herald*, the public had not even been aware of the existence of Stephens' "collections of curiosities."[88] Stephens' dream for a national museum lay in ruins.

Of all the objects destroyed in the fire, only one had been illustrated prior to its removal—a carved beam of sapote wood found at Kabah (fig. 2.11). In the interest of saving time, Catherwood had primarily devoted his energies to sketching those monuments that could not be transported; the beam's particularly fine carving, however, had prompted both the artist's and Stephens' particular interest. Whereas "the beam covered with hieroglyphics at Uxmal was faded and worn [an object also destroyed in the fire, of which Catherwood had made no illustration], this was still in excellent preservation; the lines were clear and distinct,"

2.11. CATHERWOOD, WOODEN BEAM FROM KABAH (John Lloyd Stephens, *Incidents of Travel in Yucatan,* vol. 1: 1843).

Stephens explained.[89] The unusual size, condition, and quality of the beam provide a shocking example of the rare works Stephens had removed and, at least indirectly, destroyed.

Stephens accepted no responsibility for the loss of these works, yet his reaction outlines the extent of his negligence:

> Their loss cannot be replaced; for, being the first on the ground, and having all at my choice, I of course had selected only those objects which were most curious and valuable; and if I were to go over the whole ground again, I could not find others equal to them.[90]

Justifying his initial removal of these objects, Stephens had maintained that the only way to give a true idea of their character required their physical presence. In Catherwood's illustration, however, the stolen works are ultimately reduced—like many of Catlin's Native American subjects—to a single memorialized image.[91]

The publication of Stephens and Catherwood's last collaborative work in 1843 coincided with the appearance of another best-seller devoted to the Mesoamerican past, William H. Prescott's *History of the Conquest of Mexico.* Before the appearance of this work, Americans' curiosity concerning the conquest had far outweighed their knowledge of its historical details. Not only did Prescott's enormous erudition satisfy this curiosity, but his powerful narrative style also provided a thrilling read. As one reviewer noted, the book "carries us into a new and strange world, inhabited by a peculiar people, where all the institutions and habits of life are novel. . . . It is a tale of blood and horror."[92] The impact of Prescott's work upon the popular American imagination was immediate and far-reaching. Despite its somewhat higher price, the three-volume work fared nearly as well as Stephens and Catherwood's first set, selling four thousand copies within its first month of printing.[93]

Prescott limited his investigation of this period to literary and historical, rather than archaeological, issues. Explaining this omission in an appendix, Prescott referred his readers to the work of Stephens and Catherwood: "the ground, before so imperfectly known, has now been so diligently explored, that we have all the light which we can reasonably expect to aid us."[94] Prescott's admiration for the team's work, however, did not extend to the format of their volumes. Asserting that "the limited compass of an octavo page" did little justice to the majesty of their subject, he suggested that "the exquisite illustrations of Mr.

Catherwood should be published on a larger scale, like the great works on the subject in France and England."[95]

Prescott's words could not have been better chosen to pique Stephens' sense of chauvinism. Immediately following the publication of *Incidents of Travel in Yucatan*, Stephens resolved to produce a folio edition of Catherwood's work modeled on the European publications of the 1820s. The four-volume edition would not only include hand-colored lithographs of Catherwood's original paintings but would also feature scholarly essays by Stephens, Prescott, and von Humboldt.[96] Conceived as a literary substitute for his failed museum project, the work would establish the Mesoamerican past as a prelude to U.S. history. Significantly, Stephens avoided using the term "Mexican" in his proposed title (as both Baradère's and King's works had done), preferring the more ambiguous *American Antiquities*. By 1844, however, questions of title and format became moot; priced at a hundred dollars per set, the folios would have required at least nine hundred subscribers to cover publication costs. Failing to find even three hundred advance subscribers, Stephens was forced to abandon the scheme.

Within the same year, Catherwood was able to partially salvage Stephens' project by publishing a solo work entitled *Views of Ancient Monuments in Central America, Chiapas, and Yucatan* (1844). Comprising twenty-five color lithographs and a ten-page introductory text, Catherwood's single volume represented a far more modest enterprise than Stephens' proposed *American Antiquities*. In his introduction, Catherwood presents a brief synopsis of Stephens' findings, emphasizing the ruins' indigenous authorship, their recent date of construction, and the Spaniards' supposed role in the destruction of classic Maya cities.[97] In the plates themselves, however, Catherwood departed significantly from his earlier collaborative work. Unlike his engravings for the *Incidents of Travel* series, these lithographs demonstrate a far greater sense of romanticism and a wider inclusion of indigenous "types." In another important departure, Catherwood includes numerous illustrations of Stephens himself—measuring, surveying, and securing ancient works for transport.

In plate 4 of this work, entitled *Broken Idol at Copan* (fig. 2.12), Catherwood demonstrates the full range of his romantic vocabulary. By comparing this image with his earlier engraving of the same monument from *Incidents of Travel in Central America* (fig. 2.13), it is clear that while Catherwood has retained the essential features of the monument, he has completely recontextualized the work. With its reflecting pool and wind-whipped tropical vegetation, the *Views* setting evokes a

2.12. CATHERWOOD, *BROKEN IDOL AT COPAN* (STELE C) (Frederick Catherwood, *Views of Ancient Monuments*, plate 4: 1844).

2.13. CATHERWOOD, ENGRAVING OF STELE C (John Lloyd Stephens, *Incidents of Travel in Central America, Chiapas, and Yucatan*, vol. 1: 1841).

2.14. *Left:* CATHERWOOD, STELE F AT COPAN. *Right:* Detail (Frederick Catherwood, *Views of Ancient Monuments,* plate 3: 1844).

far greater sense of drama than does the benign, grassy clearing of the engraving. Heightening this dramatic effect, Catherwood's lithograph features a flashing bolt of lightning in the background — an element that spotlights the monument while plunging the surrounding jungle into deep shadow. Finally, in order to focus the viewer's attention more completely on the central monument, Catherwood reduces the engraving's left foreground block and right-hand stele to anonymous-looking pieces of stone, while adding a pyramidal structure directly behind the broken stele.

In transforming the mood rather than the archaeological fidelity of his principal object, Catherwood reveals his particular talent as a panorama artist. To create an image worthy of a ticket-buying (or folio-purchasing) audience, he needed to maintain the esoteric character of his subject while appealing to universal emotions. In practice, this double strategy fulfilled Stephens' agenda; while reinforcing the work's indigenous authorship, Catherwood simultaneously highlighted its neglected, ownerless status. Like the shattered statue of the ruler Ozymandias in Percy Shelley's 1817 poem of the same name, this stele's "vast and trunkless legs of stone" lie in an unoccupied wilderness.

2.15. CATHERWOOD, ENGRAVING OF STELE F AT COPAN (John Lloyd Stephens, *Incidents of Travel in Central America, Chiapas, and Yucatan*, vol. 1: 1841).

Not only does Catherwood expand the role of natural settings in *Views of Ancient Monuments*, but he equally enlarges the function of indigenous portraits. Whereas the Maya figures in his *Incidents of Travel* engravings appear faceless and doll-like (if they appear at all), they form an important component of his later lithographs. In his description of plate 3, Stele F at Copan (fig. 2.14), Catherwood explains that the carving of the stele "is so graceful and pleasing, that instead of human sacrifices, it may well be supposed that nothing but fruits and flowers were offered before it."[98] To the left of the stele, Catherwood adds two Maya figures performing the act he has just described. Given the figures' absence from Catherwood's original 1841 engraving (fig. 2.15), their inclusion here represents an intentional parallel to his new text. Portraying them in a worshipful act, he conflates the site's ancient and contemporary inhabitants.

Similarly, in plate 10 (fig. 2.16), Catherwood depicts a group of Maya standing before the House of the Governor at Uxmal. Having just described the building's celebration of snakelike imagery, he illustrates the foreground figures trapping a snake—presumably, just as their ancestors had done centuries before them. In both examples, Catherwood's emphasis on cultural continuity reinforces Stephens' more recent dating for the ruins.

In addition to providing emphatic visual evidence for Stephens' agenda, Catherwood also includes several images of Stephens at work. In these behind-the-scenes glimpses of Stephens' activities, Catherwood glorifies both the explorer's investigative and acquisitive pursuits. In plate 11 (fig. 2.17), a view of the upper gateway of Uxmal's Pyramid of the Magician, Catherwood combines an indigenous genre scene with the retreating figure of Stephens. In this carefully constructed tableau, the Maya figures' oblivious attitude serves as a foil to Stephens' penetrating exploration. Framed in the blackness of an interior doorway, Stephens' covered head serves as the composition's vanishing point; his centrality is not only actual here but also metaphorical.

In plate 16 (fig. 2.18), Catherwood again uses Stephens' figure to anchor his composition. Rather than depicting the process of exploration, however, Catherwood portrays Stephens overseeing the transportation of a stone doorjamb from Kabah.[99] Here again, Maya laborers serve as a foil for Stephens; whereas they show little indication of their burden's value, Stephens looks back with an anxious eye, his gun tucked beneath his arm. This foreground image reinforces Stephens' sense of ownership in a rather obvious way, while Catherwood's panoramic background of Kabah performs the same task in a more subtle manner. Logically,

2.16. *Above:* CATHERWOOD, HOUSE OF THE GOVERNOR, UXMAL.
Below: DETAIL. (Frederick Catherwood, *Views of Ancient Monuments*, plate 10: 1844).

2.17. *Above:* CATHERWOOD, PYRAMID OF THE MAGICIAN, UXMAL.
   Below: DETAIL. (Frederick Catherwood, *Views of Ancient Monuments,* plate 11: 1844).

Stephens and his Maya team should be seen moving away from the site of the jamb's removal. By aiming Stephens' activity directly toward the ruin-dotted landscape, however, Catherwood extends Stephens' ownership from the particular to the general.

When Catherwood's *Views of Ancient Monuments* appeared in 1844, American interests south of the border hinged on political, rather than archaeological issues. In its continuing struggle with Mexico over the annexation of Texas, the United States stood on the brink of its first foreign war.[100] On his last day in office, March 3, 1845, President John Tyler signed the U.S. Congress' resolution to annex Texas, whose 1836 independence had never been formally recognized by Mexico. Following the state's admission to the Union in December, skirmishes erupted between the Mexican and American troops posted along the Rio Grande, leading to the official U.S. declaration of war in May 1846. Mobilizing a large volunteer army, the United States spent the next eighteen months engaged with Mexican forces in their northern territories. By 1847, anxious to resolve the war, President James Polk ordered General Winfield Scott to open his campaign on Mexico City itself;[101] following a heroic struggle by the Mexicans, the United States captured the capital by mid-September, effectively ending the war.

In signing the Treaty of Guadalupe-Hidalgo the following February, Mexico forfeited more than half a million square miles of territory to the United States— comprising the present-day states of Texas, New Mexico, Arizona, California, Utah, and Nevada, as well as portions of Colorado and Wyoming. In the years following this massive annexation, many Americans assumed that the remainder of Mexico would simply be absorbed by the United States as a matter of course. In his 1851 novel, *Moby Dick*, Herman Melville illustrated this contemporary American attitude toward Mexico in a metaphor drawn between whale hunting and colonialism:

> What was America in 1492 but a Loose-Fish [Melville's term for an unclaimed whale]? . . . What was Greece to the Turk? What India to England? What at last will Mexico be to the United States? All Loose-Fish.[102]

The United States' military and territorial successes in the Mexican War had rested squarely on the war's popularity with the American public. The government relied upon citizens not only to serve in its volunteer forces but also to provide the war's financial and ideological underpinnings. The source for this broad support can be directly traced to Americans' romantic interest in Mexico in this

2.18. *Above:* CATHERWOOD, PANORAMIC VIEW OF KABAH.
Below: DETAIL. (Frederick Catherwood, *Views of Ancient Monuments,* plate 16: 1844).

period, a phenomenon almost entirely attributable to the works of Prescott, Stephens, and writers like Frances "Fanny" Calderón de la Barca, who had published her *Life in Mexico* in 1843. Calderón's work, which was nearly as popular among American readers as Stephens' and Prescott's, certainly contributed to Americans' romanticization of Mexico; unlike Stephens and Prescott, however, Calderón restricted her writing to entirely contemporary themes, rather than historical or archaeological ones.

Neither Stephens nor Prescott expressed an openly jingoistic tone in his work (though Stephens had expressed his private support for the conflict during a visit with von Humboldt in the summer of 1847), yet each had helped pave the path to war.[103] In their march from Veracruz to the capital city, for example, General Scott's troops consciously reenacted the Spanish campaign that Prescott had so effectively romanticized; as for the troops in General Stephen Kearney's Army of the West, their knowledge of the Mexican antiquities they encountered increased the appeal of the region's annexation.[104] Perhaps the best example of the Prescott's and Stephens' influence is demonstrated by the opening stanza of the "Marine Hymn," written shortly after the Mexican War. In the first line, American soldiers vow to fight their country's battles "From the halls of Montezuma"—a reference that directly links the United States with Cortés' army, while substituting ancient Mexico for the modern republic.

By the mid-nineteenth century, Stephens' work had become so familiar to American audiences that it had even inspired a parody by Phineas T. Barnum, entitled *Memoir of an Eventful Expedition in Central America*.[105] Based upon Stephens' vision of the "lost city," this elaborate forty-page hoax recorded the adventures of an American writer and Canadian artist who discover a lost city called Iximaya, bringing back living specimens whom Barnum exhibited as the "Aztec Children." On the title page of his pamphlet, Barnum listed Stephens as a contributor to the tale, while he spliced together Catherwood's engravings of the Temple of the Sun and House A at Palenque to frame an internal document, "The History of the Aztec Lilliputians."

Describing the lost city, Barnum exaggerated Stephens' already romanticized vision; housing a population of eighty-five thousand, the city supposedly covered twelve square miles and was surrounded by a sixty-foot wall. While Barnum's readers undoubtedly knew they were being duped—this was, after all, the secret to his success as an entertainer—his hoax was predicated on three important assumptions: his audience's fascination with ancient Mesoamerica, their knowledge

2.19. "THE AZTEC CHILDREN: TWO ACTIVE, SPRIGHTLY, AND INTELLIGENT LITTLE BEINGS" (*New York Republic:* February 1852).

of Stephens' work, and their conflation of Aztec and Maya cultures. Exhibited as living illustrations of this travel-tale parody, the "Aztec Children" Maximo and Bartola so captured public attention that by 1852 they were being hosted at such respectable venues as the New York Society Library—whose advertisements described the pair as "Two Active, Sprightly, and Intelligent Little Beings" representing "absolutely a New and Unique Race of Mankind" (fig. 2.19).[106]

Barnum had found this pair of "Aztecs" in El Salvador in 1849, and given their small stature (both stood just over three feet tall), it is believed they were either dwarves or victims of microcephaly, a disease that would have accounted for their somewhat pointed, "Aztec"-shaped heads.[107] Though American audiences were predisposed to consider Aztecs particularly fierce, Barnum presented Maximo and Bartola as doll-like, friendly creatures. In the words of a contemporary critic, "these children are pocket editions of humanity—bright-eyed, delicate little elves."[108] By emphasizing the Lilliputian scale of the Aztec Children, Barnum not only increased their public appeal but also implied their role as collectible historical artifacts. As with the tale of Iximaya itself, the American public was aware of Barnum's deception; its delight in seeing the Mesoamerican past reduced to "pocket-sized" entertainment, however, demonstrated the extent to which Stephens' work had entered popular culture.

Though Stephens' and Catherwood's contributions to Mesoamerican scholarship are undeniable, their works must be considered within the larger framework of the United States' sense of manifest destiny. By effectively divorcing the ruins' connection to Old World antiquities and proposing a more recent date for their construction, Stephens' writings contributed to the United States' vastly increased sense of cultural and territorial self-confidence in this period. In the following decades American writers would expand Stephens' appropriation of the American past by proposing that world culture itself had originated on the American continent. As the *American Review* remarked after the close of the Mexican War, "from this year we take a new start in national development; one that must, more than ever before, draw the world's history into the stream of ours."[109]

JOSEPH SMITH AND THE ARCHAEOLOGY

OF REVELATION

The veil of obscurity that has been so long wrapt
around these relics of an unknown people, seems to
have been drawn aside, and a new era in the world's
history introduced.

—JOHN TAYLOR, *Latter-day Saints' Millennial Star*
(1851)

We have seen the plates which contain this record . . .
[a]nd it is marvelous in our eyes.

—TESTIMONY OF OLIVER COWDERY,
DAVID WHITMER, AND MARTIN HARRIS,
BOOK OF MORMON (1838)

STEPHENS' ATTEMPTS to conflate the antiquities of Mesoamerica and the
United States paralleled the efforts of his contemporary and fellow New
Yorker Joseph Smith, Jr., the founder of the Church of Jesus Christ of Latter-day
Saints. Smith, however, proposed both a historical and a *spiritual* alignment between the two archaeological traditions. The recipient of angelic visitations and
heavenly visions throughout the 1820s, Smith founded his religious movement in
1830 following the discovery of a divinely revealed account telling of ancient Israelite communities who had once flourished in the Americas. Publishing this sacred text as the Book of Mormon in 1830, Smith confirmed the document's historical validity by crediting its presumed authors with the construction of the
ancient cities and earthworks found throughout North and Central America.

Although Stephens lent no credence to Smith's revelations, he recognized the boldness of Smith's assertions in the first volume of his *Incidents of Travel in Central America, Chiapas and Yucatan*. Citing the "volumes without number that have been written about the first peopling of America," Stephens catalogues the various theories proposed by authors from the sixteenth through the nineteenth centuries; "not to be behindhand," he adds, "an enterprising American has turned the tables on the Old World, and planted the ark itself within the state of New-York"—a reference to Smith's discovery of the sacred text in the hills of his native upstate New York.[1]

However different their agendas may have been, Stephens and Smith were united in their effort to "turn the tables on the Old World" by establishing the North American continent's cultural independence from Europe. Although Smith's belief in the ancient colonization of the Americas contradicted Stephens' argument for the monuments' indigenous authorship, the Mormon leader nonetheless considered the development of Mesoamerican civilization, particularly its religious evolution, as a phenomenon distinct from Old World models. Furthermore, guided by the same sense of manifest destiny that had shaped Stephens' work, Smith sought to establish the United States as the principal heir to this archaeological legacy.

In the minds of Smith and subsequent Mormon Church leaders, the spiritual consequences of unifying ancient North and Central American cultures far surpassed the relatively modest nationalist goals of Stephens' work. Seeking nothing less than the re-creation of Zion on the North American continent, Smith founded his mission upon the belief that God had led his chosen people to the Americas in ancient times. Settling in "the Land of Bountiful," as Yucatan is described in the Book of Mormon, these Israelites represented the first stage of a divine plan for American civilization. Upon the revelation of this ancient history, and Smith's subsequent call to reunite God's American "chosen ones," the Mormon leader proclaimed that the fulfillment of God's plan for the continent was at hand.

The Book of Mormon is constructed as a historical narrative, relating the story of ancient America's colonization, the subsequent progress of civilization on the continent, and the ultimate demise of this culture around the fifth century A.D. Paralleling the structure of the Old Testament, the first half of the Mormon text establishes God's covenantal relationship with his chosen people, the descendants of a single family of immigrants from Jerusalem. Speaking through ancient

American prophets and high priests, God instructs the growing nation on the coming fulfillment of this covenant, to be signaled by the appearance of a savior and the establishment of a new spiritual order.

The second half of the Book of Mormon presents an Americanized version of the New Testament, chronicling Jesus Christ's appearance in the Americas and his establishment of the early church there. Tracing the development of this early American church through the fifth century, the Book of Mormon relates the chosen people's eventual loss of faith and ultimate annihilation. To preserve the original covenant, however, God arranges for the group's historical records to be sealed until a "latter-day" prophet would be called to restore the American church.

Though the Book of Mormon first appeared in print in 1830, Smith's testimony regarding its source remained unpublished for another eight years. In the 1838 introduction to the Book of Mormon, Smith recounted that during the night of September 21, 1823, an angel named Moroni had appeared to him, informing him of "an account of the former inhabitants of this continent, and the source from which they spring."[2] Describing this record as a hieroglyphic text written on golden tablets, Moroni explained that he had transcribed the text himself during his earthly existence and had buried the document in A.D. 421. Immediately following this visitation, Moroni conducted Smith to an earthen mound near the town of Manchester, New York, where he directed Smith to excavate the text, hidden within a small stone vault.

Following four subsequent visitations from Moroni, occurring between 1821 and 1827, Smith claimed he was endowed with the power to unseal this container and retrieve the tablets. Although the text initially appeared indecipherable to Smith, he explained, Moroni brought him two mystical stones called the Urim and Thummim to aid him in his translation. With these tools, Smith spent the next three years translating the plates, eventually returning them to Moroni for their heavenly assumption. Anticipating readers' skepticism concerning the plates, Smith provided a signed testimony by eleven chosen witnesses, whose number—adding Smith himself—equaled that of Christ's twelve apostles. In speaking of the plates, these men attested "[w]e did handle them," adding that the text had "the appearance of an ancient work, and was of curious workmanship."[3]

Smith remained silent on the precise appearance and archaeological provenience of this mysterious text, yet his descriptions of the work conform to contemporary conceptions regarding the manufacture, archaeological context, and written language systems of pre-Columbian artifacts. First, by asserting that the tablets had been crafted in gold, Smith tapped into age-old assumptions concerning the abundance of this material in ancient Mesoamerica. Second, because it was linked to an archaeological excavation, Smith's discovery resembled the similar, albeit less spectacular, retrieval of pre-Columbian artifacts from upstate New York's ancient earthworks and burial mounds.

Most important, the text that Smith translated represented a pictographic language system unlike any yet deciphered, including the Egyptian hieroglyphic system, whose legibility had been recently demonstrated by Jean-François Champollion in the 1820s. In the 1830s the only known, and *un*deciphered, hieroglyphic system was that found at ancient Mesoamerican sites in Mexico and Central America. Given the geographical links that Smith later insisted upon between the Book of Mormon and Latin America, he clearly intended readers to connect his tablets' hieroglyphs with those found in this region. Furthermore, although Smith's specific use of the Urim and Thummim stones remains unclear, readers of the Book of Mormon could easily have linked them with Champollion's Rosetta stone—a translation aid, carved in stone and written in parallel-text format.[4] In translating his own hieroglyphic text, Smith's accomplishment both equaled Champollion's and surpassed that of contemporary Mesoamerican explorers, for whom Maya writing remained a mystery (the Maya "code," in fact, would not be broken until the 1960s).

According to the account of Smith and the eleven witnesses, the plates discovered in 1827 represented two distinct groups. The largest set, consisting primarily of the plates of Nephi and Mormon, related the history of the migration and subsequent division of the family of Lehi. Conflating Lehi's mission with the Judeo-Christian narratives of both Adam's and Jesus' testing, these plates tell of Lehi's initial feat of endurance in the desert, followed by his partaking of fruit from the Tree of Life. Rather than damning Lehi and his descendants, this act confirmed their status as God's new chosen people and situated Lehi as the Adam of the New World.[5]

The Book of Mormon relates that Lehi's family, crafting divinely engineered boats "of curious workmanship" complete with navigational compasses, emigrated from Jerusalem to Central America in 590 B.C. Although Smith does not supply Lehi's precise geographical landing point in the Book of Mormon, Frederick Williams attributed a statement to Smith in 1836 that placed this point "on the continent of South America, in Chile, 30 degrees south latitude";[6] such a statement would explain the subsequent south-to-north migration of Lehi's family. In 1855,

Mormon leader Parley Pratt confirmed this location, writing that Lehi had "landed in safety on the coast of what is now called Chili [sic], in South America."[7] The Book of Mormon relates that soon after Lehi's arrival and subsequent northern migration, his family split into two opposing groups known as the Nephites and the Lamanites, whose rivalry constitutes the plates' primary narrative.

Accompanying the golden plates that Smith had discovered were the so-called Plates of Brass, presumably an Old World medium, comprising the five books of Moses that Lehi had brought with him to the New World. Smith's inclusion of this text both established the Book of Mormon's historical and textual links with the Judeo-Christian scriptural tradition and reinforced Lehi's genealogical heritage.

The second principal set of tablets, a single group known as the plates of Ether, recorded the rise and fall of the Jaredites, an ancient American civilization that had vanished before Lehi's arrival on the continent. The Jaredites, according to the Book of Mormon, had emigrated from the Near East to North America following the fall of the Tower of Babel described in the Bible's book of Genesis.[8] The destruction of Babel is traditionally dated to 600 B.C., or immediately prior to Lehi's arrival, although the Jaredites' abandoned settlements were not discovered by Lehi's descendants until several centuries later.[9] It was on the site of the abandoned Jaredite communities in upstate New York, the Book of Mormon relates, that the Lamanites ultimately destroyed the Nephites in A.D. 421. At this final battle the Nephite prophet-historian Moroni had hidden the plates on the hilltop near present-day Manchester, consigning his people's history to obscurity until Smith's 1827 revelation.

Smith's belief that Mesoamerica had been colonized by the Israelites belonged to a long tradition of similar origin theories proposed by North American scholars, although Smith's particular characterization of this migration represents a marked departure from earlier theories. From the first period of English colonization on the continent, Puritan settlers had metaphorically identified with the Jews of the Old Testament, citing their similar search for a "promised land" in which they could worship without the threat of persecution. In the latter seventeenth and eighteenth centuries, this association evolved into a more literal interpretation supported by Roger Williams, William Penn, the Mather brothers, and even President Ezra Stiles of Yale—all of whom believed that the lost tribes of Israel had founded ancient North American civilization.[10] The crucial difference between their belief and Smith's proposed Israelite migration, however, lies in Smith's dating of Lehi's departure from Jerusalem.

Historically, the disappearance of the ten lost tribes followed their abduction by the king of Assyria in 721 B.C. Of the twelve original tribes, all of whom were descended from the sons of Jacob, there remained only the tribes of Judah, Benjamin, and a portion of Manasseh, all of whom continued to live in Jerusalem until the city's fall in 586 B.C.[11] According to Smith's reckoning, Lehi had embarked upon his voyage more than 130 years following the Assyrian captivity—consequently, his family belonged not to the ten lost tribes abducted by the Assyrians but rather to the *surviving* tribes of Judah and Benjamin.

Lehi's connection to these two tribes bore specific ideological implications. By aligning ancient American civilization with the surviving branches of Israel rather than with the lost tribes, Smith invested his charge for the reconciliation of God's "chosen peoples" with a greater sense of immediacy. Because his church belonged to the genealogical lineage of Jacob, Smith's latter-day reestablishment of Israel was characterized as a new stage within a continuous, living tradition. The "literal gathering of Israel" that Smith had been called to accomplish depended upon the American church's unbroken line of succession from Jacob and, by extension, from Abraham himself.

Smith's establishment of an ancient pedigree for the Mormon Church must be seen in light of contemporary efforts to "primitivize" American Christianity through the rejection of European theological models. Gathering momentum in the 1820s, the American evangelical movement known as the Second Great Awakening had achieved its greatest success in the upstate New York region of Smith's upbringing. It was there that the itinerant preacher Charles Grandison Finney had established his Utica-based revival movement in 1826, aimed at the dismantling of Calvinist, European-derived Protestantism.[12] By the middle of the next decade the region had hosted so many revivals, and had witnessed such an intense uprising of religious fervor, that the area became known as the "burned-over district."

New York revivalists believed that the Reformation had failed to correct the corruptions of medieval Catholic doctrine, and they therefore called for a restoration of Christianity as it had been lived in the time of the apostles.[13] Because this evangelical movement shunned religious orthodoxy of any sort, it proved particularly supportive of any sect falling outside the Protestant denominational framework; even the protoreligious practices of American Freemasonry, which had fallen under general attack by mainstream Protestants in the 1820s, were encouraged by the primitivists.[14] The early and rapid acceptance of Mormon revelation in New York, then, derived from the restorationists' embrace of any doctrine that promoted personal experience of the gospel, a return to early historical models of the church, and the rejection of Old World Protestantism. Codifying these tenets in the Mormon Articles of Faith, composed in 1842, Smith called on Latter-day Saints to profess: "[W]e believe in the same organization that existed in the primitive church. . . . We believe in the literal gathering of Israel, and that Zion will be built on this continent."[15]

Smith's reconstitution of American Christianity was founded upon the belief that Christ had appeared in the Americas immediately following his crucifixion and resurrection in Jerusalem. Representing the Mormon Church's central Article of Faith, Christ's American visitation paralleled his messianic mission in Israel. As the Book of Mormon relates, Christ appeared at the Nephites' Tower of Sherrizah in A.D. 34, following the proclamations of the Mormon prophet Samuel (the ancient American counterpart to John the Baptist). During his residence among the Nephites, Christ redelivered his Sermon on the Mount, gave instructions for conducting baptism and Holy Communion, and adopted a group of twelve American apostles.[16]

Contemporary editions of the Book of Mormon include illustrations of Samuel's proclamation and Christ's appearance to the Nephites, as envisioned by Mormon artist Arnold Friberg. In each of these scenes, Friberg contextualizes the narrative within an architectural setting based upon well-known models of Puuc-style Maya and Teotihuacano architecture. In the image depicting Samuel's proclamation, the temple before which the prophet stands features the characteristic stone latticework and centralized Chac mask of Uxmal's Nunnery complex; similarly, Friberg models the Tower of Sherrizah, upon which Christ appears to the Nephites, on the stepped masonry platforms of Teotihuacan's Avenue of the Dead.[17] Although these illustrations belong to the modern era rather than to the nineteenth century, they parallel the nineteenth-century Mormons' connection between specific archaeological sites and events described in the Book of Mormon. Specific textual confirmations for such correspondences are discussed below.

The Book of Mormon relates that the spread of Christianity in the Americas, as in the eastern Mediterranean, was apostolically driven and characterized by clashes with traditional Jewish and pagan cultures—specifically, the Nephites' struggle to proselytize their unbelieving and increasingly idolatrous Lamanite brothers. Although the evangelical experience of the first-century Nephites mirrored that of the New Testament church, however, their constituency did not. In contrast to the Jewish and gentile membership of the early Pauline church, the Nephite faithful all claimed direct descent from Israel—representing an independent, and implicitly superior, branch of Christianity.

Such descriptions of pre-European apostolic activity in the Americas were not without precedent. Throughout the sixteenth and seventeenth centuries, missionaries in New Spain had often expressed the belief that St. Thomas had preached the gospel in the Americas.[18] By the end of the eighteenth century, this belief fueled a Mexican nationalist agenda in the sermons of Dominican friar Servando Teresa de Mier; revising the story of the Virgin of Guadalupe's miraculous visitation, Mier asserted in a 1794 sermon that the recipient of the vision had been St. Thomas, rather than the *indio* Juan Diego, and that the miracle had occurred in ancient times—when St. Thomas and his four apostles had undertaken an evangelical mission to the Americas.[19] By relying upon Mexicans' fervent devotion to the Guadalupana, Mier thus established a regional connection to the early Christian church that, like the Mormons' account, bypassed the postconquest establishment of Mesoamerican Christianity.

By proposing that American Christianity had developed in isolation from Europe, Smith's religious agenda neatly mirrored Stephens' later archaeological claims. For both, Mesoamerican ruins provided evidence of the North American continent's—and by extension, the United States'—connection to an ancient culture rivaling that of the Old World. Assigning distinct geographical zones to each of the Book of Mormon's principal groups, Smith claimed the widest possible range of archaeological sites as confirmation for his divine revelation. Although the Book of Mormon provides no precise mapping of these groups' settlements, its descriptions of their distinctive geographical features and differing architectural styles are clearly intended to imply specific known sites and archaeologically substantiated building types.

In a passage from the eighth chapter of Mosiah, the Book of Mormon relates the Nephites' discovery of the Jaredite settlements that had flourished before their arrival. Exploring the "north country" near "the land of many waters," the Nephites found "a land which was covered with bones of men . . . and with ruins of buildings of every kind"; from these ruins the Nephites learned to create round earthworks ringed with stone "pickets," defensive ditches, low mud towers, and burial mounds.[20] Noting the direct correspondence between Jaredite building techniques and the ancient mounds discovered in the Great Lakes and Mississippi Valley regions, Vermont's *Battleboro Messenger* stated in 1830 that "the Book of Mormon could have been designed to explain the ancient fortifications and other things seen in the west."[21]

By the 1820s, numerous pre-Columbian mounds had been discovered near the New York towns of Onondaga, Pompey, Manlius, Oxford, Jamesville, Ridgeway, and Canandaigua—all of which conformed to the general description of Jaredite ruins in the Book of Mormon. At least eight of these mounds, in fact, could be found within a twelve-mile radius of the Smith family's farm near Palmyra.[22] An ancient burial mound near Canandaigua serves as an illustrative example of these works. Located less than ten miles from the presumed site of the golden tablets' discovery, this earthen enclosure was described by Ephraim Squier in his 1851 *Antiquities of the State of New York* as "circular in plan with a single opening," featuring a ring of post holes and containing "human bones in considerable quantities."[23] Squier's description of the site's silhouette, which appeared at first glance to be the "brow of a hill," equally conformed to Smith's descriptions of the earthen mound from which he had retrieved the tablets.

Not only did such mounds provide an architectural record of the Jaredite civilization, but the skeletal remains at these sites also seemed to support Smith's location of the Nephite Armageddon. In at least two instances, authors writing before the publication of the Book of Mormon had also hypothesized that these burial mounds represented the aftermath of a large-scale battle. In 1817, for example, former New York governor DeWitt Clinton had written that a mound in New York's Genesee County contained piles of skeletons "deposited there by their conquerors."[24] Later, John Yates and Joseph Moulton had written in their 1824 *History of the State of New-York* that the area's mounds represented the work of light-skinned peoples destroyed by ancient Native American tribes. The ethnic distinction that these authors drew between conqueror and conquered is noteworthy, given Smith's later characterization of the Nephite-Lamanite conflict.

Yates and Moulton's work also lent credence to Smith's assumption that New York's mounds formed the first part of a chain of antiquities running down through Mexico.[25] Revealing a certain regional chauvinism, perhaps, Smith assigned the greatest antiquity to those mounds near "the great waters" (presumably the Great Lakes)—not only glorifying his native New York but also firmly anchoring the first American civilization within the borders of the United States.[26]

The Book of Mormon cites the Jaredites as the continent's first true architects, yet it credits the Nephites with constructing the great cities and religious centers of Mesoamerica, which, according to Mormon tradition, were built between the mid-fifth century B.C. and the fourth century A.D. Smith's text provides detailed descriptions of the Jaredite fortifications, yet its references to the Nephites' stone buildings and vast temples tend to be more impressionistic—largely because the archaeology of this region was only slightly known in the United States prior to Stephens' 1841 publication.[27] Smith's geographical siting of these works is equally vague. Settling in the "Narrow Neck of Land" later identified by Mormon leaders as the Isthmus of Tehuantepec, the Nephites colonized eastward toward the "Land of Bountiful," or present-day Yucatan, establishing settlements in the "Land Southward," corresponding to lower Central America.[28]

Unlike the Jaredites, the Nephites built in stone, excelled in the use of cement, and established large urban centers characterized by platform towers.[29] The first construction in the region, directed by the prophet Nephi, had been built "after the manner of the Temple of Solomon"—a reference that, given the nineteenth-century's differing versions of this lost structure, could have suggested a range of visual possibilities.[30] In their colonization of the "Land Northward," by contrast, the Nephites favored "tabernacles of clay," a possible reference to the Pueblo tradition of building in adobe.[31]

Aided by angel-architects, the Nephites built masonry fortifications to defend themselves against the Lamanites, the cursed branch of the family of Lehi.[32] Described as "a dark, filthy, and loathsome people," the Lamanites are denounced for their failure to build permanent structures; "they lived in the wilderness and dwelt in tents," the Book of Mormon explains, adding that "they were spread throughout the wilderness on the west."[33] It was the Lamanites, the Mormon Church maintains, from whom all later North and Central American ethnic groups are descended—a factor that propelled the Mormons' later nineteenth-century missionary efforts in Mexico and among native North American groups. Smith's descriptions of Lamanite shelters as "tents" were no doubt intended to evoke images of the contemporary Plains Indian tipi; added to the Jaredites' earthwork fortifications and the Nephites' stone palaces and "clay tabernacles," these tents completed Smith's inventory of all known indigenous American architectural types.[34]

As the Nephites prospered and "spread forth into all parts of the land," described in the third chapter of the Book of Helaman, they banished the nomadic Lamanites ever farther northward—a reservationist policy resembling that of the mid-nineteenth-century United States toward Native American groups. All along their approach to the region of the Great Lakes, the Nephites continued to build fortifications to protect outpost settlements from the Lamanites, often using the abandoned Jaredite settlements as an architectural palimpsest for their own works.[35] Ultimately, the two groups fatally clashed at the battle of Cumorah, in present-day upstate New York—the so-called Land of Desolation, named for the bone-strewn former homeland of the Jaredites. Following this battle, the victorious Lamanites represented the sole survivors of Lehi's original family.[36]

Significantly, the fourteen-century period between the destruction of the Nephites in A.D. 421 and Smith's revelation of 1827 directly corresponds to the fifteen-hundred-year development of Christianity in Europe. For Smith and his followers, this period marked the corruption of the early apostolic Church, leading to the excesses of Catholicism and the perceived failures of the Reformation. By eliding this period between the fifth and nineteenth centuries and allying the contemporary faithful with the last members of the early American church, Smith's revelations ensured the Latter-day Saints' independence from the historical framework of European Christianity. Owing nothing to the Old World, the Mormon Church would rise directly from the ashes of Cumorah itself.

The fifteen-hundred-year lapse in the Mormon historical narrative is partially bridged by the Book of Mormon's occasional allusions to the continent's post-421 history—most importantly, its apparent predictions of the Spanish conquest and the establishment of the United States. While God promises the Nephites that their land will be "kept from the knowledge of other nations" and that "there shall be none to molest them, nor to take away the land of their inheritance," he requires in turn that they keep his commandments.[37] Predicting a time when "their land will be full of idols," however, Nephite prophets foresaw that God would "bring other nations unto them, and He will give unto them power, and He will take away from them the lands of their possessions" such that "many houses shall be desolate and great and fair cities without inhabitant."[38] Though these Nephite prophecies may also refer to the future Lamanite occupation of the Nephite territories, they appear to imply an invasion by a new group, a country formerly ignorant of these lands. Following this period of punitive occupation, the Book of Mormon asserts, God would create a new nation on the continent, a great "land of liberty where no king shall rule," a powerful country that God would "fortify against all other nations."[39]

Though these prophecies are intentionally vague, their implication is clear. The future, foreign occupation of the Nephite territory is characterized as retributive intervention, a period when their culture would suffer the same fate as that of the Jaredites. By contrast, the ultimate creation of the "land of liberty," Smith's thinly disguised reference to the United States, represents the fulfillment of God's original promise to his chosen people. By casting Spain and the United States in opposing villain/savior roles, Smith echoed Stephens' characterization of the conquest. For both, the Spanish occupation is perceived as an anomalous interruption of local culture that only the enlightened United States could restore.

The publication of Stephens and Catherwood's *Incidents of Travel in Central America, Chiapas, and Yucatan* in 1841 provided the Mormon Church with spectacular confirmation for the existence of the Nephites' civilization. Within the same year, Charles Blancher Thompson published his *Evidence in Proof of the Book of Mormon,* the first in a long line of Mormon-authored works situating Stephens' discoveries within their presumed Nephite contexts. For Thompson and subsequent Mormon scholars, the explorer's writings and Catherwood's powerful images provided proof "sufficient to show the public that the people whose history is contained within the Book of Mormon are the author of these works."[40]

In the year following Thompson's publication, the editor of the Mormon Church's newspaper *Times and Seasons* cited Stephens' work as well, proposing the first tentative correspondence between a Nephite settlement and a specific Mesoamerican site:

> The [Nephite] city of Zarahemla, burnt at the crucifixion of the Savior, and rebuilt afterwards, stood upon this land. . . . We are not going to declare positively that the ruins of Quirigua are those of Zarahemla, but when the land and the stones and the books tell the story so plain, we are of the opinion that it would require more proof than the Jews could bring to prove the disciples stole the body of Jesus from the tomb, [than] to prove the ruins of the city in question are not those referred to in the Book of Mormon.[41]

Not only did the Mormons establish a correspondence between Nephite sites and those discovered by Stephens, but they also began to favor his geographical labels over the Book of Mormon's more vague terminology. Writing for the Mormons' *Millennial Star* in 1848, for example, Orson Pratt first cited the Nephites' occupation of *Yucatan*—rather than the "Land of Bountiful."[42]

In the next decade Mormon leader John Taylor addressed Stephens' supposed archaeological confirmation in a way that extended not only Stephens' dating of the ruins but the chronology of the Book of Mormon itself. In a lengthy 1851 essay for the *Millennial Star,* entitled "The Discovery of Ruins," Taylor asserted that "there is the most incontrovertible evidence exhibited in the symbolic writings and inscriptions upon every part of these dilapidated monuments," adding that they were erected in "a period in the age of the world of which all history is silent."[43]

Arguing that the ruins represented a far greater antiquity than had previously been believed, Taylor asserted that the peoples from the Book of Mormon "existed not only for a great length of time since the building of the Egyptian pyramids, but contemporary with them, and what is more wonderful still, far back and yet farther into the mazes of antiquity."[44] A high-ranking member of the Mormon Church and Brigham Young's eventual successor as its president, Taylor was supported by the full weight of church authority—justifying his claims, as Smith had before him, on the basis of spiritual rather than archaeological evidence.[45]

Having survived its stormy first decades and the 1847 establishment of the "New Jerusalem" in Salt Lake City, Utah, the Mormon Church turned its attention in the 1850s to recalling its Lamanite brethren. Parley Pratt's "Address to the Red Man," printed in the *Millennial Star* in 1852, declared to Native American tribes that "you are a Branch of the House of Israel, you are descended from the Jews," and that, following Smith's revelation, "your history, your Gospel, your destiny is revealed."[46] Heeding Pratt's call, the frontiersman and Mexican-American War veteran Daniel Jones led the church's mission to the Native American tribes. His efforts later resulted in a commercially popular, Catlinesque narrative entitled *Forty Years among the Indians* (1890), yet Jones' activities failed to secure the general support of either Native American tribes or the Mormon Church's membership—each ultimately considering the other a culturally incompatible partner.[47]

Jones's proselytizing efforts among the Lamanites' descendants embraced the indigenous peoples of Mexico and Central America as well, where the Mormon Church had attempted to establish missionary ties as early as the 1850s. By reuniting the continent's "remnants of the House of Jacob," Mormon leaders believed they would hasten Christ's Second Coming and his establishment of the New Kingdom.[48] During the bitter political and military struggles that took place between Utah and the federal government in the 1850s and 1860s, however, Mormon president Brigham Young recalled all of the church's missionaries to defend Salt Lake City in the so-called Utah War. The mission to Mexico remained stalled until 1874.

In that year, Young announced that the time had arrived to reclaim Lehi's

Mexican descendants.[49] Sending the first Mormon delegation to Mexico with Jones in 1876, Young embarked on an intensive program of Mormon colonization and proselytizing in Latin America. The missionaries' reception in Mexico, unlike that among Native American tribes, proved particularly warm. Not only did post-Reform Mexico encourage the establishment of non-Catholic churches, but, following the humiliating French occupation of the country in the 1860s, Mexican liberals embraced the image of historical legitimacy offered by the Mormons.[50]

Adopting potent symbols of the Aztec past, the church glorified ancient Mesoamerican culture in ways that flattered their new converts. Establishing religious chapters in Mexico City, for example, church leaders chose such Nahua-associated names as "Moctezuma," "Aztecas" and "Netzahualcoyotl." In a more overt gesture in 1881, Mormon missionaries celebrated the fifty-first anniversary of the Mormon Church in a formal prayer ceremony atop the sacred Aztec volcano Popocatépetl.[51] Capitalizing on the location's powerful religious significance, the missionaries thus cemented the church's connection to the Mesoamerican past while implying the supremacy of their new, American, religious order.

In its eagerness to encourage settlement of its sparsely populated northern territories, the Mexican government supported Young's efforts to establish permanent Mormon communities in the region—a policy that led to the rapid development of Mormon missions in the Casas Grandes area in the 1880s. The arrangement proved mutually beneficial, for both the Mormon Church and the Mexican republic were united in their distrust of the U.S. government. By creating a safe haven for Mormons and a strengthened buffer zone for the Mexicans, these mission communities represented a rather benign form of manifest destiny. As Jones explained to a Mexican customs officer in 1876, "the Mormons had sent us to look for land to settle, as we were growing and wished new country," adding that, in contrast to the U.S. federal government, the Mormons were "friends to the red man" who hoped to live in peace with their new neighbors.[52]

Addressing his fellow Americans' distrust of the Mormon mission to Mexico in 1876, Young asserted the church's commitment to religious and territorial colonization throughout North America:

> It has been the cry of late, through the columns of the newspapers, that the "Mormons" are going to Mexico! That is quite right, we intend to go there. . . . We intend to hold our own here, and also penetrate the north and the south, the east and the west . . . and to raise the ensign of truth; we will continue to grow, to increase and spread abroad, and the powers of earth and hell combined cannot hinder it.[53]

Young's words reflect the Latter-day Saints' particularly aggressive, and success-ful, efforts to penetrate the farthest reaches of the continent in this period, just as they believed their Nephite ancestors had done. From a relatively small sect in the 1830s, the Mormon Church had grown to nearly sixty thousand members by the close of the 1870s.[54]

Although the Mormon Church's rapid growth had led to its persecution in the United States, marked by Smith's assassination in 1844 and the Utah Wars of the 1850s and 1860s, the Latter-day Saints' missionary philosophy mirrored the nine-teenth-century U.S. program of territorial expansion. In their crusade to reunite the "remnants of Jacob" in North America, Mormon leaders scripturally con-firmed the United States' sense of precedence on the continent while creating a membership that transcended national boundaries.

Like Stephens before him, Smith succeeded in subsuming Mesoamerican an-tiquities within a broader, North American historical narrative that not only ex-cluded European influence but also divorced contemporary Latin Americans from any direct link to the monuments.[55] Furthermore, each supported the United States' sense of manifest destiny on the continent by contextualizing this monumental past as the first strata of "American," or U.S., civilization—an epoch that constituted the country's cultural or, in Smith's case, religious, foundation. While Stephens' argument for cultural consolidation derived from the geographic proximity of the United States to the ruins, however, the Mormon Church claimed this shared culture on the irrefutable grounds of spiritual destiny. It is for this reason that, even in the wake of twentieth-century professional archaeology, the strength of Mormon claims to the region has grown proportionally with its increase in membership.[56]

4

THE TOLTEC LENS OF DÉSIRÉ CHARNAY

[I]t shall be found that I have resolved this vexed
American Question, so hotly controverted hitherto.

—DÉSIRÉ CHARNAY,
The Ancient Cities of the New World (1887)

FOLLOWING the annexation of Mexican territories in 1848 and Stephens' death in 1852, popular American interest in pre-Columbian ruins noticeably cooled. The Mormon Church's belief in a divinely established, ancient North American civilization was publicly maintained throughout the nineteenth century, yet even this phenomenon was a fairly esoteric outgrowth of the nation's archaeological chauvinism. Beginning in the 1860s, however, Stephens' perception of a unified, national antiquity was adopted and transformed by Désiré Charnay, a French explorer working under American patronage. Charnay's work was particularly important in that he both recast the ethnic history of ancient Mesoamerica and harnessed powerful new photographic and casting technologies to record the ruins he investigated. The technological sophistication of Charnay's surveys, combined with the racial bias of his theoretical perspective, forms a vital link between Stephens' interpretations of the ancient "American" past and the later institutionalization of this vision at the 1893 World's Columbian Exposition in Chicago.

Charnay confirmed Stephens' insistence upon American rights in Mesoamerican archaeology by implicitly aligning the region's history with that of the United States. For Charnay the ruins pointed to a single cultural fountainhead, the Toltec civilization, a group that he ethnically linked to the ancestors of northern Europe — and, by extension, to the majority population of the nineteenth-century United States. Furthermore, in claiming the Toltecs' diffusion throughout the North American continent, Charnay reinforced Stephens' conflation of Mesoamerican antiquities with those found in the Ohio and Mississippi River Valleys.

Unlike the Mormon Church, which had based similar archaeological conclusions upon divine inspiration, Charnay drew his assumptions from observed archaeological evidence — publishing his explorations in travel narratives modeled upon Stephens and Catherwood's work. Whereas all previous explorers had relied upon accompanying artists to record their discoveries, Charnay's pioneering use of photography allowed him to serve as both author and illustrator. Not only did the process invest his work with greater pictorial fidelity, solving earlier problems associated with artists' interpretations of the sites, but it also allowed the explorer to record a greater number of monuments within far shorter periods of fieldwork.

Aside from his achievements in photography, Charnay's greatest technological contribution lay in his development of an efficient system for plaster-casting the monuments he encountered. By creating lightweight paper molds of the ruins, rather than producing heavy plaster copies on-site, he dramatically increased both the range and the size of potentially reproducible works. Because these new photographic and casting technologies replaced the need to physically dismantle works for acquisition, a practice that had never proved logistically or politically viable anyway, Charnay escalated the possibilities for re-creating Mesoamerican monuments within American museological contexts. Without these two developments, the tremendous visual and ideological impact of the Mesoamerican exhibits at the 1893 World's Fair in Chicago could never have been achieved.

Beginning in 1857, Charnay embarked on a two-year photographic survey of Mexico's ancient monuments. With the publication of this work in 1862, a folio entitled *Cités et ruines américaines,* Charnay established himself as the latter-nineteenth century's preeminent authority on Mesoamerican antiquity.[1] Over the next three decades Charnay's only serious American competitor was Augustus Le Plongeon, another photographer and cast maker, whose work forms the subject of chapter 5.

Political disruptions in Mexico prevented Charnay from capitalizing on the success of his first volume, but his return to Mexico in the early 1880s marked a period of intense activity—resulting in his more theoretical work of 1887, *The Ancient Cities of the New World*.[2] Financing this second photographic expedition through patrons in France and the United States, Charnay was charged with the acquisition of artifacts and architectural plaster casts for French and American museums. Over the space of two years, he amassed a collection of casts and pre-Columbian artworks that outstripped even Stephens' projected inventory for his national museum of American antiquities. In addition, Charnay had devised a theoretical framework that justified these activities on the basis of pseudoscientific racial theory.

Born near Lyons, France, in 1828, Charnay had emigrated to the United States at the age of twenty-two, settling in New Orleans, where he taught French at a local preparatory school.[3] Fascinated by Stephens' accounts of Central American antiquities, the schoolteacher dreamed of conducting his own explorations in Mexico; the opportunity came in 1857 when Charnay, like Stephens before him, secured a diplomatic posting to Mexico from France's Ministry of Public Instruction (although the explorer's diplomatic duties on this expedition appear to have been negligible).[4] Blaming the public's diminished enthusiasm for Mesoamerican antiquities on the "lax manner" in which archaeology had been conducted following Stephens' death,[5] Charnay hoped to revive popular interest in the ruins through the new medium of photography.

Although Stephens and Catherwood had produced daguerreotype images of the ruins on their 1841 expedition, Charnay's 1863 work represented the first widely available photographic images of the ancient Mesoamerican monuments. Because the daguerreotype process yielded unique images on nonreproducible metal plates, Stephens and Catherwood's photographs had functioned solely to supplement engravers' renderings of Catherwood's field drawings. Within just a few years of Stephens and Catherwood's final voyage, however, William Henry Fox Talbot's perfection of the glass-negative process eventually allowed for the multiple production of photographic images. By 1851, Talbot's invention had, in turn, led to Frederick Archer's introduction of the "wet plate" process—which re-

placed Talbot's silver-treated glass negative with a damp, more light-sensitive collodion emulsion plate.[6] The resulting images represented both a dramatic im-
provement in clarity and a reduction in necessary exposure time.

Although the technological developments of the 1850s had revolutionized
photography's reproductive possibilities, the "wet plate" process still posed enormous obstacles for field photographers like Charnay. Because the collodion emulsion dried so rapidly, the plates required on-site treatment prior to their exposure, followed by their immediate development. The process presented little
difficulty within a photographic studio, yet it proved especially arduous for photographers working in remote and semitropical environments. Battling insects,
severe humidity, and the unstable nature of photographic chemicals, Charnay
faced a constant series of challenges—not least of which was the tremendous
weight of the equipment itself.[7] When Charnay arrived in Veracruz in 1858, his
cargo included a cumbersome field camera, a tripod, dozens of fourteen-by-
eighteen-inch glass plates, hundreds of gallons of developing chemicals, a dark-
room tent, and other supplies. In all, the equipment weighed more than four
thousand pounds.[8]

His field camera should have allowed Charnay to record a greater variety of
monuments in far less time than his explorer-artist predecessors had required,
yet the transportation of his photographic supplies consumed the majority of this
first trip. Traveling in advance of his equipment, Charnay was often forced to wait
several months for its arrival. Once the material had arrived, Charnay frequently
faced further delays caused by broken glass plates or spoiled developing chemicals. Over a period of two and a half years, Charnay traveled to the sites of Mitla,
Palenque, Izamal, Chichen Itza, and Uxmal. In total, however, his on-site photography amounted to scarcely six weeks' work, an average of just over a week at each
site. Although he spent almost two weeks at Mitla, Charnay's work periods grew
increasingly shorter at subsequent sites: nine days at Chichen Itza, eight days at
Uxmal, nine days at Palenque, and a week at Izamal.[9]

Added to the hazards of transportation was the time-consuming process of
individually preparing and developing images in the field. During a week's work
at Izamal in April 1860, for example, Charnay produced only three acceptable images.[10] Increasingly aware of his limited time and funding, Charnay neglected to
perform even the most cursory surveys of the monuments he photographed; furthermore, because of his already overburdened supplies, he was unable to produce architectural casts or collect artifacts on this expedition.[11] In speaking of

this first trip, Charnay later explained that "from want of technical knowledge, I was unable to carry out the great schemes I had imagined."[12]

The striking set of forty-seven images that Charnay published in *Cités et ruines américaines* amply compensated for the shallow nature of his fieldwork. In comparing his 1860 photograph of the so-called Iglesia at Chichen Itza with Catherwood's earlier drawing of the same monument (fig. 4.1), the superior descriptive quality of Charnay's work is immediately apparent. Catherwood's image correctly records the building's proportions and decoration, yet Charnay's photograph conveys information previously available only to the site's visitors. The astounding clarity of the photographic plate not only expresses the differing textures of the monument's stonework but also illustrates the exact manner in which the masonry had been laid. Far from a strictly mechanical facsimile, however, Charnay's photograph exhibits a strong sense of mood; by presenting the structure in raking sunlight and filling the entire pictorial plane with his subject, Charnay created an image of tremendous, almost threatening, power.

In his larger, panoramic formats Charnay demonstrated the full range of the camera's possibilities. Without sacrificing any of the visual detail of his close-up shots, Charnay's panoramic views captured entire facades within a single frame, often exposing previously unnoticed or incorrectly illustrated compositional features. Charnay's photograph of the eastern side of the Nunnery Quadrangle at Uxmal, for example, records the facade's subtle deviations from perfect symmetry—a factor that Catherwood either corrected or failed to notice in his elevation of the same structure (fig. 4.2). Furthermore, rather than presenting works in isolation, Charnay's panoramic images contextualized the relationships of structures to one another; his image of the Nunnery Quadrangle, for example, correctly shows the looming pile of the Pyramid of the Magician in the distance—a stacking of images that Catherwood avoids in his own engraving.

In both tone and format, Charnay's 1863 work consciously followed the model Stephens had established with his 1841–1843 *Incidents of Travel* series. For the title of this work, Charnay favored the more continentally inclusive adjective "American" over "Mexican," a choice that reflected Stephens' taxonomy, rather than that of Baradère, Charnay's countryman and Stephens' predecessor. Charnay's frequent usage of the modifier "American" mirrored Stephens' reliance upon this term's dual national and geographical significance, while foretelling Charnay's later insistence on pan-American unity. In his organization of the volume Charnay combined Stephens' approach with that of King—interspersing his illustrations with a run-

4.1. *Above:* CHARNAY, IGLESIA, CHICHEN ITZA, 1860 (Désiré Charnay, *Cités et ruines américaines:* 1863).
Below: CATHERWOOD, IGLESIA, CHICHEN ITZA (John Lloyd Stephens, *Incidents of Travel in Yucatan,* vol. 1: 1843).

4.2. *Above:* CHARNAY, EASTERN FACADE OF NUNNERY COMPLEX, UXMAL, 1860 (Désiré Charnay, *Cités et ruines américaines:* 1863).
    Below: CATHERWOOD, EASTERN FACADE OF NUNNERY COMPLEX, UXMAL (John Lloyd Stephens, *Incidents of Travel in Yucatan*, vol. 1: 1843).

ning narrative as well as appending an analysis of the monuments by an "expert" in the field, the French medievalist Eugène-Emmanuel Viollet-le-Duc.

Charnay had originally hoped to reach Stephens' broad, middle-class reading audience, yet his volume failed to equal the popularity of the *Incidents of Travel* series. Composed of large, individually printed plates, his photographic album proved nearly as prohibitively expensive as the early nineteenth-century lithographic works had been. Because of the great cost of the folio and its perceived nonmarketability, the text did not appear in English until after the proven success of the author's later *The Ancient Cities of the New World* (1887). It was only through the subsequent development of photogravure, a process that allowed for inexpensive photographic reproduction, that *Ancient Cities* was able to match the economy, and the wider readership, of Stephens' works.

Uncannily, both Charnay's and Stephens' publications appeared on the eve of military actions involving their native countries and the Mexican government. Whereas the publication of Stephens' last volumes had directly preceded the U.S. invasion of Mexico, Charnay's folio appeared in the same year as France's so-called Mexican "intervention" of 1863 — an event that resulted in France's suppression of the Mexican republic and installation of Emperor Maximilian. Though Charnay's 1858–1860 trip had involved no overtly political agenda, his work proved advantageous to his sponsors in the French government, who presumably sought the public's support for their expansionist policies. Charnay's romantic images of Mexico, like those of Stephens and Catherwood, seemed to whet France's popular desire for territorial conquest.[13]

Both Stephens and Charnay supported their countries' military aggression, although the latter exhibited none of Stephens' discretion in speaking of the French invasion.[14] Glorifying the French coup in *Cités et ruines américaines*, Charnay wrote that "it was France's duty to rouse Mexico from its numbness," adding, "America will not protest; paralyzed by the horrible [Civil] war that devours her . . . [and] reduced to powerlessness, she will only be able to watch jealously the birth of the magnificent empire that escaped her."[15] Charnay's strident chauvinism and his apparent disdain for the United States would later return to haunt him. Following the expulsion of France and the execution of Maximilian in 1867, Charnay was barred from fieldwork in Mexico for nearly two decades.[16] Furthermore, following his return to Mexico in the 1880s, Charnay found it difficult—if necessary—to favor his American patrons with the first rights to his work.

The immediate impact of Charnay's *Cités et ruines américaines* was more visual than political. In the photographs' radical sense of authenticity, seemingly divorced from artistic subjectivity, Charnay provided viewers with the experience of an eyewitness—and thereby increased his audience's sense of interpretive agency. Perceived as a kind of fact-gathering machine, the camera substituted actual experience with a transparently "real" document, a precious commodity in this era of increasingly objective investigation.[17] Given his near silence regarding the works he encountered on this first trip, Charnay himself appears to have been muted by the photographs' visual fidelity. As Walter Benjamin has noted, in this period "the process of pictorial reproduction was accelerated so enormously that it could not keep pace with speech."[18]

Charnay bolstered the sparse text of *Cités et ruines américaines* with a lengthy introduction by Napoleon III's minister of fine arts, Eugène-Emmanuel Viollet-le-Duc. Although Viollet-le-Duc had never traveled to Mexico, the documentary power of Charnay's photographs apparently provided all of the information this architectural historian required for his analysis. Running more than a hundred pages, Viollet-le-Duc's introduction was primarily concerned with the ethnic origins of the monuments' architects. "To what race do these people belong," he asked; "to purely white races, or to a race mixed with the white?"[19] Answering this question, he asserted that whereas most Mesoamerican ethnic groups represented a mélange of "white" and "yellow," certain peoples had once existed in the region whose ethnic character recalled "the most beautiful of white types, however far removed from the Celtic-Iberian or Spanish race."[20]

Viollet-le-Duc's particular interest in skin tone, a theme to which he repeatedly returned within his introduction, sprang from his racially determined theory of architectural evolution, a system ultimately derived from Joseph Arthur Gobineau's *Essai sur l'inégalité des races humaines* (1855). Attributing the human instinct for masonry building to ancient Aryan groups of the Himalayas, Viollet-le-Duc sought Aryan traces in nearly every monumental building tradition he examined. Mesoamerican architecture proved no exception. "It would be difficult to deny today the existence of relations between the Scandinavians and America from the ninth century of our era," Viollet-le-Duc asserted, having explained Scandinavians' derivation "from the high northern plateaus of India."[21]

Alluding to Viking contact in North America, Viollet-le-Duc explained that Mesoamerican settlement had resulted from a north-to-south migration pattern. "In admitting a priori that the Americas had been colonized by peoples from the north," Viollet-le-Duc asserted, this group, "always seeking sweeter skies, descended through the state of Ohio, occupying the coasts of the Carolinas, extending all the way to the Floridian coast, eventually spying the island of Cuba and soon Yucatan."[22] By thus linking the ancient earthworks of North America with the ruins of Mesoamerica, Viollet-le-Duc confirmed Stephens', and the Mormons', conflation of these cultures.

Given Charnay's theoretical reticence in *Cités et ruines américaines,* it is uncertain whether he ascribed to Viollet-le-Duc's migration theory at this stage. It is clear, however, that Viollet-le-Duc's subsequent work, *Habitations of Man in All Ages* (1876), shaped Charnay's views of the Toltec civilization, whose primacy in Mesoamerican culture formed Charnay's thesis in *The Ancient Cities of the New World.*[23] Narrated by fictional, time-traveling culture critics named Epergos and

Doxus, *Habitations of Man in All Ages* constituted Viollet-le-Duc's fullest treatment of architecture's Aryan origins. Beginning their journey with a visit to the "family of Arya" in the Himalayas, Doxus and Epergos witness the first construction of a stone shelter. Over the course of the following centuries, the pair observes the descendants of Arya's industrious family, described with "fair hair, white skin, and blue eyes," as they migrate east, west, and south, conquering weaker cultures and introducing their own masonry traditions.[24]

In the twenty-second chapter of the book, Viollet-le-Duc related Doxus and Epergos' arrival in "Yucatheca," where they encounter two distinct ethnic groups, the Nahuas and the Toltecs (here, Viollet-le-Duc incorrectly applies the term "Nahua"; the Nahua-speaking peoples of central Mexico are ethnically and geographically distinct from the Maya of Yucatan). Like the conquering Aryans, the Toltecs are described as "men of great stature from the north," with "whiter skin than the Nahuas"; the Nahuas, by contrast, are described as "an inferior class, brown-skinned, short, robust, and subjected to labor of all kinds."[25] Prior to the Toltecs' arrival, Viollet-le-Duc explained, the Nahuas had developed their own building traditions—yet "what they produced was irregular and unworthy of their conquerors." He continued, "The latter [Toltecs] have brought these artisans to work voluntarily or by force, and so have had temples, cities, and palaces built for them, worthy of the race."[26] Although Viollet-le-Duc's characterization of the Toltec invasion conformed in an impressionistic way to their historical conquest of Yucatan, he clearly viewed the Toltecs as the New World's Aryan culture bearers—a fiction that Charnay attempted to confirm in his later work.

In the 1870s, knowledge of the Toltec civilization was almost entirely based upon Aztec narratives recorded in postconquest chronicles. The Aztecs ascribed an ancient lineage to the Toltecs and claimed their cultural inheritance from this group, yet the Toltec empire had represented a relatively late development in Mesoamerican culture. Flourishing between A.D. 800 and 1200, the period when the nearly thousand-year-old Maya civilization had begun to dissolve, this warrior society of Central Mexico had established an empire that included parts of northern Yucatan by the end of the 900s. Following the destruction of its capital, Tula, in 1100, Toltec control of both central Mexico and Yucatan came to an end. Within another two hundred years, this civilization, like that of the classic Maya before them, had disappeared.

It was not until the fourteenth century, when the Aztecs had assumed power

in central Mexico, that the vanished Toltecs and their abandoned capital were historically rehabilitated, providing this successive warrior society with a convenient
cultural pedigree. As Mary Miller has noted, the Aztecs "telescoped all past glories
into the Toltec era," while retaining the term "Toltec" and "Tula" as labels for contemporary persons and cities.[27] Skilled Aztec craftsmen were described as
"Toltecs," for example, and their city, Tenochtitlan, as "Tula" (hence the later confusion concerning Tula's geographical location).

Viollet-le-Duc's and Charnay's belief in a single, Mesoamerican diffusion culture bears the stamp of another French scholar from this period, the abbot
Charles-Étienne Brasseur de Bourbourg. Having rediscovered a series of important ancient Mesoamerican texts in the 1850s and early 1860s, Brasseur de Bourbourg had published a twenty-six-hundred-page treatise entitled *Histoire des nations civilisées du Mexique et de l'Amérique centrale* between 1857 and 1863. A
work of tremendous scholarship, Brasseur de Bourbourg's *Histoire* represented
the most comprehensive treatment of ancient Mesoamerican sources yet written.
Throughout the 1860s the abbot continued his remarkable pace, translating the
Popol Vuh, the Quiché Maya's sacred text, as well as Friar Diego de Landa's crucial
sixteenth-century document, *Relación de las cosas de Yucatán.*[28] Following his rediscovery of Landa's manuscript, however, Brasseur de Bourbourg's scholarship
slipped into the dubious realm of Atlantis theory and cultural diffusionism.

Using Landa's recording of a Maya "alphabet," Brasseur de Bourbourg claimed
that he had unraveled the mystery of the Maya's ethnic origin. In attempting to
codify the local Maya's pictographic writing system, Landa had sought to corre-
late Maya glyphs with the letters of the Roman alphabet, relating the sound of
each letter to a specific glyph or series of glyphs. Failing to understand the radical
differences between written Roman and Mayan characters, Landa provided a visual primer linking the two systems, explaining, "Here begins their *a, b, c.* . . ."[29]
This system has yielded invaluable phonetic information for twentieth-century
Maya epigraphers, despite its misplaced method, yet it hardly provided Brasseur
de Bourbourg (as he claimed) with the tools to read Maya glyphic inscriptions.

Given his tremendous stature in ancient Mesoamerican scholarship, Brasseur
de Bourbourg provided the first academic confirmation for the theory of New
World diffusion. Publishing his treatise *Quatre lettres sur le Mexique* in 1868, the
abbot asserted that the Maya had descended from the Toltecs—who, he claimed,
had constituted the surviving population of the civilization of Atlantis.[30] This

vanished land mass, he asserted, had extended in a crescent from North America
to Africa; moreover, he suggested that the direction of cultural exchange had run
from west to east, preceding Atlantis' destruction around 4000 B.C.[31]

Brasseur de Bourbourg's insistence on the cultural primacy of the Toltec civilization confirmed Viollet-le-Duc's, and later Charnay's, characterizations of this
group. Not only did Brasseur de Bourbourg claim that the Toltecs represented Atlantis' last remnants, but, like Viollet-le-Duc, he also implied their connection to
Scandinavia—locating Tula, the Toltec capital, in northernmost Europe.[32] Charnay's correct identification of Tula, located in the state of Hidalgo north of Mexico City, disproved Brasseur de Bourbourg's latter claim, yet Charnay shared the
abbot's beliefs in a lost Atlantic land mass and in the diffusion of Toltec culture.[33]

In the decades that elapsed between Charnay's two Mexican expeditions, his
belief in the Toltecs' primacy grew from theoretical assumption to scholarly cer-
tainty. Upon his return to Mexico in 1880, all that remained was the collection of
data to confirm his theory.[34] The more leisurely tenor of this expedition, in
marked contrast to his hurried recording mission of the 1850s, was largely due to
new developments in photographic and casting technologies since midcentury.
Most important was the invention of the dry-plate negative process in the 1870s,
which freed Charnay from individually preparing and developing photographic
plates in the field. The new process not only lightened his equipment load but also
allowed him to document a far wider range of monuments within short, intensive
periods of work. Second, through the development of new casting techniques,
Charnay was able to create lightweight paper molds of architectural works. Essentially sculptural negatives, these paper molds obviated the need to transport
large quantities of plaster to the sites. With this expedition the process of visually
re-creating Mesoamerican monuments, in both two-dimensional and three-dimensional form, shifted from the field to Charnay's Paris studio.

The collecting activities of this second expedition, as outlined by Allen
Thorndike Rice in the *North American Review* in 1880, reflected Charnay's new
nationalistically driven agenda. In this article, Rice states that "we are happy that
it should be in our power to signalize the departure of an expedition to Central
America . . . [supported] through the united efforts of two powerful governments," the United States and France. Charnay's mission may have enjoyed joint
sponsorship, yet Rice insists that "in fairness to France, we must state that the pre-
dominance of American interests has been fully recognized by her."[35] Explaining
this arrangement, Rice notes that the expedition's "many valuable and interesting

accessions," primarily in the form of plaster casts, would be first presented to the Smithsonian Institution in Washington, D.C. The remaining artifacts, and second-generation casts, would be given to the Trocadéro Museum in Paris.[36]

The United States' preferential rights to Charnay's "accessions" derived not only from the greater American financial support of his expedition but also from the United States' perceived historical connection to the Mesoamerican past. By insisting upon the special relationship between "Americans"—meaning the citizens of the United States—and ancient Mesoamerica, Rice indicated that the U.S. sense of cultural inferiority had remained largely unchanged since Stephens' time.

Though Charnay would eventually donate the fruits of his expedition to the Smithsonian, his American sponsorship came primarily from a private, rather than an institutional, source. Before his departure in 1880, Charnay had enlisted the financial support of New Yorker Pierre Lorillard, owner of the Continental Tobacco Company.[37] Placing considerable financial resources at Charnay's command, Lorillard extended his generosity to his own native France; it was he, in fact, who had suggested the placement of secondary artifacts and casts in the Trocadéro—an arrangement that the French government, because of its nominal support of Charnay's expedition, could hardly have insisted upon.[38] In recognition of his patronage, the collection in the Trocadéro would bear Lorillard's name, as would the Central American site today known as Yaxchilán, which Charnay temporarily claimed for his patron in 1881.

In his dedication to Lorillard in *Ancient Cities,* Charnay implied that he and his American patron shared a belief in the unity of ancient American civilization:

> I strove, during the progress of these studies, to carry out the program *laid down by you* [my italics] toward the reconstruction of civilizations that have passed away. I think I have succeeded, and I hope to have sufficiently demonstrated that these civilizations had but one and the same origin—that they were Toltec and comparatively modern. . . . If it shall be found that I have resolved this vexed American Question, so hotly controverted hitherto, it will be mainly due to your generous support.[39]

Charnay's mission to solve the "American Question" appears to have been theoretically supported by Lorillard himself. Furthermore, in his allusion to the "comparatively modern" date of Mesoamerican civilization, mentioned here for the first time in Charnay's writings, the explorer both affirmed Stephens' dating system and neatly solved the problem of the Toltec/Maya chronological gap. Correctly assigning the Toltec empire to the end of the first millennium, Charnay nonetheless came to the false conclusion that all subsequent Mesoamerican cities, both central Mexican and Maya, postdated this Toltec foundation period.

Between May and October of 1880, Charnay focused his energies in central Mexico, the seat of the former Toltec empire. At the site of the ancient Toltec capital, Tula, in Hidalgo, Charnay determined the shape of his subsequent explorations in central Mexico, Chiapas, and Yucatan. Thoroughly sounding Tula's overgrown structures for hidden treasure caches, Charnay subsequently turned to the excavation and photographing of the large multichambered residential complex northeast of site's ceremonial center. Although Tula's architecture represents a rather lackluster example of ancient Mesoamerican craftsmanship, Charnay's thesis had predisposed him to lavish praise on the works he excavated there.[40] "We are filled with admiration for the marvelous building capacity of the people who erected them," he writes; "they were acquainted with pilasters, caryatids, square and round columns; indeed, they seem to have been familiar with every architectural device."[41]

In his analyses of Tula's architecture, Charnay often reverts to classical terminology—a device intended to imply the Toltecs' position as the Greeks of the New World. Referring to the characteristic central Mexican *talud-tablero* system, a distinctive profile created by capping a slanted wall with a slightly overhanging, vertical frieze, Charnay credits the Toltecs with creating a "North American order" equivalent to the Doric order of the Greeks.[42] Furthermore, asserting that "the degree of culture of a nation" could be read in its specialized building typologies, Charnay notes that "as the Greek discoursed upon philosophy walking under noble porticoes, so did the Toltec offer prayers in appropriate temples."[43]

Charnay's insistence upon an analogous relationship between the Toltecs and the Greeks is most clearly seen in his hypothetical illustration of a seated "Toltec king" (fig. 4.3). In this image Charnay intentionally recalls the pose, costume, and throne of Phidias' cult image at the Temple of Zeus at Olympia—also the source, noted previously, for Thomas Gage's illustration of the Aztec war god Huitzilopochtli (see fig. 1.3 and corresponding text). Given his characterization of the Toltecs as "nearly white," it is curious that Charnay presents a dark-complected Maya in this image; apparently, Charnay either photographed a local figure in this fantastic setting or had the costume and throne added in the photograph's subsequent engraving.

4.3. CHARNAY, "TOLTEC KING" (Désiré Charnay, *The Ancient Cities of the New World:* 1887).

Though Charnay intentionally linked the Toltecs and the Greeks in his writings, he by no means ascribed to the classical-contact theories that had preceded Stephens' work. Rather, Charnay accepted the theory that native North American populations had migrated from Asia, across the Bering Strait—a belief that did not exclude his adherence to Viollet-le-Duc's theory of Aryan contact in North America. While Viollet-le-Duc had suggested Mesoamerica's derivation from Scandinavian/Viking contact in *Cités et ruines américaines,* his narrative of Aryan diffusion in *Habitations of Man* had also explained the group's colonization of Asia. By extending the trajectory of this latter migration pattern to the Americas, Charnay was able to support his Bering Strait thesis while still preserving the Toltecs' supposed Aryan ethnicity.

Describing the ancient Toltecs as above middle height, with light complexions and thick hair, features that "distinguished [them] in later times from the other aborigines," Charnay clearly echoed Viollet-le-Duc's earlier Aryan-based distinction between the Toltecs and the Nahuas.[44] At Teotihuacan, just north of Mexico City, Charnay found archaeological confirmation for this ethnic distinction in the hundreds of molded clay heads he excavated there (fig. 4.4). A mixture of presumed "Caucasian" and "Greek-profiled" portraits with more numerous "Indian types," this group of artifacts indicated for Charnay the ethnic heterogeneity of ancient central Mexico, while providing evidence of a small, Caucasian elite.[45]

Charnay first tested his thesis of Toltec diffusion at Teotihuacan. Culturally and temporally distinct from Tula, the enormous city of Teotihuacan had been founded nearly a thousand years before Tula by a group whose precise ethnicity remains a mystery. Sacked and abandoned by the year 750 A.D., the site had collapsed almost two hundred years before the establishment of Tula. Nevertheless, Charnay found abundant evidence to support the ancient city's presumed Toltec

4.4. MOLDED CLAY HEADS, TEOTIHUACAN (Désiré Charnay, *The Ancient Cities of the New World*: 1887).

origin. In uncovering one of the grand apartment complexes at Teotihuacan, for example, he exclaimed, "[W]hy, it is our Tula palace over again!" — a correspondence simply based, apparently, on the structures' similar use of heavily battered cement walls and right-angled corners.[46] Furthermore, in Teotihuacan's numerous examples of *talud-tablero* temple construction, Charnay perceived the Toltecs' application of their distinctive architectural "order" (this profile at Teotihuacan had, in fact, served as the source for the later Toltec constructions).

At Tula, Teotihuacan, and other sites in central Mexico, Charnay carried out a particularly aggressive campaign of artifactual acquisition, forming collections for the Smithsonian and the Trocadéro while hoping to make his own fortune. In four days of excavations at Nahualac and Tenenepanco, for example, Charnay unearthed more than eight hundred pieces of pottery and stonework. Despite the archaeological value of his findings, he expressed with regret that he had found "few jewels and no precious stones."[47] Censuring the destructive acts of "treasure-seeking looters" at Tula, Charnay himself was one of the worst offenders; hearing rumors that a local shepherd had discovered a buried vase at Tula filled with five hundred ounces of gold, Charnay nearly destroyed Structure 2 at the site while looking for a similar cache.[48] Justifying such acts as necessary for the enrichment of Washington and Parisian collections, Charnay bristled at the Mexican government's insistence upon claiming "one third from the best of our finds." In the future, Charnay warned would-be explorers, they should "do their work quietly, offering nothing to the Republic."[49]

Though he found no buried gold, Charnay considered all of his excavated artifacts as "priceless in every respect, because of their analogy and intimate connection with all those we shall subsequently discover, forming the first links in the chain of evidence respecting our theory of the unity of American civilisation."[50] To demonstrate this perceived artifactual unity, and to augment his collection of copied works, Charnay carefully mined the collections of the National Museum in Mexico City. Finding that "the Museum was not in working order" and furthermore that "nothing was classified," Charnay illustrated the museum's haphazard stacking of Aztec works (fig. 4.5) as an example of the institution's lack of organization.[51] Officially founded by the Mexican National Congress in 1831, the museum had faced a series of shutdowns and rather haphazard management until the 1870s; by the time of Charnay's visit in 1880, however, the museum's apparent chaos actually derived from an ambitious reorganization campaign.[52] Claiming to find "nothing remarkable" here, Charnay nevertheless ordered the casting of three

4.5. AZTEC "IDOLS" AT THE MUSEO NACIONAL IN MEXICO
CITY (Désiré Charnay, *The Ancient Cities of the New World*: 1887).

hundred vases from the collection that he "caused to be placed in the Trocadéro during the [1889] Paris Exhibition."[53]

Moving east to the site of Palenque in December 1880, Charnay continued to seek evidence for Toltec migrations. Though he conceded that the sophisticated reliefs and architectural refinement of Palenque surpassed the efforts of Tula's builders, he asserted that the "earlier" works at Tula and Teotihuacan had represented "the parent samples" of Palenque's later, more highly evolved style.[54] Furthermore, citing the excellent preservation of Palenque's stucco figures and the lack of wear on the site's numerous flights of stairs, he insisted that the city could not have been more than a few centuries old—a conclusion that erroneously situated Palenque's construction after that of Tula.

Despite their apparent stylistic congruence, Charnay did draw certain distinctions between Tula's and Palenque's building typologies. Asserting that Palenque represented a holy city or a pilgrimage site, rather than a strictly urban center like Tula or Teotihuacan, Charnay characterized its ruins as exclusively religious in nature—a false assumption later echoed by many twentieth-century Mayanists.[55] Furthermore, in his analysis of Palenque's temples, Charnay demonstrated their more direct link to Asian traditions, confirming his theory that the Toltecs had arrived on the continent via the Bering Strait. Juxtaposing his illustration of Palenque's Temple of the Sun with an image of a contemporary Japanese teahouse (fig. 4.6), Charnay asserted that "anyone who is acquainted with Japanese architecture would be struck by the resemblance of this temple to a Japanese sanctuary."[56]

For Charnay, the resemblance between these geographically and culturally distinct traditions derived from his belief in their shared architectural and ethnic ancestry. In Mesoamerica, as in Japan, India, Cambodia, and Java, he explained, "a foreign race [presumably Viollet-le-Duc's wandering Aryans] introduced and implanted a ready-made civilisation in the invaded country, using the conquered race for the construction of its buildings."[57] The similarity between the Japanese teahouse and the Temple of the Sun, then, was the result of a single foreign influence tempered by differing local labor forces. "These monuments, as also those of Yucatan and lower Mexico," he explained, belonged "to a branch of the southern Malay civilisation, separated from the parent stock, and crossed many times with whites."[58]

In the ruined cities of Yucatan, Charnay continued to seek out the Toltecs' influence—a task that proved easier at sites like Uxmal and Chichen Itza, where the Toltecs *had* established a stronghold between the tenth and eleventh centuries. Ignoring all evidence of the region's fully developed pre-Toltec culture, Charnay characterized the architecture of these ancient cities as no different from that of the works he had seen at Tula and other central Mexican sites. Following his survey of Yucatan, Charnay categorically stated that "we are in a position to affirm that there was no other civilization in Central America except the Toltec civilization, and that if another existed, our having met with no trace of it gives us the right to deny it altogether."[59]

As Charnay neared the end of his second expedition, he stated that the physical hardship of his field research "sinks into utter insignificance as compared with the great joy of our discoveries, the ever fresh interest of our photographs, [and] the looking forward with immense satisfaction to the time when we shall produce the splendid squeezes of these grand, mysterious inscriptions, not yet found in any museum."[60] The pride that Charnay felt for his papier-mâché molds, which would give rise to later casts or "squeezes," reflects the tremendous importance he placed on architectural molding during this second expedition. Initially considered a corollary activity to his photographic documentation, mold making ultimately formed the primary part of Charnay's work at Palenque and subsequent sites in Yucatan. By the summer of 1882, Charnay had produced more than three hundred square feet of molds from Palenque's temple facades, as well as eight hundred square feet from Uxmal and Chichen Itza.[61]

Charnay's unparalleled production of architectural casts depended upon newly developed paper-molding processes.[62] Rather than casting the ruins on site, as previous explorers had attempted to do, Charnay simply created papier-mâché molds from which he could produce a limitless number of plaster reproductions. Applying six layers of newspaper or packing tissue onto the surfaces he wished to reproduce, he would brush the paper with a thin water-and-flour mixture until it fully adhered to the stone or stucco surface; squeezing the excess moisture from this overlaid paper, he would remove the application while it remained wet, carefully drying it near a banked fire.[63] Once the mold had reached its proper firmness, yet before it had lost its elasticity, it was rolled and tied for transport.

Molds of the temples' sculptures and architectural elements were not as easily produced nor as visually faithful as photographs. Although Charnay praised the efficiency and economy of this new paper-mold system, he explained that "it would be impossible to give an idea of the immense and minute brushwork required to cover 325 square feet of paper six sheets deep."[64] Added to this labor-intensive process were problems in achieving clear impressions; clinging debris, crumbling stucco, and even windy conditions made applying the paper a sometimes impossible task. Charnay, too, appears to have mistaken the monuments' authentic stucco exteriors for a later Spanish addition—a misunderstanding that led him, before making some of his impressions, to attempt the removal of the reliefs' topmost layer. "We try with small success to undo their savage work [the presumed Spanish stucco]," he explained, "by means of daggers, brushes, and repeated washes, taking up much time, but in most cases the relief is lost to science, being too much defaced to allow us to make squeezes."[65]

By eliminating plaster casting from his fieldwork, Charnay was able to mold far more extensively than his predecessors, assuming he did not destroy the works in the process. Charnay's speed proved remarkable as well; when his first set of Palenque molds was destroyed by an accidental fire, he was able to replace the entire group—all 325 square feet—within just ten days.[66] Estimating that the molds he had taken would have weighed close to thirty thousand pounds as plaster copies, Charnay exultantly explained that his collection of paper molds weighed no more than five hundred pounds.[67] Furthermore, by creating molds rather than reproductions, Charnay was spared the protest of local authorities who had asserted that Stephens' casts "at first sight . . . may be taken, surely, for second originals."[68] Charnay's paper molds, like his photographic negatives, "conveyed no picture to their eyes"—leaving officials "well convinced of the utter lack of value in the treasures that I carried."[69]

In envisioning the final context of his cast and reassembled temple fragments, Charnay fully understood the radical sense of fidelity they would convey in a museum setting. Charnay writes, for example, that once he had established his casts

4.6. *Left:* TEMPLE OF THE SUN, PALENQUE.
Right: JAPANESE TEMPLE (Désiré Charnay, *The Ancient Cities of the New World:* 1887).

from Copan at the Smithsonian Institution, his work would form a substitute for the experience of traveling to the site:

> It is true that the quiet student at Washington will, of necessity, remain cold to . . . the feelings which have moved enthusiastic travelers. But, though the future investigator may have no share in the genial enthusiasm of the explorer . . . he will, in effect, have before his eyes Copan, with all its mysteries, its columns scored with hieroglyphs, its rows of death's heads on sculptured walls, its nameless kings and gods.[70]

The revolutionary verisimilitude of the cast, then, would replace the objective reality of the original. Stephens' earlier attempt to purchase Copan, and to reassemble the city within the United States, would have essentially been effected through Charnay's scheme.

By obviating the need to purchase or dismantle sites, Charnay's casting potentially distanced him from the claim-staking agenda that had fueled Stephens' work, yet Charnay proved equally susceptible to the temptations of proprietary acquisition. In March 1881, Charnay arrived at the ancient city of Yaxchilán, on Usumacinta River, seeking what he believed to be Stephens' "lost city."[71] Although he found the English explorer Alfred Maudslay already established there, Charnay promptly asserted his own rights to the site and named it in honor of his American patron.[72] Mapped in *The Ancient Cities of the New World* as the "Villa Lorillard," the site retained the name of Charnay's benefactor well into the twentieth century.[73]

Describing the Villa Lorillard as lying in a "region hitherto unclassified," Charnay implied the area's political, as well as its archaeological, lack of affiliation.[74] Situated just southwest of the territory held by the Santa Cruz Maya, this area of Chiapas bordered the battle zones of the bloody Caste War, begun in 1847. By the 1870s the Mexican government had divided Yucatan in half, creating a north-south border running between Chichen Itza and Valladolid; the area to the west, including the capital city Mérida, remained under federal control, while the region to the east was surrendered to the Maya rebels. Traveling to archaeological sites within rebel-occupied territory, Charnay protected himself with a guard of nearly a hundred men (a small army similar to the one Stephens had wished for).[75] The so-called Villa Lorillard belonged within federally controlled territory, yet Charnay echoed Stephens' earlier prediction that even the officially recognized government was poised on the edge of political anarchy; in mapping this region, Charnay labeled the entire eastern half of Yucatan with the words "Re-volted Indians."

Whereas Charnay's casts and photographs represented the most significant material achievements of his expedition, his publication of *The Ancient Cities of the New World,* in French in 1885 and in English in 1887, represented his greatest contribution to the travel literature of this region. Not only was the work well received in American scholarly circles, hailed by both the *North American Review* and the American Antiquarian Society, but it also reached the largest reading audience since Stephens' publications of the 1840s — to the great satisfaction of his American publishers, Harper and Brothers, who continued to reap profits from Stephens' reprinted works. Benefiting from the new process of photographic engraving, Charnay ensured that his photographs would be economically and accurately reproduced. Not only did this allow him to serially publish his work in newspapers and scholarly journals, but, because these images were unprotected by copyright restrictions, subsequent authors also endlessly recycled his images in later nineteenth- and early twentieth-century tourist guides.[76]

By providing the United States with casts and photographs of the monuments, in addition to a popular travel narrative that established the unity of "America's" ancient past, Charnay had accomplished nearly all of the projected goals of Stephens' earlier work. Charnay's Toltec-diffusion theory linked the antiquities of the United States and Mexico in no uncertain terms, while presenting an ethnic profile of this ancient civilization that mirrored the ancestry of the nineteenth-century U.S. white population. Referring to the Toltecs as the "first Americans," Charnay asserted that "we might pronounce with safety that all the monuments in North America were of Toltec origin."[77]

5

BORDERING ON THE MAGNIFICENT

AUGUSTUS AND ALICE LE PLONGEON

IN THE KINGDOM OF MÓO

> Life stirred within a beauteous Maya queen
> Of noble deeds, of gracious word and mien . . .
> Within her being Past and Future slept,
> And into guileless mind no phantom crept.
>
> —ALICE LE PLONGEON,
> *Queen Móo's Talisman* (1902)

IN HIS 1880 review of Charnay's *Cités et ruines américaines,* the *North American Review*'s editor Allen Thorndike Rice envisioned an end to the archaeological insecurities that had plagued the United States since the 1820s. "America, it has been said, is without traditions, has no past," he wrote, continuing:

> [B]ut just as geology shows that this Western Continent [North America] is really the "Old World", so archaeological research will perhaps show that man and human civilization are as ancient here as in Europe. However that may be, these venerable monuments appeal with special force to Americans of the present day, not only on account of their value as purely scientific data, but because they supply the links which connect us with the past.[1]

Acknowledging efforts made by earlier archaeologists and writers to supply these links, Rice also warned Americans to exercise discretion—cautioning that "theories of origin of the American races from an Israelitish [*sic*] stock . . . may be safely dismissed as the fruits of misguided enthusiasm and perverted ingenuity."[2] Within five years of this review, American archaeologist Augustus Le Plongeon not only proclaimed a far greater antiquity for the North American continent than Rice projected but also contextualized these findings with a "misguided enthusiasm and perverted ingenuity" far surpassing any claims made by colonial authors, Waldeck, or even the Mormon Church.

The last of the great amateur archaeologists from this period, Le Plongeon was also the most consistent promoter of ancient Mexico's ties to "American" history. In Le Plongeon's mind, however, this history was founded upon an intensely personal vision. For him and for his wife, Alice Dixon Le Plongeon, the remains of ancient Mexico and Central America represented nothing less than the seeds of world civilization, the birthplace of Freemasonry, and the former kingdom of their own reincarnated souls.

The period of Charnay's and Le Plongeon's most intense activity, the 1870s and 1880s, had witnessed tremendous advances in archaeological technology, particularly in terms of field photography and plaster casting, without any corresponding increase in the knowledge of ancient Mesoamerica's ethnic origins, writing systems, or dating. Stephens had been closer to understanding the works of the ancient Maya, in fact, than had any of his latter nineteenth-century successors. His correct assumptions concerning the ruins' indigenous authorship and the historical content of their glyphic inscriptions, however, were not widely accepted until the twentieth century, when the archaeological evidence for these assumptions was more firmly established.

Compounding the dearth of reliable historical information in this period, and inviting further chauvinistic distortions of the ruins, were the dual phenomena of Mexico's unprecedented political instability and the equally unprecedented industrial and economic strength of the post–Civil War United States. At no other point in their histories had Mexico been so vulnerable to cultural claim staking, or the United States so invested in its own national mythology.

Conditions, then, were particularly ripe for any American archaeologist driven to prove the specious diffusion theories of Brasseur de Bourbourg—whose *Quatre lettres sur le Méxique* (1868) promoted North America as the world's "mother-continent." Given the extraordinary license that Le Plongeon was afforded in war-torn Yucatan, as well as his penchant for photographic manipulation, he was able to "prove" the French scholar's theories, producing the most bizarre record of ancient American civilization ever written.

Born on the Isle of Jersey to French parents, Le Plongeon had emigrated to the United States as a young man in the 1840s; by the next decade, he had gained permanent U.S. citizenship and established a photography studio in San Francisco. Le Plongeon's first interest in archaeology dates to the 1860s, when he was asked to accompany Ephraim Squier — previously noted in connection with the archaeology of upstate New York (see chapter 3) — on an expedition to document the ancient ruins of Peru. An ultimately fruitless partnership, the eight-year expedition ended in acrimony between Le Plongeon and Squier, whom Le Plongeon accused of absconding with his photographic negatives and refusing to publish the results of their investigations.[3] According to Lawrence Desmond and Phyllis Messenger, it was during his stay in South America that Le Plongeon first embraced Brasseur de Bourbourg's diffusion theory.[4]

The shape of Le Plongeon's future professional and personal life were determined in January 1873. That month, addressing the American Geographical Society, Le Plongeon formally announced the agenda of his proposed trip to Yucatan; entitled "Vestiges of Antiquity: On the Coincidences between the Monuments of Ancient America and Those of Assyria and Egypt," the lecture outlined his plans to gather evidence for Brasseur de Bourbourg's thesis, proving the theory of Bering Strait migration to the Americas — but in *reverse* (the ancient Maya, Le Plongeon believed, had traveled westward across Asia before founding the "outpost civilization" of ancient Egypt).[5] Later that month Le Plongeon married Alice Dixon, a British woman twenty-five years his junior, who would become his closest working partner and eventually his only academic defender.

In July 1873 the Le Plongeons embarked on their first expedition to Yucatan, a period of investigation that would last, with intermittent returns to the United States, for nearly a decade. Declaring the archaeological field as uncharted as at the start of the nineteenth century, Le Plongeon wrote:

> When Mrs. Le Plongeon and I landed in 1873 . . . we thought that because we had read the works of Stephens, Waldeck, and carefully examined the photographic views of Mr. Charnay . . . [that] we knew all about them. Alas! Vain presumption! When in presence of the antique shrines of the Mayas, we soon saw . . . how little those writers had seen of the monuments they pretended to describe.[6]

Throughout the 1870s the couple negotiated an area of northern Yucatan that, though archaeologically rich, was also the geographic center of Mexico's Caste War — a violent, twenty-five-year-old conflict between the area's indigenous

Maya and the region's sometimes-ruling federal government. Successfully avoiding armed threat from either the recognized government or from the rebel leaders (the Le Plongeons' strategies are discussed below), Augustus Le Plongeon initially had a promising career in the region. His many important findings from the sites of Chichen Itza and Uxmal, for example, were regularly featured in such periodicals as *Harper's Weekly, Scientific American,* and *North American Review,* while his patronage derived from the august American Antiquarian Society, by way of the society's president Stephen Salisbury. Salisbury maintained his financial and personal relationship with Le Plongeon long after the archaeologist had been discredited in scholarly circles and abandoned by patrons like Pierre Lorillard, Charnay's primary supporter.[7]

Following their arrival in Mérida, the region's capital city, Augustus and Alice Le Plongeon immersed themselves within the politics and culture of contemporary Yucatan. Soon conversant with the issues underlying the region's Caste War, particularly the injustices suffered by the Maya under the hacienda system, the Le Plongeons—and Alice in particular—took up their cause in passionate letters to the United States and through sincere, if limited, local advocacy. Undertaking instruction in Yucatec Maya, the Le Plongeons were the first American explorers, amateur or otherwise, to communicate with local guides, workers, and government officials in their own language.[8]

Such instances of political and cultural engagement, along with Augustus Le Plongeon's recognition of indigenous Maya authorship of the ruins, contributed to the Le Plongeons' acceptance by the Santa Cruz Maya—the rebel group in control of eastern Yucatan. The Le Plongeons' informal alliance with the Santa Cruz Maya, or at least their recognition by this group as neutral parties in the Caste War, proved particularly important at the site of Chichen Itza, which had fallen under rebel control soon after the Le Plongeons' arrival in Mérida. For the Santa Cruz Maya, designating Chichen Itza as their capital had been an act of self-conscious political symbolism—echoed in the 1990s by the Chiapas rebels' selection of Palenque as a symbolic rebel stronghold. Aside from the exceptional (and jealously regarded) liberty they were granted at Chichen Itza, and their relative freedom at federally occupied sites in the western Puuc region, the Le Plongeons had to curtail the remainder of their itinerary in eastern Yucatan, skipping Postclassic sites like Tulum altogether—an omission that particularly piqued Pierre Lorillard, who had hoped Le Plongeon would claim Tulum in his name, as Charnay had done at the site now known as Yaxchilán.[9]

Arriving at Chichen Itza in May 1875, the Le Plongeons took the precaution of traveling with an armed guard, under the directorship of a Colonel Díaz;[10] friendly relations with the Santa Cruz Maya apparently remained tenuous, however. Le Plongeon's primary objective at the site, from the very beginning, was to furnish evidence for Brasseur de Bourbourg's diffusion theory and to establish the advanced state of ancient Maya civilization. This mission took an immediate and characteristic turn for the bizarre when Le Plongeon encountered the building now known as the Akab Dzib, a Classic-era Maya structure whose stone friezes, Le Plongeon believed, held the key to understanding Maya history.

Inspired by a story Le Plongeon had heard from Mariano Chablé, an elderly man from the town of Espita, Le Plongeon sought proof that the "ancient cord" that Chablé described in this structure's friezes — a typical Maya rope motif — was in fact an ancient representation of a telegraph system.[11] Though the assertion struck even Le Plongeons' contemporaries as absurd, the incident perfectly illustrates Le Plongeon's insistence that world culture, and even the inventions of the modern era, depended entirely upon the mother culture of the Maya. Writing about the incident years later, Le Plongeon despaired that its importance — and that of other examples like it — had been overlooked by scholars, claiming that the works "will reveal the history of the mighty nations that have dwelt on this Western continent — they will tell of the origin of all our ... traditions."[12]

Le Plongeon's inventive reading of the archaeological record was not restricted to his anachronistic projection of nineteenth-century technologies. In a pivotal episode in 1875, Le Plongeon projected *himself* into the Mesoamerican past as well. Seeking to establish his own connection to the site of Chichen Itza, a sacred city to the Santa Cruz Maya, Le Plongeon not only attempted to convince his workers that he had occupied the site in a former life but also that his image had been placed on the city's largest temple, the pyramid known as El Castillo. In the following passage, Le Plongeon explained the scene of this discovery in language that suggests, at least at this early stage, that Le Plongeon was aware of the deception he was perpetrating:

> On one of the antae [pillars] at the entrance on the north side [of El Castillo] is the portrait of a warrior wearing a long, straight, pointed beard. . . . I placed my head against the stone so as to represent the same position of my face ... and called the attention of my Indians to the similarity of his and my own features. They followed every lineament of the

faces with their fingers to the very point of the beard, and soon uttered an exclamation of astonishment: "Thou! Here!"[13]

It is difficult to understand the workers' astonishment at this presumed coincidence, if we are to trust Le Plongeon's account at all. Le Plongeon wore a long, pointed beard, it is true, although one must imagine that such beards were not a particularly unusual style in the 1870s (and yet they are, in fact, relatively rare in pre-Columbian imagery). Furthermore, the schematic, central Mexican style of the relief he describes could hardly have constituted an individualized portrait.

If Le Plongeon's ruse was as successful as he claimed — and there is evidence that it was — the reason may lie in the archaeologist's uncanny success at finding buried or hidden artifacts, all of which he claimed were related to the cult surrounding his former self (and which, time has shown, are almost all of authentic ancient origin). In 1931, Edward Thompson, the U.S. consul at Mérida, related a secondhand account of one of Le Plongeon's workers from this period. The grandson of Desiderio Kansal, who had participated in Le Plongeon's digs at Chichen Itza, related to Thompson his grandfather's belief that "the bearded white one" [Le Plongeon] had special powers of divination, always knowing exactly where to dig; "the figures of *bacabes* [sculptures of minor gods]," he told Thompson, "rose out of the ground as if to meet the bearded white one. . . . [A]s he looked at the *bacabes,* we saw that his lips were moving. . . . [D]oubtless he was speaking to them."[14]

Le Plongeon's unusual archaeological technique was confirmed by his contemporary Juan Péon Contreras, director of the Museo Yucateco in Mérida. Contreras explained in 1877 that Le Plongeon's discoveries were the result of "abstruse archaeological reasoning and . . . meditation," an image that Le Plongeon himself fostered in staged photographs portraying these deep reveries.[15] Characterizations of Le Plongeon's "psychic archaeology" dovetail neatly with his wife's profound interest in mesmerism, séances, and the occult. Her own first book, *Here and There in Yucatan* (1886), for example, featured lengthy sections devoted to local Maya "magic" practices, including an expanded treatment of a *Harper's Bazaar* article she had previously written about the "evil eye" in Yucatan.[16] By 1888, word of Le Plongeon's inexplicable success had even reached the leader of the Theosophical movement in New York, Madame Helena P. Blavatsky, who cited the work of the Le Plongeons as proof of "metaphysical archaeology."[17]

Immediately following his demonstration at El Castillo, Augustus Le Plongeon made the most important discovery of his career—a stone figure found nearly seven meters underground, beneath the structure now known as the Platform of the Eagles. Le Plongeon stated that after the bearded-relief episode, "every word of mine was implicitly obeyed"; according to him, the workers "returned to the excavation and worked with such good will that they soon brought a ponderous statue to the surface."[18] The statue, a spectacularly preserved depiction of a reclining male, appeared unlike any ancient Maya work known to contemporary archaeologists (fig. 5.1). For modern archaeologists, this work is an important visual indicator of the Toltecs' presence in Yucatan; in type and composition, it is easily identifiable as central Mexican—yet elements of its style, and certainly its location, speak of Maya origins.[19] Since the discovery of this work, fourteen similar figures have been found at Chichen Itza,[20] each showing a reclining male figure holding an offering bowl. None have been found, however, of the same quality and scale as the first.

Unaware of the work's historical importance, yet anxious to assign it an immediate narrative, Le Plongeon named the figure "Chaac mool," meaning "red or great jaguar paw" in Yucatec Maya—a romantic label intended to link the work with a fictional former ruler of the site.[21] Speaking of this figure, Le Plongeon insisted: "it is not an idol, but a true portrait of a man who has lived an earthly life; I have seen him represented in battle, in councils, and in court receptions."[22] This invented royal personage, Le Plongeon explained, was closely associated with the

5.1. LE PLONGEON'S CHACMOOL FIGURE, CHICHEN ITZA (labeled "Prince Coh")
(Augustus Le Plongeon, *Sacred Mysteries among the Mayas*: 1886).

archaeologist himself—a fact immediately registered, he says, in his workers' response to the statue:

> So, they said, thou art one of our great men, who has been disenchanted. Thou, too, wert a companion of the great Lord Chaacmol [*sic*]. That is why thou didst know where he was hidden; and thou hast come to disenchant him also. His time to live again on earth has arrived.[23]

In his first photograph of the chacmool[24] following its excavation (fig. 5.2), Le Plongeon deploys this self-projection in visual terms. Seated in a pose mirroring that of the reclining chacmool figure (also referred to, as above, as "Lord Chaac Mool"), Le Plongeon conflates himself with this ancient Maya "ruler" (ironically,

5.2. LE PLONGEON POSED WITH CHACMOOL, CHICHEN ITZA, 1875 (Augustus Le Plongeon, *Queen Móo and the Egyptian Sphinx:* 1896).

as Mary Miller has argued, the figure may actually represent a humiliated captive rather than a person of rank).[25] To the left of Le Plongeon, a member of his excavation team strikes a pose that was most likely orchestrated by the archaeologist himself; crossing his chest with his arm and clutching his shoulder, this contemporary Maya re-creates a classic Maya gesture of submission to a great lord or captor—a sign that Le Plongeon, at least, would have known from Maya vases and relief sculpture. The final effect of this *tableau vivant* was to convince Le Plongeon's audience—as he claims to have convinced his workers—that the royal legacy of Chichen Itza had been transferred to a white, middle-aged French émigré from San Francisco.

The importance of the chacmool's discovery, for Le Plongeon, did not end with his identification as its subject. Hoping to fully capitalize on his discovery, the archaeologist was determined to send the work to the 1876 Centennial Exposition in Philadelphia. At the nation's first world's fair, and the first public celebration of its all-too-brief history, the statue would have provided an international audience with evidence of the continent's "former grandeur"—proof that the American Antiquarian Society had been seeking since the 1820s. For Le Plongeon in particular, the work's presence at Philadelphia would have justified Stephen Salisbury's continued support for his excavations and, Le Plongeon hoped, would have gained the archaeologist a wider and badly needed sponsorship base.

Knowing that the Mexican government might take exception to this plan, the Le Plongeons conveyed the statue on a wooden cart to a hidden location near Piste, covering it in oilcloths and tree branches "so that a casual traveler, ignorant of the existence of such an object, would not even suspect it."[26] Knowledge of the statue's whereabouts eventually reached President Tejado and other local Yucatec politicians, however, who banned the work's export—citing an 1827 law that forbade foreign ownership of Mexican antiquities.[27] Tejado's enforcement of this rarely invoked law, an unusual instance of local protest, transformed the statue's custodianship into a cause célèbre—a symbol of the cultural power struggle that Stephens had initiated in the 1840s.

In a desperate appeal to Tejado, Le Plongeon asked how the president could allow "the greatest discovery ever made in American archaeology, to remain lost and unknown to scientific men, [and] to the choicest of nations," adding, "No! I do not believe it!"[28] To the archaeologist, displaying the work solely within Mexico's borders was tantamount its reconsignment to the ground. Deaf to Le Plongeon's appeals, Yucatec politicians brought the recovered statue to Mérida by

wagon, staging a parade and declaring a public holiday in the statue's honor—
only to have the work confiscated in turn, two months later, by Mexican president
Porfirio Díaz and the federal government in Mexico City.[29] Taken from Mérida
aboard the Mexican gunboat *Libertad,* the chacmool was installed in the National
Museum of Mexico, where officials replaced the work's inscription, "Discovery of
the wise archaeologist, Mr. Le Plongeon, in the ruins of Chichen Itza," with a text
praising President Díaz for bestowing the treasure upon a grateful nation.[30]

The controversy generated by the chacmool's discovery, and the enormous
cultural power with which Le Plongeon, Tejado, and Díaz invested this work, illu-
minate the roles that nationalism played in Mesoamerican archaeology during
the Porfiriato period. To Le Plongeon, the discovery of the work constituted his
ownership; given his presumption of American precedence at these sites, and his
elastic view of the American past, he believed that the chacmool's surrender had
robbed the United States of an important cultural legacy. To Tejado and his Yucatec constituency, retaining the statue became a token of regional pride—a
symbol of the area's distinction from central Mexico and from the federal government it resented. Finally, to Díaz and his cultural ministers, confiscation of the
work acted in two ways; Yucatan's forfeiture placed its archaeological legacy
under federal jurisdiction, while Le Plongeon's loss sent the clear message that
Mexican national interests trumped the rights of American discovery. Following
this episode, American claims on the Mesoamerican past—whether actual or
ideological—could no longer be made without a challenge from Mexico.

Despite his profound and lasting disappointment over the chacmool's confiscation, Le Plongeon subsequently enlarged the scope of his archaeological activity as well as the fictional narrative with which he invested it. Discovering a well-
preserved mural in the Temple of the Jaguars, a structure overlooking Chichen
Itza's Great Ball Court, Le Plongeon claimed to have found the key to understanding the chacmool's historical narrative. The meaning of this mural, a complex battle scene featuring scores of individual figures, still eludes modern scholars—although it may represent the ninth-century sacking of the Classic Maya city
Piedras Negras.[31] Undaunted by the mural's inscrutability, Le Plongeon formu-
lated an authoritative interpretation of the work. The story he invented would inform the rest of his archaeological career, while sounding the death knell of his
scientific credibility.[32]

Isolating a single warrior in this mural (fig. 5.3), Le Plongeon identified the
figure as "Prince Coh" (a label he had also applied to the chacmool figure).[33] In

this scene, Le Plongeon explained, Coh is shown in mortal combat with his evil brother, Prince Aac, lord of Uxmal. Following Coh's defeat, and his posthumous ennoblement as Lord Chaac Mool, his widow—the former Kinich Kakmo, now known as Queen Móo[34]—was commanded to marry her villainous brother-in-law. Escaping to Egypt, she consigned this so-called kingdom of Móo (its name deriving from the fact she, rather than Aac, legitimately succeeded Coh) to descend into ruin under Aac's poor management.

As Desmond and Messenger have remarked, the narrative that Le Plongeon extracted from this mural soon "gain[ed] a momentum that would be difficult to curtail."[35] In her adoptive land, Le Plongeon explained, Queen Móo had chosen a new identity—that of the goddess Isis—and, despite her taxing journey, had managed to found Egyptian civilization.[36] Her last gesture on American soil, Le Plongeon asserted, had been to erect a memorial to her slain husband: the chacmool statue. In Egypt, Móo's/Isis' acts of memorialization continued, including her commission of the Sphinx itself.[37] Móo's obsessive memorializing activities, part of her connection to the Isis/Osiris narrative discussed below, also bear comparison to the ubiquitous commemorative works Queen Victoria commissioned to honor her husband, Prince Albert, in this decade. The cultural impact of these works, and of the widowed monarch's very public grief—even for those living outside the British Empire—cannot be discounted in understanding Le Plongeon's narrative.

Approximately 115 centuries after Queen Móo's departure, by Le Plongeon's reckoning, she had returned to her native continent[38]—as Alice. To mark his wife's distinction as the former queen of Yucatan and culture goddess of Egypt, Le Plongeon presented her with a small, jadeite tube he had extracted from the Platform of the Eagles (fig. 5.4). Mounted as a brooch in gold brackets, it was reverently referred to by the Le Plongeons as "Queen Móo's Talisman." The artifact is clearly visible in published images of Alice following the 1870s (fig. 5.5) and served as the central motif in her epic 1902 poem, *Queen Móo's Talisman: The Fall of the Maya Empire* —"a documentation of their [her and Augustus'] ancient memories" presented in a thousand lines of rhymed verse.[39] Three years after Augustus' death in 1908, Alice, with the help of Brooks Betts, converted the poem into a play entitled *The Fall of Maya: A Tragic Drama of Ancient America*. Alice characterized the work as a "tragic musical"; critics agreed.

Published versions of the fantastic and often convoluted story of the Le Plongeons' kingdom of Móo were not restricted to Alice's intentionally fictional works

5.3. "PRINCE COH," DETAIL FROM THE TEMPLE OF THE JAGUARS MURAL, CHICHEN ITZA (Alice Le Plongeon, *Queen Móo's Talisman:* 1902).

of the early 1900s. Rather, they formed the core of Augustus Le Plongeon's three major accounts of the ruins, all published in the years following the couple's first travels in Yucatan. The first of these appeared within a year of the Le Plongeons' return in 1880, with a rambling title that reflected the esoteric, and often profoundly confusing, arguments contained within the book: *Vestiges of the Mayas, or, Facts Tending to Prove That Communications and Intimate Relations Must Have Existed, in Very Remote Times, between the Inhabitants of Mayab and Those of Asia and Africa* (1881). Five years later, this treatise was followed by the even more

5.4. QUEEN MÓO'S TALISMAN (Alice Le Plongeon, *Queen Móo's Talisman:* 1902).

5.5. ALICE LE PLONGEON WEARING QUEEN MÓO'S TALISMAN (Alice Le Plongeon, *Here and There in Yucatan: Miscellanies:* 1886).

arcane *Sacred Mysteries among the Mayas and the Quichés 11,500 Years Ago: Their Relation to the Sacred Mysteries of Egypt, Greece, Chaldea, and India; or, Free Masonry in Times Anterior to the Temple of Solomon* (1886). A decade later, this work was succeeded by Le Plongeon's final and most bizarre work, *Queen Móo and the Egyptian Sphinx* (1896). Repetitive, ponderous, and always confidently authoritative in tone, these works insisted upon North America's central role in the founding of world civilization. Brasseur de Bourbourg's hypothesis was "proved" not only by the remains of the kingdom of Móo but also, as Le Plongeon's titles suggest, by evidence that Freemasonry had been invented by the Maya.

Unlike the popular works of Stephens and Catherwood, the relatively well-known Book of Mormon, or either of Charnay's well-received photographic publications, Le Plongeon's works failed to reach a popular, or even an academic, audience. Following Le Plongeon's first work, one publisher told him, somewhat baldly, that "American readers do not care for this subject."[40] Le Plongeon's last work, *Queen Móo and the Egyptian Sphinx,* found no financial supporters, despite Alice's appeals to William Randolph Hearst's wife, Phoebe, whom Alice knew through Theosophical circles. Augustus' work, Alice assured Phoebe Hearst, would "give America its true place amongst the nations."[41] Ultimately, he was forced to produce the book at his own expense.

Le Plongeon's failure to attract a wide reading audience, and his loss of credibility in scientific circles, raise the question of his importance within nineteenth-century Mesoamerican archaeology. His fantastic narratives of the kingdom of Móo and of "Maya" Freemasonry have certainly compromised the reception of his work, yet it is his very combination of the fraudulent with the authentic that captures the essence of this period. Although others before him may have presented the ruins with greater scientific integrity, their cultural agendas were often no more substantial than the bogus story of Queen Móo's flight to Egypt. The eventual "literary" context of Le Plongeon's discoveries does not diminish their value, then, but reveals the ruins' enduring potential for cultural manipulation.

Le Plongeon's casting activities in Yucatan provide a good example of his work's real value and seriousness, apart from the theories that brought him such professional obloquy. A more careful practitioner of Lotin de Laval's mold-making process than Charnay, Le Plongeon did not, as Charnay had done, hack off layers of stucco before producing his paper "squeezes." Carefully and systematically reproduced, Le Plongeon's countless molds of relatively small, overlapping sections were the three-dimensional equivalents to his trademark serial photographs. Le Plongeon produced molds at nearly all the sites he visited, especially Uxmal and Chichen Itza, though his molds at Uxmal were by far the most numerous — including seventeen molds of its Nunnery Quadrangle, forty-three of the Pyramid of the Magician, and a staggering eighty-three taken at the Governor's Palace.[42] For Le Plongeon, as for his contemporaries, these molds surpassed even his photographs in their scientific value; their eventual loss, discussed below, was one of the great tragedies of his career.

Le Plongeon's mixture of the real and the improbable, so well captured by his discovery and subsequent interpretation of the chacmool figure, was nowhere more apparent than in his photographs of the ruins. In terms of quantity, and even in terms of quality, Le Plongeon's photographic record of the ruins was unparalleled in the nineteenth century.[43] Initially employing the same cumbersome, wet-plate process that Charnay had used in the 1860s, Le Plongeon meticulously established his shots, often using scaffolds or ladders for head-on images — whereas Charnay had used lens boards to avoid this, inviting distortion.[44] Le Plongeon was also particularly adventurous in photographing from dangerous, or previously unreachable, vantage points. His images of the upper temple at Uxmal's Pyramid of the Dwarf, for example, required him to stand on a ladder perched over a fifty-five-foot drop.[45]

Le Plongeon spent a great deal of time capturing small, tightly focused details of the monuments — including, for example, his documentation of the entire upper frieze on the House of the Governor at Uxmal. No matter how oddly he interpreted it, this uninterrupted, sixteen-plate series provided an important and hitherto unavailable study document. Not only did Le Plongeon pioneer this type of archaeological close-up, but he also used a wide variety of photographic formats, including serial panoramas and, most typically, stereoptic views of the ruins. The advantage of the latter format was the startling three-dimensional effect it allowed, dramatically increasing the structures' immediacy (an effect that is, unfortunately, lost on modern viewers of the photographs).

The advantages of Le Plongeon's photographic techniques were ultimately compromised by the images' appearance in his publications. Printed images of ancient buildings, for example, often gave no visual or textual indication of the structures' locations, and isolated details are often shown without any reference to the corresponding structures from which they were photographed. Most confusing of all are Le Plongeon's doctored or "collaged" images, which he presented as unretouched field shots. His heavily redrawn photograph of a "Queen Móo" relief, taken at Uxmal (fig. 5.6), leaves little hint of the original work—while his re-creation of Chichen Itza's Platform of Venus, a line drawing sandwiched between photographic images of sky and ground, is entirely invented (fig. 5.7). In works like these, Le Plongeon's photographs approach the fantastic nature of Waldeck's distorted images; and, as Waldeck had attempted to do, Le Plongeon placed these distortions at the service of a specific narrative.

Le Plongeon's primary invented narrative, the kingdom of Móo saga, is inti-mately connected in all of his writings to the ritual practices, or Sacred Mysteries, of Freemasonry. "We are bound to admit," he wrote in *Sacred Mysteries among the Mayas,* "that a line exists between the ancient mysteries [shared, he believed, by Central America and Egypt] and Free Masonry. It is for us to try to discover when that link was riveted, and by whom."[46] In Le Plongeon's narrative this riveter was, of course, Queen Móo herself—whose secondary identity as Isis and whose role as a tragic widow reconfigure the Egyptian myth of Isis and her husband, Osiris. In this traditional narrative, following Osiris' murder by the hand of his evil brother Typhon, Isis had wandered throughout Egypt commissioning memorial obelisks in her husband's honor—an activity that was linked, of course, with the actual practice of masonry.

Central to the rituals of Freemasonry, whose members claimed their symbolic descent from Osiris, this story was transformed in Le Plongeon's writings to imply an earlier and, more importantly, an "American" setting for the drama. Sin-gular as it is, Le Plongeon's story belongs to a long tradition of Masonic variants of the Isis/Osiris saga. Each constitutes a Sacred Mystery of its own, typically in-volving a central hero's murder and subsequent apotheosis[47]—a formula ulti-mately derived from the story of Christ's passion. As with Móo and Coh's story, these Sacred Mystery narratives often served nationalist ends; following France's occupation of Egypt under Napoleon, for example, the French Freemasons de-clared ancient Egypt as the sole source of the order's Sacred Mysteries, while British Freemasons traced their sacred rites to those of the Druids.

Le Plongeon's insistence upon conflating the narratives of Móo/Coh and Isis/Osiris represents only one aspect of his nearly obsessive arguments concern-ing the origins of Freemasonry. Beginning with his first published works, Le Plongeon had situated Maya building practices, ritual spaces, and even ceremo-nial dress all within the context of Masonic symbolism. In an 1881 article for *Harper's Weekly,* entitled "An Interesting Discovery: A Temple with Masonic Sym-bols in the Ruined City of Uxmal," Le Plongeon cited the presence of triangular

5.6. *Above:* NORTH WING, HOUSE OF THE GOVERNOR AT UXMAL; PROFILE OF
"QUEEN MÓO" SEEN AT LOWER LEFT-HAND CORNER.
   Below: LE PLONGEON'S ENLARGED, RETOUCHED IMAGE OF THIS DETAIL
(Augustus Le Plongeon, *Queen Móo and the Egyptian Sphinx:* 1896).

arches, quincunx formations of wooden beam holes, symbolic numbers of temple steps, and, most important, a fragmented figure's "Masonic apron" bearing what appeared to be the depiction of a human hand as examples of the ancient Maya's participation in the arcane rituals of Freemasonry.[48]

Like Waldeck before him at Uxmal, Le Plongeon claimed to be the only witness to many of these interesting discoveries. Of the "Masonic" apron, for example, he says that "after carefully taking a mould of it, I had it placed in one of the rooms in the south wing of the building, to save it, as much as possible, from being injured...." Photographing the object apparently proved impossible, but he assured readers that "as soon as convenient, photographs will be taken from the cast."[49] Today the location of this fragment, or even of Le Plongeon's cast, is unknown.

By coincidence or design, Le Plongeon's article in *Harper's Weekly* appeared on the same page as the obituary of James M. Austin, who had served as the grand secretary of the New York Freemasons for nearly thirty years. Given Le Plongeon's thorough knowledge of Masonic symbols and imagery, and his insistence upon seeing them everywhere in Yucatan, it is not surprising that Le Plongeon was, himself, a high-ranking Mason in New York. What is unusual about his promotion of Freemasonry, however, is his insistence upon its actual practice in

5.7. LE PLONGEON'S COMPOSITE PHOTOGRAPH/RECONSTRUCTION DRAWING, PLATFORM OF VENUS, CHICHEN ITZA (Augustus Le Plongeon, *Queen Móo and the Egyptian Sphinx:* 1896).

ancient history—an assertion that, even in regard to Egyptian antiquity, was dismissed by most nineteenth-century Masons as absurd.[50]

For Americans in Le Plongeon's generation, Freemasonry represented the chief fraternal organization within an ever-increasing number of secret and/or fraternal societies. As Lynn Dumenil has pointed out, American Masonic lodges' sharp increase in membership paralleled the spectacular growth of urban areas in the second half of the nineteenth century. Freemasonry's stability, regimented hierarchy, and quasi-religious values, she argues, addressed white, middle-class men's fears of the disorder caused by immigration and a heavily industrialized economy.[51] Between 1850 and 1870 the number of Masons in America rose from sixty-six thousand to more than half a million—and by 1880 it boasted the current or former membership of seven U.S. presidents, eight governors of New York State, and most of the great "robber barons" of the Gilded Age, including John Wanamaker, William H. and William K. Vanderbilt, and J. C. Penney.[52] By the last quarter of the nineteenth century, American Freemasonry had become a seemingly unstoppable, and highly visible, social force.

Le Plongeon's insistence upon the presence of Freemasonry in ancient America reflected the order's growing presence in contemporary life. His reasons for situating Masonic practices among the Maya, however, could also have stemmed from other motives. In Le Plongeon's eyes, the increasing social and political clout of American Freemasonry belied its underlying cultural debt to England—home of the first Masonic lodge, founded in 1717.[53] If London's eighteenth-century lodges had first suggested Freemasonry's connections to ancient Egypt, then Le Plongeon's subordination of Egypt to the ancient American continent elevated contemporary American Freemasonry at England's expense. Without erasing the group's traditional associations, and only elaborating them, Le Plongeon effectively declared the independence of American Freemasonry.

Reconfiguring an Old World tradition with a more uniquely American model, Le Plongeon's strategies bear more than a passing resemblance to Joseph Smith's divine revelations. For both men, the truth of their assumptions lay rooted in evidence to which only they—or a small handful of believers—were privy. Despite the emerging secularization of latter nineteenth-century archaeology,[54] Le Plongeon and the Mormon Church continued to exploit religious or pseudoreligious models to explain the role of Divine Providence in the development of ancient Mesoamerican civilization.[55]

Le Plongeon's Sacred Mysteries and Smith's Book of Mormon provide documentary evidence that is irrefutable by virtue of its divine or, in Le Plongeon's case, paranormal source of origin. Whereas Smith had received the ancient record of the Nephites and Lamanites on golden plates, Le Plongeon explained that in 1885 he had discovered a similar set of ancient tablets detailing the Mesoamerican rites of Freemasonry—consisting of "two stones fitly cemented together" from a cache "in the mausoleum of the high pontiff Cay [brother to Prince Coh], in the city of Chichen-Itza, in Yucatan."[56] In an earlier article from 1880, Le Plongeon even echoed Smith's revelations of historical destiny, claiming to have found a manuscript that "has lain dormant during all these centuries, to be resurrected at a time when the world is better prepared to appreciate it than at any other time since it was written."[57]

American Freemasonry, then, was not only elevated but also sanctified by the story of Queen Móo and Prince Coh. The story served another important purpose as well, one that was related to Freemasonry's Sacred Mysteries—the establishment of an ancient, nationally grounded literary tradition. Le Plongeon's "translated" glyphic passages relating to Queen Móo, as well as Alice Le Plongeon's epic 1902 poem about the doomed Maya couple, were attempts to create a heroic saga equal to the stature of, for instance, the *Song of Roland* within French culture. In a well-known scandal of the preceding century, Scottish poet James Macpherson had been proven guilty of a similar fraud. Claiming to have translated two poems by a third-century Gaelic bard named Ossian, *Fingal* (1761) and *Temora* (1763), Macpherson had invented a complete hero cycle around this lost figure intended to demonstrate the glories of ancient Irish culture.[58] Like Macpherson, Augustus and Alice Le Plongeon also attempted to fill the need for a "national" epic—yet failed to do so, largely because of the poverty of the writing they attributed to this ancient culture.

A direct contemporary of the Le Plongeons, and a figure whose career succeeded in all of the ways that their own did not, also conceived of the archaeological past in literary terms. Heinrich Schliemann, the archaeologist who rediscovered ancient Troy in the 1870s, often explained that his entry into the field had been based upon a single engraving from the *Iliad* he had owned as a child.[59] Whether the story is apocryphal or not, Schliemann certainly entered into his excavations with a preconceived notion of what he might find, based on Homer's epic. Making spectacular discoveries between 1872 and 1873 at Hissarlik, in Turkey—the presumed former site of Troy[60]—Schliemann demonstrated great talent in the public staging of his finds. In one of the most famous archaeological

5.8. SOPHIE SCHLIEMANN WEARING KING PRIAM'S TREASURE, CA. 1872
(C. Schuchhardt, *Schliemann's Excavations:* 1891).

images of the nineteenth century, Schliemann photographed his wife, Sophie, wearing "King Priam's Treasure"—the purported jewels of Helen of Troy (fig. 5.8). In this image Schliemann intended his audience to associate, rather than conflate, his wife with the historical figure of Helen, though the effect of the image was very similar to Le Plongeon's later chacmool tableau and his images of Alice wearing the far more modest "jewel" of Queen Móo.

Instructive parallels can also be drawn between the staging of Schliemann's and Le Plongeon's field shots, especially those images featuring their wives. Comparing an engraving of Sophie Schliemann at the Tomb of Clytemnestra, from a photograph taken in 1876, with a photograph of Alice at Uxmal's House of the Governor, taken in 1881, one is struck by the images' resemblance (figs. 5.9 and 5.10). In both, the archaeologists' wives stand outside large, corbelled arches sheltering local workers. In each the woman, literally as well as figuratively, is part of a triangulation involving the site's history; they role-play as grieving figures but also act as contemporary mediators between the archaeologist and the structure, as well as between the archaeologists and the indigenous workers.

5.9. SOPHIE SCHLIEMANN, FOREGROUND, AT TOMB OF CLYTEMNESTRA,
1876 (Heinrich Schliemann, *Mycenae:* 1878).

5.10. ALICE LE PLONGEON AT HOUSE OF THE GOVERNOR, UXMAL, 1873
(Augustus Le Plongeon, *Queen Móo and the Egyptian Sphinx:* 1896).

Given Le Plongeon's profound familiarity with Schliemann's work, and the probability he knew this engraving or others like it (the composition is a recurring trope in both men's work), one wonders what would have motivated Le Plongeon to restage such an image. It appears that Le Plongeon was attempting to establish his own work as Schliemann's parallel, hoping perhaps that the German archaeologist's greater reputation and the authentic literary tradition within which he performed his work would elevate Le Plongeon's own work by association.

Schliemann's attempts to establish a large national collection of antiquities were perfectly mirrored in Le Plongeon's career. "What have we in New York, in the United States, in fact," Le Plongeon asked, "to offer students of American archaeology?" His answer was, of course, that the United States was devoid of "anything that may throw light on the history of our ancient inhabitants of this Western continent."[61] Le Plongeon's solution to this problem was the full-scale re-creation of ancient Mesoamerican sites within New York City, a scheme that both echoed Stephens' vision for a national museum of American antiquities and foreshadowed Frederick Putnam's installation of plaster-cast Maya temples at the 1893 World's Columbian Exposition in Chicago. In his introduction to *Sacred Mysteries among the Mayas,* Le Plongeon explained:

> In New York, perfect facsimiles of the palaces and temples of the Mayas could be erected in Central Park, both as ornament to the place, and object of study for the lovers of American archaeology who may not have the means, nor the time, nor the desire, to run the risk of submitting to the privations and hardships that those who wish to visit the ruined cities, must inevitably encounter. But alas! All in vain.[62]

Le Plongeon's desire to see Maya temples erected in Central Park, specifically, undoubtedly arose from his resentment that the Metropolitan Museum of Art had recently installed an ancient Egyptian obelisk, known as Cleopatra's Needle, in that same location in 1881.[63] The erection of this Eighteenth Dynasty monument, a gift to the museum from the Egyptian government, had been accompanied by parades, concerts, lectures, and thousands of curiosity seekers. Tickets to the event went so far as to proclaim the installment "The Greatest Achievement of the Nineteenth Century!"[64]

New York Freemasons considered the obelisk's arrival a particularly important event as well, including William Henry Vanderbilt, who had financed the obelisk's transport from Alexandria.[65] Prior to the obelisk's foundation-laying ceremony on October 10, 1880, nine thousand Freemasons had marched up Fifth Avenue to the monument's intended site in Central Park.[66] The next day, attired in Masonic aprons, their highest-ranking members had laid the obelisk's foundation and lectured the assembled crowd on the Sacred Mysteries that Freemasonry had adopted from ancient Egypt. Curiously, given his views on the subject, Le Plongeon made only a brief reference to the famous obelisk in his *Sacred Mysteries among the Mayas*—briefly noting, predictably, its symbolic confirmation of Freemasonry's ancient history.[67]

Le Plongeon may have taken a far greater interest in Cleopatra's Needle than this passing remark would indicate, however. In August 1880, six months prior to the obelisk's installment, New York's *Daily Graphic* printed an anonymous story announcing the "true" American origin of the Metropolitan's new acquisition. Although I have not found conclusive evidence to link Le Plongeon and this document, the circumstantial evidence for his authorship is strong; Le Plongeon was back in New York by this date, and his particular rhetorical style is unmistakable in the article. Even without conclusive proof of Le Plongeon's hand, the unnamed author's theories so closely resemble Le Plongeon's that they would merit consideration alongside his own.

The lengthy, sensational title of the article—a hallmark of Le Plongeon's—reads: "Our American Obelisk, the Most Important Archaeological Discovery of the Age; An Ancient Manuscript Found in Sicily Gives a Translation of the Hieroglyphic Inscriptions; The Builders of the Obelisk Descendants of Men from Mexico or Yucatan."[68] Explaining the unattributed authorship of the article, its writer asserts that he "dislikes notoriety and will not consent to having his name published."[69] Though Le Plongeon was hardly reluctant to be associated with improbable treatises, his choice of anonymity here (as I believe it to be) may reflect a growing recognition of his dismissal by academics.

Citing an obscure source that had been languishing in the library of a Sicilian monastery—a discovery that recalls Brasseur de Bourbourg's great archival finds in Europe—the *Daily Graphic*'s informant claims to know the correct translation of the hieroglyphs found on the Egyptian obelisk, which had not yet even appeared in New York:

> They tell of long wanderings of a race . . . through extensive plains and mountains and deserts, to their ultimate resting place on the Nile, where they are contented and powerful, but where they cannot help looking back with wistful eyes to the ancient home of their race in a faraway country. They even perceive in the dim future

that this—a relic of their greatness—will be transported to the land of their origin, which they may never behold again.[70]

The author states not that the obelisk had been erected by these wandering "Americans" after their arrival in Egypt, however, but that they had brought the monument with them as a reminder of their former home. The author's evidence for the work's transportation is even murkier than the existence of the rediscovered Sicilian manuscript. The obelisk had been illustrated, he argues, in ancient inscriptions found in Iowa and Alaska (of earlier and later dates, respectively) and so on through Asia to Egypt (fig. 5.11)—a western course that proved the reverse Bering Strait theory that Le Plongeon had offered at the American Geographical Society seven years before and that provided a possible overland itinerary for Queen Móo's flight to Egypt. Significantly, the obelisk's stopping points in North America included only locations within U.S. borders.

In the year after the installment of Cleopatra's Needle, Le Plongeon sold his enormous collections of molds from the site of Uxmal to the Metropolitan Museum[71]—hoping still, perhaps, to see his ancient "city" eclipse the attraction of Cleopatra's Needle. At the museum, however, he reported that after three years had gone by "the [molds] have been placed in the cellar, out of the way, for want of space, against a wall," adding that "these things are not appreciated . . . they are

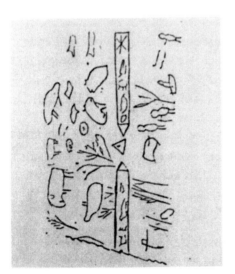

5.11. DRAWINGS DERIVED FROM THE IOWA AND ALASKA "INSCRIPTIONS" (New York *Daily Graphic:* July 1880).

looked upon as of no value."⁷² The molds were never used in making casts for the museum's collection.

Given their obvious value, and the enthusiasm with which Charnay's, and later Frederick Putnam's, casts were received, the Metropolitan's attitude toward Le Plongeon's molds seems curious. By the 1880s, the director of the Metropolitan, Luigi Palma di Cesnola, may have viewed Le Plongeon's molds as suspiciously as he did Le Plongeon's scholarship—although there is no evidence to suggest Le Plongeon may have doctored these works. A second set of Le Plongeon's molds, offered to the Museum of Natural History in New York, were ultimately rejected and subsequently turned down, again, by the Smithsonian Institution in Washington.⁷³ In the case of the Smithsonian, cheaper molds from the Trocadéro, presumably Charnay's, were purchased in their place.

The eventual fate of Le Plongeon's molds is, sadly, unknown. Their loss is particularly tragic, not only because of the Herculean effort they represented but also because this collection would have provided a three-dimensional document of the works' condition nearly 125 years ago. Ironically, because their loss has never been officially declared, speculation about the molds' current whereabouts has invested them with same "lost treasure" mystique that once surrounded the buildings they were intended to reproduce. They may yet be found.

The loss of Le Plongeon's material legacy does not erase the value of his long career or his importance for scholars of ancient Mesoamerican history. That he and his wife were able to accomplish so much that was important, while writing so much that was fraudulent, is a testament to the period in which they operated. Within half a generation, no archaeologist would be given such free reign at a site nor the license to claim, figuratively or actually, its ancient artifacts. Time itself— or at least its accurate reckoning, in Maya inscriptions—would no longer allow it.⁷⁴ (Le Plongeon's belief in the tremendous age of ancient American civilization—estimated at twelve thousand years old—was based, like so many of his assumptions, upon flimsy linguistic evidence and invented natural history.)

The legacy of Móo scholarship following the Plongeons' deaths fell to the even more speculative scholar James Churchward, to whom Alice had bequeathed Augustus' papers in 1911. Churchward's works, including *The Lost Continent of Mu* (1926), *The Children of Mu* (1931), and *The Cosmic Forces of Mu* (1936) equaled, and often surpassed, the bizarre nature of Le Plongeon's writing. Not only did Churchward alter the spelling of Queen Móo's former kingdom, but he also, in a move that Le Plongeon would have considered a profound betrayal, relocated the continent of Mu/Móo to the Pacific Ocean—thereby divorcing its connection to ancient Mexico or the Maya and extinguishing Le Plongeon's short-lived vision of an ancient American diffusion culture.

Le Plongeon's bizarre assertions concerning Freemasonry, diffusionism, and the return of lost Maya souls provided, as he believed, "a key that will unlock the door of that chamber of mysteries." Despairing at his compatriots' lack of interest in their presumed ancient past, he added, "Will no efforts be made by American students to unlock it?"[75] The next generation of archaeologists would certainly unlock many of these mysteries, but in the process, the Le Plongeons themselves would be locked out.

EPILOGUE

THE PERIOD between 1893 and 1915 marked both the dramatic culmination and the eventual eclipse of Stephens' vision. At Chicago's World's Columbian Exposition of 1893, Stephens' concept of a unified, national historical narrative, stretching back to the Mesoamerican past, was briefly realized. At this fair, the United States presented a seamless history of its hegemony in the New World, contextualizing the pre-Columbian past as prologue to its contemporary cultural achievements. By the time of San Diego's Panama-California Exposition of 1915, in contrast, fair organizers characterized the ancient American past as an essentially "Indian" legacy, divorced from the cultural traditions of Anglo-America.

Whereas the 1876 Centennial Exposition in Philadelphia had celebrated the first century of U.S. nationhood, the World's Columbian Exposition in Chicago looked back to the discovery of the North American continent itself—thereby situating the United States as the ultimate product of Columbus' voyage to the New World. Representing the triumph of Anglo-American culture and industry

Fig. 6.1. THOMPSON'S PLASTER RECONSTRUCTION OF THE ARCH OF LABNÁ, CHICAGO WORLD'S COLUMBIAN EXPOSITION OF 1893 (Walter Bancroft, *The Book of the Fair*, vol. 7: 1893).

Fig. 6.2. PLASTER FRAGMENTS OF THE GOVERNOR'S PALACE AND NUNNERY, UXMAL, CHICAGO WORLD'S COLUMBIAN EXPOSITION OF 1893 (*The World's Columbian Exposition Reproduced*, plate 13: 1894).

in North America, the Chicago exposition provided an illusion of national unity through carefully ordered governmental, technological, artistic, and ethnographic displays. In its central core of buildings known as White City, the fair projected a visual as well as a cultural unity. An assemblage of enormous steel sheds with classically inspired facades, this group of buildings confirmed the United States' self-perception as the continent's custodian of Western culture.

Because it cast the nation's historical progress back to the period of earliest European contact, the fair invested the monuments and artifacts of the continent's pre-Columbian civilizations with special importance. Fair organizers placed Frederick Putnam, director of Harvard University's Peabody Museum, in charge of the fair's anthropological and ethnographic exhibits. In regard to civilization in the Americas, Putnam's charge was to display its systematic development in precontact times, using an extensive collection of Mesoamerican antiquities and reproductions. Putnam's Anthropology Building formed the centerpiece of these displays, providing fairgoers with an array of sculptural casts, photographs of Mesoamerican ruins, and a spectacular installment of life-size reproductions of Maya temple facades. While the national pavilions of Latin American countries also included exhibits devoted to Mesoamerican and South American antiquities, Putnam's displays in the Anthropology Building constituted their most comprehensive representation.

The ambitious assemblage of cast temple façades that Putnam displayed at the fair represented the heroic achievement of archaeologist Edward Thompson. In the 1880s the American Antiquarian Society had commissioned Thompson to create a plaster copy of the palace façade at Labná. The result, a particularly elegant reproduction cast in plaster, fiber, and paper pulp, was so admired in Worcester that Putnam had asked Thompson to prepare a large number of molds for the upcoming exposition.[1] Spending more than a year in Yucatan with a workforce of forty men, Thompson fought driving rains, malaria, and even temporary blindness while casting façades from Uxmal, Chichen Itza, Labná, Kabah, and other sites. By the close of this project, Thompson had reproduced a staggering ten thousand square feet of the ancient temples — far more, and in a shorter space of time, than either Le Plongeon or Charnay had produced over the course of their careers.

Using Thompson's molds, Putnam cast and erected six of his monumental temple facades in a circular arrangement outside the Anthropology Building (figs. 6.1 and 6.2). In its placement at the edge of the exposition's south pond, this grouping resembled an enormous garden folly—a romantic backdrop situated below the gleaming buildings of the Court of Honor. Standing at the center of this arrangement, visitors to the fair were provided a 360-degree view of temple façades from the Puuc region of northern Yucatan; like the neoclassical buildings of White City, this assemblage of plaster temples was intended to provide the illusion of cultural uniformity. The temple fragments Putnam chose for this display represented works from Uxmal and Labná—including the Arch of Labná, portions of its Palace, and segments of the Palace of the Governor from Uxmal. Belonging to the northwestern region of Yucatan and dating from roughly the same period, they failed to represent the enormous range of ancient works found in Yucatan.

Although Charnay had noted earlier that, despite the fidelity of his casts, museumgoers would "of necessity, remain cold to . . . the feelings which have moved enthusiastic travelers," Putnam's installation presented an unparalleled simulation of real experience. Artificially aging the casts and landscaping them with clinging, tropical plantings, he attempted to re-create their original archeological contexts. The resulting effect transformed Catherwood's romantic engravings into a living tableau, allowing the fairgoer to sense the drama of exploration within familiar surroundings. The experience, of course, was greatly distorted. The works represented small fragments of much larger structures, their placement was arbitrary, and the casts provided no sense of plan, volume, or interior space—to say nothing of the temples' original function. In essence, Putnam had created a panoramic theme ride for the armchair explorer—the archaeological equivalent of the exposition's newly invented Ferris wheel.

Contained inside the Anthropology Building, guidebooks to the fair explained, was "a more complete collection of Central American archeology than ever before available for the study of these old ruins and their unknown builders."[2] Collections of casts, some of them Charnay's, were supplemented by forty large photographs taken by the English explorer Alfred Maudslay at sites in Guatemala, Honduras, Chiapas, and Yucatan.[3] Although photographs of Mesoamerican ruins had been accessible, if not widely available, since Charnay's first work was published in the 1860s, Putnam's installation marked the first public exhibition of such images. The extraordinary fidelity of Maudslay's work (fig. 6.3) provided fairgoers with yet another means of re-creating the explorers' experience.

Putnam's anthropological exhibits were intended to demonstrate the development of human civilization in the Americas, and though he did not always main-

6.3. ALFRED P. MAUDSLAY, EASTERN WING OF THE NUNNERY (CASA DE LAS MONJAS),
CHICHEN ITZA (Alfred P. Maudslay, *Biologia Centrali-Americana:* 1889–1902).

tain a physical separation between exhibits devoted to ancient and contemporary
cultures—the "ethnological grounds" outside the Anthropological Building included some living displays of native North Americans along with Thompson's
casts, for example—he nonetheless perceived a clear distinction between the
two, particularly in regard to the monumental architecture of ancient American
cultures and the dwellings of contemporary Native Americans. In planning for
contemporary "Indian encampments" along the Midway Plaisance, a mile-long
avenue extending west of the fair's center, Putnam intended for the villages to
serve as a dramatic foil to the more "civilized" neoclassical structures of White
City.[4] By contrast, the re-creation of an ancient Anasazi cliff dwelling, placed on
the western side of the Anthropology Building, shared the role of Thompson's
temple casts as a prelude to White City.[5]

Although Putnam's distinction between ancient and living indigenous cultures may appear unsurprising, this arrangement contradicted the beliefs of contemporary ethnologists who asserted the unity of all American indigenous
groups, both living and extinct. Chief among this group was Lewis Henry Morgan, whose 1876 essay "Montezuma's Dinner" had proposed that the Aztecs were
simply a southern extension of the Iroquois nation.[6] Although Morgan's theories

eventually fell out of favor, at the time of the 1893 fair his ideas still dominated the Smithsonian Institution's Bureau of American Ethnology.[7]

The placement and scale of the cliff-dweller and Maya temple reproductions demonstrates their alliance with White City, rather than with the fair's exotic, nonhistorical Midway zone (fig. 6.4).[8] Placed on the south side of the fair's primary exhibition spaces, these monumental examples of the continent's ancient past marked the starting point in the spatial progression toward nineteenth-century American civilization. Though the Agriculture Building screened these works from the center of White City, an unobstructed axis connected the Anasazi and Maya casts with the far eastern end of the Court of Honor. It is worth noting the location of the fair's Indian School along this axis, as well; placed halfway between the Anthropology Building and the eastern end of the Court of Honor, the school's location reflected Anglo-America's belief in the Native American's "semicivilized" status.

Far removed from the fair's Midway zone, which was the site of the exposition's foreign exhibits and public amusements, the Anthropology Building and its outdoor displays were implicitly included within the continuum of American culture. In this liminal position between the fair's edge and center, these "ancient American" exhibits anchored the southeastern corner of the fair—providing a visual foundation for the neoclassical emblems of America's progress.

Not only did the Anthropology Building serve as a prelude to the exhibitions at the center of White City, but it mirrored the placement of the Palace of Fine Arts, located on the north side of the fair's Manufactures and Liberal Arts Building. The Palace of Fine Arts showcased the greatest contemporary U.S. achievements in painting and sculpture, an assemblage of works that essentially conformed, like the structures of White City itself, to traditional European standards. Acting as a historical foil to the Palace's exhibits, the Anthropology Building's collections of ancient Mesoamerican casts and other artifacts constituted the continent's pre-European artistic legacy. Situated at opposite ends of the fair's elevated railway, these structures formed the two poles of cultural achievement in the New World; in traveling from one end of the railway to the other, visitors to the exposition figuratively moved through the progressive stages of American civilization.

Though the structures mirrored each other's locations along the railway and represented a similar cultural agenda, the primacy of the Palace of Fine Arts was made clear in both its context and its size.[9] Built as a permanent structure that would eventually house the Art Institute of Chicago, the Palace of Fine Arts in-

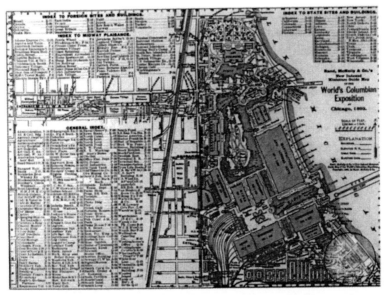

6.4. *Above:* PLAN, FAIRGROUNDS OF WORLD'S COLUMBIAN EXPOSITION, CHICAGO
(Midway at left; White City, center right; anthropological exhibits, lower right, circled).

Below: DETAIL, SHOWING THOMPSON'S "RUINS OF YUCATAN" CASTS (Rand
McNally map, 1893).

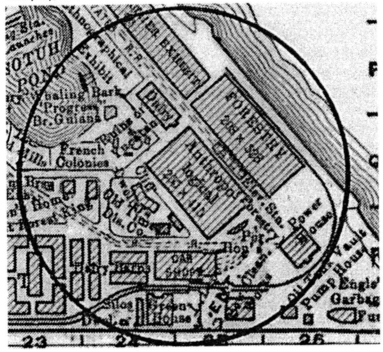

cluded 260,000 square feet of exhibition space; the Anthropology Building, on the other hand, contained only 103,750 square feet of exhibition space.[10] Furthermore, whereas the Palace neighbored the fair's state and federal government buildings, the Anthropology Building was situated above the stockyards and service buildings—a location that reinforced its secondary status within the hierarchy of American culture.

Following the close of the exposition, Putnam planned for the permanent installation of the fair's anthropological exhibits in a grand museum of natural history. With the aid of department store magnate Marshall Field, the project eventually materialized as Chicago's Field Museum of Natural History. Putnam's initial plan called for the museum "to be patterned after a prehistoric building of Mexico or Central America," a scheme that, if executed, would have represented the first example of a Mesoamerican revival-style building in the United States.[11] It was not to be. At Field's insistence, Daniel Burnham designed the new museum building in the same beaux arts, neoclassical idiom he had employed for the fair's White City. Putnam's suggestion, however, remains remarkable. In proposing an ancient Mexican style to house his ethnographic and anthropological exhibits, he confirmed the placement of ancient Mesoamerican cultures at the center of America's prehistory.

In the period between the World's Columbian Exposition and the 1915 Panama-California Exposition in San Diego, two key developments changed the way in which the ancient Maya, and modern Mexico itself, was perceived in the United States. In 1905, archaeologist J. T. Goodman provided the first correct correlation of the Maya and Christian calendars, establishing that the Maya had created their great urban centers between the fourth and ninth centuries A.D.[12] By assigning a fixed date to their cities, Goodman invested the ancient Maya with a sense of historical identity. Moreover, his dating system either contradicted or modified most nineteenth-century chronologies of the ruins—demonstrating, most importantly, the temporal gaps that existed between the Classic Maya and later groups such as the Toltecs and the Aztecs.[13]

Within five years of Goodman's discovery, a second event altered U.S. perceptions of Mesoamerica: the eruption of the Mexican Revolution in 1910, a conflict that led to seven years of virtual anarchy in the country. Throughout this period, groups in the United States alternately viewed Mexico as a potential military threat or as an exciting theater of social reform; for Mexicans, the struggle represented the final resolution of its century-long search for a national identity.[14] With the close of the revolution in 1917 and the birth of modern Mexican nationhood, the United States could no longer view Mexico's territory—either geographically or archaeologically—as a negotiable commodity.

The 1915 Panama-California Exposition in San Diego clearly reflected the changing relationship of the United States to the Mesoamerican past.[15] In his 1916 analysis of the San Diego fair, Edgar Hewett demonstrated that the archaeological recognition of Maya culture had proved a mixed blessing. Although Maya ruins were no longer considered the work of "unknown builders," as they had been described in 1893, at San Diego they were erroneously conflated with the cultural achievements of contemporary native North American tribes. "It is necessary to repeat again and again," Hewett explained, "that all native American remains, whether of Plains tribes, mound-builders, cliff-dwellers, Pueblo, Navaho, Toltec, Aztec, Maya, or Inca are *just* [my italics] the works of the Indian."[16] Furthermore, Hewett asserted, this pan-American indigenous culture represented a distinct, and essentially foreign, development from the "Caucasian" culture of the United States—the very culture from which, Charnay believed, the ancient Mesoamerican city builders had descended. "Between us and the Indian," Hewett insisted, "is a racial chasm which no mind can quite bridge. No Caucasian will ever see with the eyes or think with the brain cells of the Indian."[17]

Exhibits of Maya art and architecture at the 1915 fair were housed within the California Building, a location that, though central to the theme of the fair, collapsed Mesoamerican antiquity with that of the ancient Southwest and reduced its diverse civilizations to a form of exotic regionalism. The arrangement goes far in explaining how Frank Lloyd Wright, whose interest in the Maya exhibits at this fair has been documented by Anthony Alofsin and others, perceived pre-Columbian architecture as a type of Californian vernacular—an attitude that shaped Wright's romantic, Maya-inspired designs for projects he completed in California in the 1910s and 1920s.[18]

The California Building's Maya exhibits ranged from sculptural casts to a series of frescoes depicting six of the principal cities of ancient Central America. In addition, fair exhibitors provided several large architectural models representing individual buildings from Maya urban centers. In contrast to the monumental, life-size casts at the 1893 fair, however, these models presented fully restored versions of the structures—highlighting their original method of construction, rather than their contemporary, archaeological contexts. This emphasis upon design was reflected in Hewett's assessment of the works. The great pyramid at

Chichen Itza, known as El Castillo, was "a . . . design of exceptionally high order, indicating great progress in architecture," while the House of the Governor at Uxmal was described as the "last word in the building art of ancient America."[19] The San Diego fair's emphasis on the architectural legacy of the Maya, "whose design and construction commands the admiration of master-builders today," reflected the new interest in the Mesoamerican past shown by Wright and his contemporary architects.[20] The short-lived "Mayan revival" style, exemplified in works by Wright, Paul Cret, and Robert Stacy-Judd, placed the Maya past within a distinct historical and regional framework.

By the second quarter of the twentieth century, Americans no longer looked to the Mesoamerican past to bolster their own sense of national confidence. Increasingly, rather, Mexico's antiquities were admired as part of a constellation of Latin America's exotic attractions.[21] Tourism replaced exploratory travel, while the monumental forms of the Mesoamerican past were reduced to "south of the border" kitsch. Addressing this new audience of American travelers, George Crawford wrote in his 1890 tourist's guide to Mexico:

> A prominent guide-book writer says, "the shape of Mexico is that of a cornucopia turned the wrong way"—the cornucopia is there, but it is by no means turned the wrong way; the big end is toward the United States, and there is naught for us to do but pour out its treasures of climate, scenic beauty, antiquity, legends, and commercial wealth for our delectation.[22]

NOTES

INTRODUCTION

1. John Noble Wilford, "Splendid Maya Palace Is Found Hidden in Jungle," *New York Times*, September 8, 2000, pp. A1 ff. Wilford's use of the term "Maya" rather than "Mayan" is the currently accepted adjectival form of the word ("Mayan" indicates the language the Maya speak), as well as its plural noun form ("Maya" rather than "Mayas"). Throughout this book I follow current usage, although I occasionally include titles or quotations that feature older forms.

2. Obviously, these conclusions are not Wilford's but those of the archaeologist who discovered the site, Dr. Arthur A. Demarest of Vanderbilt University, and of his colleague Dr. Tomas Barrientos of the Universidad del Valle in Guatemala.

3. Fantastic theories regarding the ruins are not restricted to the nineteenth century; in the twentieth century, Erich von Däniken famously claimed that the classic Maya city of Palenque had been built by space aliens in his best-selling *Chariots of the Gods?* (Putnam, New York: 1968).

4. Significantly, after the publication of Stephens' discoveries the church modified Smith's original claim that this group of Israelites had landed on the coast of present-day Chile. From the 1850s onward, church leaders spoke of a landing point closer to Central America.

5. Adding another level of complexity to the issue, the term "Mexican" also connotes the Nahua-speaking *Mexica* peoples, the Central Mexican group from whom the Aztecs derive.

6. Thomas Patterson dates the advent of professional archaeology in the United States to the 1870s, asserting that by the early 1930s the discipline had become fully institutionalized. Patterson, *Toward a Social History of Archaeology in the United States* (Harcourt, Brace College Publishers, New York: 1995), p. 12.

7. One such example was Edward Thompson's dredging of the Sacred Cenote at Chichen Itza in 1904; the spoils were sent to Thompson's sponsoring institution, Harvard's Peabody Museum, until their repatriation in the 1980s.

8. Wilford, "Splendid Maya Palace," p. A24.

CHAPTER 1

1. The 1650 publication *Annals of the Ancient and New Testaments*, by Archbishop James Ussher, furthermore established the biblical date of Creation at 4004 B.C. Until the advent of stratigraphic geology in the second quarter of the nineteenth century, Ussher's calculation remained authoritative. See Glyn Daniel, *The Idea of Prehistory* (C. A. Watts and Co., London: 1962), p. 42.

2. The two most important illustrated records, ironically, were intended as instruction manuals for the policing and eradication of "pagan" activities in former Aztec areas. Fray Bernardino de Sahagún's multivolume *Historia General de las cosas de Nueva España* (1579; also known as the *Florentine Codex*) and Diego Durán's *Historia de las Indias de Nueva España* (ca. 1579–1581) represent a near-encyclopedic effort to record the daily life and religious practices of preconquest times.

3. René Descartes, *Oeuvres Philosophiques* (Garnier frères, Paris: 1963), 1:77; cited and translated in Michel Foucault, *The Order of Things* (Vintage Press/Random House, New York: 1994), p. 51.

4. Hernando Cortés, *Five Letters of Cortés to the Emperor*, trans. J. Bayard Morris (W. W. Norton, New York: 1928), p. 90.

5. In full, Díaz' first impression of the sacred precinct reads: "*Y así dejamos la gran plaza sin más verla y llegamos a los grandes patios y cercas donde está el gran cu; tenía antes de llegar a él un gran circuito de patios, que me parece que eran más que la plaza que hay en Salamanca, y con dos cercas alrededor, de calicanto, y el mismo patio y sitio todo empedrado de piedras grandes, de losas blancas y muy lisas . . .*"; Bernal Díaz del Castillo, *Historia Verdadera de la Conquista de la Nueva España* (Editorial Porrua, Mexico: 1968), 1:279. For the English version provided in the text above, I have used Alfred Maudslay's translation of Díaz' passage; Díaz del Castillo, *The Discovery and Conquest of Mexico*, trans. Alfred P. Maudslay (Noonday Press, New York: 1965), p. 217.

6. José de Acosta, a Jesuit missionary based in Lima between 1570 and 1587, published his *Historia natural y moral de las Indias* in 1590; covering subjects from religious philosophy to social customs, geography, and natural history, the volume provided a rich source of information for De Bry's subsequent engravings. In 1601, following De Bry's death, his family issued portions of Acosta's text, along with De Bry's illustrations, in the posthumous ninth volume of the artist's *Grands Voyages* series (this volume entitled *De novi orbis natura . . .*).

7. Acosta's text and the accompanying De Bry image appear in Théodore De Bry and J. I. De Bry, *De novi orbis natura . . .* (Francof., Apud M. Beckerum, Amsterdam: 1601), plate 102. For the English version of Acosta's text, I have used Michael Alexander's translation; Alexander, *Discovering the New World* (Harper and Row, New York: 1976), p. 163.

8. Díaz, *Discovery and Conquest of Mexico*, p. 220.

9. Thomas Gage, *Le Voyage de Thomas Gage* (Paul Marret, Amsterdam: 1720), 1:iii. My translation.

10. Friar Diego de Landa, *Yucatan before and after Conquest*, trans. William Gates (Dover Publications, New York: 1978; orig. *Relación de las cosas de Yucatan*, 1566), p. 85. Although written in the sixteenth century, Landa's manuscript was considered lost until the Mesoamerican historian Charles-Étienne Brasseur de Bourbourg rediscovered the work in 1863.

11. The most famous of Aztec artifacts, the colossal Calendar Stone, was cemented into the wall of Mexico City's cathedral following its rediscovery in 1790.

12. Landa noted the continued practice of human sacrifice at Chichen Itza's sacred cenote (Landa, *Yucatan before and after Conquest*, p. 90), while in 1841 John Lloyd Stephens observed that the worship

of "El Demonio" had continued at Uxmal through the start of the eighteenth century. See Stephens, *Incidents of Travel in Yucatan* (Harper and Brothers, New York: 1843), 1:198.

13. Claude Baudez, *Lost Cities of the Maya* (Harry N. Abrams, New York: 1992), p. 32.

14. T. R. Fehrenbach, *Fire and Blood: A History of Mexico* (Da Capo Press, New York: 1995), p. 296.

15. Baudez, *Lost Cities,* p. 32.

16. Baudez notes this omission in *Lost Cities,* p. 33.

17. Estachería's list of inquiries was formally prepared for Bernasconi but no doubt echoed the directives of Calderón's mission. In light of Bernasconi's failures, Estachería must have charged the leader of the third investigation, Captain Antonio Del Río, with completing Bernasconi's investigation. See Robert L. Brunhouse, *In Search of the Maya: The First Archaeologists* (Ballantine Books, New York: 1990), p. 7.

18. Although Almendáriz' name does not appear in the final plates of Del Río's work, nor does Del Río specifically mention Almendáriz within the text, William Bullock named him as the artist when he saw the original report in Mexico City. See Bullock, *Six Months' Residence and Travels in Mexico* (John Murray, London: 1824), 2:68.

19. Antonio Del Río, *Description of the Ruins of an Ancient City Discovered near Palenque in the Kingdom of Guatemala in Spanish America* . . . (Henry Berthoud, London: 1822), p. 3.

20. Ibid., p. 5.

21. Ibid., p. 12.

22. Ibid.

23. Ibid., p. 19.

24. Howard Cline notes that the originals, thought to be lost until 1946, were eventually found in a Madrid archive. To date, however, the fourteen plates in the 1822 editions of Del Río's report are the only published versions. Cline, "The Apocryphal Early Career of J. F. Waldeck Pioneer Americanist," *Acta Americana* 5 (The Inter-American Society of Anthropology and Geography, Los Angeles: 1947), p. 297.

25. Von Humboldt particularly focused on three Aztec sculptures rediscovered in the 1790s (the Calendar Stone, the Stone of Tizoc, and the cult image of Coatlicue), believing that these monuments contained the keys to deciphering Aztec cosmology. Alexander von Humboldt, *Views of the Cordilleras and Monuments of the Indigenous Peoples of America* . . . , trans. Helen Maria Williams (Longman et al., London: 1814, 1:262.

26. Given contemporary ascriptions of the site's authorship, however, von Humboldt's assessment of a Toltec origin was astute — and remained the common wisdom until the mid-twentieth century. For a complete discussion of von Humboldt's contributions to Mexican anthropology, see Jaime L. LaBastida, ed., *Alejandro de Humboldt: Aportaciones a la Antropología Mexicana* (Editorial Katún, Mexico: 1986). Von Humboldt's erroneous belief in the Toltec authorship of Cholula is discussed on pp. 31 and 49 of his text.

27. Von Humboldt had met Dupaix traveling in Mexico, explaining that Dupaix "had sketched with great accuracy the reliefs of the pyramid of Papantla [currently known as the Pyramid of the Niches at El Tajín], on which he intends to publish a very curious work." Von Humboldt, *Views,* 1:43.

28. Henri Baradère, ed., *Antiquités Mexicaines: Relation des trois expéditions du Colonel Dupaix ordonnés en 1805, 1806, et 1807 par le Roi Charles IV* . . . (Firmin Didot frères, Paris: 1844), 1:xiii. This and all subsequent quotations from the Baradère edition are my own translations.

29. Ibid., 2d expedition, p. 16.

30. Ibid., pp. 16–17.

31. Dupaix insists, for example, that the builders of Palenque represented "a race of men unknown to ancient or modern historians, who existed in a time far earlier than our own era." Ibid., 3d expedition, p. 20.

32. Ibid., p. 7.

33. Ibid., 2d expedition, p. 32.

34. Ibid., 3d expedition, p. 17.

35. Ibid., 2d expedition, p. 25.

36. The "Greek" character of this bust is especially noted in Alexandre Lenoir's essay "Parallel of the Ancient Mexican Monuments with Those of Egypt, India, and the Rest of the Ancient World," in Baradère, *Antiquités Mexicaines*, vol. 1, appendix, p. 26.

37. In describing the piece, Dupaix emphasizes the figure's admirable modesty, writing: "Here, the sculptor has artistically disposed the arms and hands of this female figure, in order to hide the parts he wants to take away from view, which gives the figure a certain resemblance to the Medici Venus. This is not astonishing—the artist could have, with his similar sensibilities, conceived and produced the same idea as that of the Greek artist." Baradère, *Antiquités Mexicaines*, vol. 1, 2d expedition, p. 53.

38. Charles Farcy, "Monuments Americains," in Baradère, *Antiquités Mexicaines*, vol. 1, sec. 9, p. 51.

39. Baradère, *Antiquités Mexicaines*, vol. 1, 2d expedition, pp. 55–56.

40. Ibid., 3d expedition, pp. 24–26.

41. Ibid., p. 26.

42. Fehrenbach, *Fire and Blood*, p. 316.

43. Ibid., p. 342.

44. According to Baradère, *Antiquités Mexicaines*, 1:viii.

45. Berthoud credits the theft to a shadowy figure named "Dr. McQuy," although Howard Cline postulates that this name may be a bastardization of "MacQueen." James MacQueen owned the lithography company that produced Del Río's reengraved plates and was known to be in the West Indies during the revolutionary period in Guatemala. See Cline, "The Apocryphal Early Career of J. F. Waldeck," p. 299.

46. Del Río, *Description*, p. ix. In the wake of independence from Spain, Guatemala initially remained under Mexican administration. Mexico's demands for the return of Del Río's papers are noted in Baradère, *Antiquités Mexicaines*, 1:viii.

47. Bullock, who claims to have seen Almendáriz' originals, concluded that Waldeck had taken a certain amount of liberty with them (see note 18 for chapter 1).

48. Cabrera's account centers upon a trans-Atlantic traveling hero named Votan, whose descendants supposedly included the peoples of Palenque, the Hebrews, and several minor Greek deities.

49. Baradère, *Antiquités Mexicaines*, 1:viii.

50. José Alcina Franch, in "Los viajes de exploracíon arqueológico por Mexico de Guillermo Dupaix," *Anuario de Estudios Americanos* 12 (Seville: 1965), p. 10, names Latour-Allard as King's source. This collection of drawings is disparaged, however, in Baradère's introduction; "not only are they less beautiful," he insists, "but less accurate than what we are offering to the public." See Baradère, *Antiquités Mexicaines*, 1:ix.

51. Edward King, Lord Kingsborough, ed., *Antiquities of Mexico* (Robert Havell, London: 1831),

6:230–401. His "racial" evidence and references to Levitical law occur repeatedly throughout this essay, as well as in more than three hundred pages of similarly themed essays that he includes in volume 8.

52. Baradère, *Antiquités Mexicaines,* 1:x.

53. Jean-Frédéric Waldeck, "Extrait d'une lettre . . . à M. Jomard," *Foreign Quarterly Review* 18 (London: 1836), p. 250. Text in English.

54. Jean-Frédéric Waldeck, *Voyage pittoresque et archéologique dans la province d'Yucatan pendant les années 1834 et 1836* (Bellizard Dufour et cie., Paris: 1838), p. b. My translation.

55. His engravings of the museum's collection of preconquest artifacts were published in 1827 under the English title *Collection of Mexican Antiquities.*

56. Coauthored with the French Mesoamericanist Charles-Étienne Brasseur de Bourbourg, this work did not appear until 1866 (full title: *Monuments anciens du Méxique: Palenque et autres ruines d'ancienne civilisation du Méxique;* Arthus Bertrand, Paris: 1866). The images included in the volume, however, date from Waldeck's travels in 1834–1836.

57. Since he was registered with a British company, Waldeck may have claimed British citizenship on his passport for expediency's sake. A facsimile of his passport is included in Waldeck, *Voyage pittoresque,* appendix A.

58. Cline, "The Apocryphal Early Career of J. F. Waldeck," p. 290.

59. Brunhouse notes this inventory in *In Search of the Maya,* pp. 55–56.

60. Waldeck, "Extrait d'une lettre," p. 250.

61. Waldeck, *Voyage pittoresque,* p. 95. This and all subsequent translations from this work are my own.

62. Waldeck, *Monuments,* p. vii. Again, although this volume did not reach a publisher until 1866, the images and Waldeck's notes date from the same period as *Voyage pittoresque.* My translation.

63. The ancient presence of elephants, Waldeck insists, is "proven by the existence of several bones, nearly fossils, found near Lake Chalco, and by the fragment of tusk that I saw at the University of Mexico." See Waldeck, *Voyage pittoresque,* p. 100.

64. Ibid., p. 71.

65. Ibid., p. x.

66. Ibid., p. 95.

67. At the time of Waldeck's visit, the pyramid's dilapidated condition would have made any clear illustration of its elevation an impossibility. Frederick Catherwood's more faithful illustrations of the 1840s imply, however, that the regularity of the structure's rounded corners indicate a nonrectangular plan. The 1970 reconstruction of the pyramid, in elliptical form, is accepted by most scholars as accurate—although the debate continues. See Augusto Molina-Montes, "Archaeological Buildings: Restoration or Misrepresentation," in Elizabeth H. Boone, ed., *Falsifications and Misreconstructions of Pre-Columbian Art* (Dumbarton Oaks, Washington, D.C.: 1982), p. 136.

68. Waldeck, *Voyage pittoresque,* p. 34.

69. As evidence, Waldeck cites the destruction of Mayapan in 1420 "by the indians," slaves to the city founders; ibid., p. 23.

70. Waldeck's confusion is somewhat complicated in this passage. The Quiché Maya also speak of a pilgrimage to "the seven caves" in their sacred text, the Popol Vuh, but the label "Chicomoztoc," the Aztec place of origin, occurs solely in Central Mexican codices. See Waldeck, *Voyage pittoresque,* p. 45; his references to the "Hebrew traces" at Palenque appear on p. 46.

71. Ibid., p. 97.

72. Immanuel Kant, "What Is Enlightenment?" trans. Peter Gay, in *Introduction to Contemporary Civilization in the West* (Columbia University Press, New York: 1954), 1:1071.

CHAPTER 2

1. For the sake of brevity, the titles of the two-volume works of 1841 and 1843 will hereafter be referred to in the notes as *Central America* and *Yucatan,* respectively.

2. *North American Review* 57 (David H. Williams, Boston: 1843), p. 88.

3. In *Central America*, 2:296, Stephens relates that "so little notice was taken of [the Del Río work] that in 1831 the *Literary Gazette,* a paper of great circulation in London, announced [Palenque] as a new discovery made by Colonel Galindo."

4. *North American Review* 51 (Ferdinand Andrews, Boston: 1840), p. 397, and *North American Review* 57 (David H. Williams, Boston: 1843), p. 89.

5. Isaac Goodwin, "An Address, Delivered at Worcester, August 24, 1820, before the American Antiquarian Society . . . ," in American Antiquarian Society, *An Account of the American Antiquarian Society, 1812–1854* (Manning and Trumbull, Worcester, Mass.: 1820), p. 12.

6. *North American Review* 3 (Oliver Everett, Boston: April 1821), p. 225.

7. Fehrenbach, *Fire and Blood,* p. 296.

8. American Antiquarian Society, *Archaeologica Americana: Transactions and Collections of the American Antiquarian Society* (Worcester, Mass.: 1820), p. 245.

9. By the mid-1830s the regions of Yucatan and Chiapas separately sought full independence from the central government in Mexico City. Until the end of the nineteenth century, the political status of these areas vacillated between full diplomatic separation from Mexico and territorial affiliation with the central government. At the time of Stephens' and Catherwood's first journey, Yucatan and Chiapas required passports for travelers arriving from Mexico; by the time of their second trip, a beleaguered Yucatan had hired the Republic of Texas' naval forces to protect the region from reabsorption. Both Yucatan and Chiapas eventually lost this struggle.

10. Michael D. Coe, *Breaking the Maya Code* (Thames and Hudson, London: 1992), p. 93.

11. Stephens' familiarity with these authors' works was impressive, given their relative inaccessibility in this period. In *Central America,* Stephens specifically mentions von Humboldt's work (1:99) and reveals his ownership of Del Río's book (2:352). Van Hagen confirms that the New York bookseller John R. Bartlett had shown Stephens copies of Dupaix's expedition (the Baradère edition) as well as Waldeck's *Voyage pittoresque* prior to his first trip. See Victor W. Van Hagen, *Maya Explorer: John Lloyd Stephens and the Lost Cities of Central America and Yucatan* (University of Oklahoma Press, Norman: 1947), p. 70. By the time of his second trip, Stephens owned his own copy of Waldeck (*Yucatan,* 1:175).

12. John Lloyd Stephens, *Incidents of Travel in Egypt, Arabia Petraea, and the Holy Land* (Harper and Brothers, New York: 1837), 1:iii–iv.

13. Stephens, who proved a hopeless diplomat, nevertheless understood the political situation of the area better than most of his contemporaries. In *Central America,* 1:193–209, he offers a full treatment of the region's complicated rivalries.

14. Victor Van Hagen, *Frederick Catherwood, Architect* (Oxford University Press, New York: 1950), p. 10.

15. A full treatment of Catherwood's initial involvement with the Leicester Square Panorama, and an informative general analysis of London's panoramas in this period, is given in John Davis' *The Landscape of Belief: Encountering the Holy Land in Nineteenth-Century American Art and Culture* (Princeton University Press, Princeton, N.J.: 1996), pp. 59–64.

16. In Van Hagen's biography of Catherwood, he notes that Catherwood's Panorama (which charged the relatively steep admission price of twenty-five cents) proved even more successful than its Broadway competitor, George Catlin's Indian Gallery. See Van Hagen, *Frederick Catherwood,* p. 50. Although Catherwood's architectural practice seems to have blossomed after his Latin American travels, there is little indication that his firm, Catherwood and Diaper, gained any significant commissions before 1839.

17. Stephens, *Central America,* 1:96.

18. Ibid., 1:119.

19. Ibid., 1:115.

20. Ibid., 1:127–128.

21. Ibid., 1:128.

22. Ibid., 2:124.

23. Ibid., 2:363–364.

24. Ibid., 2:433.

25. Quoted in Eric Foner and John Garraty, eds., *The Reader's Companion to American History* (Houghton Mifflin Co., Boston: 1991), p. 743.

26. Ibid., 1:115–116.

27. Ibid., 2:124.

28. Ibid., 2:474.

29. Ibid., 1:138.

30. Catherwood's knowledge of casting techniques had been acquired in Greece, where, during the country's fight for independence from the Turks, the artist had occupied himself with making architectural casts. See Van Hagen, *Frederick Catherwood,* p. 175.

31. The letter, which also denies Stephens' right to purchase the site, appears in full in Stephens' appendix. See Stephens, *Central America,* 2:470.

32. Ibid., 2:474.

33. Ibid., 1:98. Stephens' reference to the authorship of Copan appears on p. 102.

34. Ibid., 1:79.

35. Ibid., 1:103–104, 128.

36. Ibid., 1:160.

37. Ibid., 2:363.

38. Ibid., 2:361.

39. Van Hagen, *Maya Explorer,* p. 231.

40. Stephens, *Central America,* 1:148, 2:52.

41. Ibid., 1:248. Subsequent to Stephens' failed mission, Carrera assumed the presidency of the new republic—a position he held from 1840 until his death in 1865.

42. Stephens' characterizations of the government are found in ibid., 1:324 and 2:127; his letter to Forsyth is also included in 2:127.

43. In his conflation of political and archaeological ruin, Stephens closely echoes European perceptions of the ancient Mediterranean in this period.

44. Stephens, *Central America,* 1:119, 2:348, 2:429–430.

45. Ibid., 2:442.

46. Ibid., 2:413.

47. Ibid., 2:146. Stephens' analogy to ancient Greece, rather than Rome, is telling; as Mary Miller and Linda Schele have observed, in the nineteenth century "the Maya were considered the Greeks of the New World, and the Aztecs were seen as the Romans — one pure, original, and beautiful, the other slavish, derivative, and cold." See Miller and Schele, *The Blood of Kings: Dynasty and Ritual in Maya Art* (George Braziller, New York: 1986), p. 21.

48. Stephens, *Yucatan,* 2:309.

49. Catherwood's working conditions in this temple are described in Stephens, *Central America,* 2:342. Although Waldeck drew the tablets in the 1820s, he failed to publish the drawings until 1866; his illustration, however, does not begin to approach the fidelity of Catherwood's — including, among other inaccuracies, the appearance of "elephant-head" glyphs.

50. Catherwood's instructor Sir John Soane, a great admirer of Piranesi's work, introduced his students to works such as *Antichità Romane* and *Della magnificenza ed architettura de Romana;* Victor Van Hagen asserts that it was these images, in fact, that inspired Catherwood's initial journey to Rome. Van Hagen, *Frederick Catherwood,* p. 12.

51. Stephens, *Yucatan,* 1:247.

52. Ibid., 1:53.

53. Stephens, *Central America,* 2:358.

54. Stephens, *Yucatan,* 1:167.

55. Ibid., 2:310.

56. Quoted in Fredrick B. Pike, *The United States and Latin America: Myths and Stereotypes of Civilization and Nature* (University of Texas Press, Austin: 1992), p. 99.

57. It should be noted that at the time of Stephens' work in Mesoamerica, the term "Maya" applied exclusively to the language spoken by contemporary Indians. Stephens never uses the word as an ethnic label for these groups.

58. Stephens, *Yucatan,* 1:50. While local Maya had indeed been enlisted in the construction of the colonial city's buildings, Stephens argued an unbroken craft tradition from the classic Maya civilization — collapsed in the tenth century — to the construction of Mérida in the sixteenth century.

59. Ibid., 1:198.

60. Stephens, *Central America,* 2:195.

61. Van Hagen, *Maya Explorer,* p. 139.

62. Stephens, *Central America,* 2:197.

63. Ibid., 2:457.

64. Ibid., 2:197.

65. Stephens, *Yucatan,* 2:107.

66. Ibid., 2:310.

67. Stephens, *Central America,* 1:26.

68. Stephens, *Yucatan,* 2:316.

69. Stephens' claims for the "virgin" state of his discoveries first appears in *Central America,* 1:119.

70. Ibid., 1:137.

71. Van Hagen, *Maya Explorer*, p. 196.

72. *Knickerbocker Magazine* 16 (June 1841), p. 364.

73. *New York Review* 9 (August 1841), p. 228.

74. *Knickerbocker Magazine* 16, p. 367.

75. Stephens, *Yucatan*, 1:226.

76. Ibid., 1:v.

77. Ibid., 2:32.

78. The full title of Catlin's work: *Letters and Notes on the Manners, Customs, and Conditions of the North American Indians: Written during Eight Years of Travel amongst the Wildest Tribes of Indians of North America in 1832, '33, '34, '35, '36, '37, '38, and '39* (David Bogue, London: 1841).

79. Ibid., 1:3.

80. Whereas Catlin's program of acquisition paled by comparison to Stephens' agenda, Catlin too collected Native American artifacts for display in his traveling exhibition — including weapons, clothing, tipis, and human remains. Kathyryn S. Hight's 1990 article "'Doomed to Perish': George Catlin's Depictions of the Mandan" provides the best analysis of Catlin's premature memorializations (*Art Journal* 49 [summer 1990], pp. 119–124).

81. Van Hagen's claims for Stephens' professionalism appear in Van Hagen, *Maya Explorer*, p. 112. The "excavation" near Maxcanú is sited in Stephens, *Yucatan*, 2:128.

82. Stephens, *Yucatan*, 2:254.

83. Ibid., 1:258.

84. Stephens, *Central America*, 2:473.

85. Susan Stewart, *On Longing: Narratives of the Miniature, the Gigantic, the Souvenir, and the Collection* (Duke University Press, Durham, N.C.: 1993), p. 141.

86. Catlin's words appear in *Letters and Notes*, 1:120.

87. Stephens, *Yucatan*, 1:136.

88. "Fire at Catherwood's," *New York Herald*, August 1, 1842, p. 2.

89. Stephens, *Yucatan*, 1:252.

90. Ibid., 1:103.

91. Ibid., 1:252.

92. *North American Review* 58 (Otis, Broaders and Co., Boston: 1844), pp. 159–160.

93. Van Hagan, *Maya Explorer*, p. 256.

94. William H. Prescott, *History of the Conquest of Mexico* (Modern Library, New York: 1936 [orig. 1843]), p. 688.

95. Ibid.

96. Van Hagen, *Maya Explorer*, p. 259.

97. Frederick Catherwood, *Views of Ancient Monuments in Central America, Chiapas, and Yucatan* (F. Catherwood, London: 1844), p. 1.

98. Ibid., p. 12.

99. The doorjamb depicted in this image, which eventually made its way to the Smithsonian Museum of Natural History in Washington, D.C., had originally been shipped to Catherwood's Panorama in New York (arriving, fortuitously, after the disastrous fire). Having abandoned his project for a national museum, Stephens later gave the work to his friend John Church Cruger for use as a garden

folly (mentioned earlier in chapter 2), from whose descendants Sylvanus Morley purchased the work in 1918 for the Washington museum. See Van Hagen, *Maya Explorer*, p. 231.

100. Although the War of 1812 technically constituted the United States' first foreign war, this conflict had essentially represented a continuation of lingering revolutionary hostilities with Great Britain. The Mexican War, by contrast, represented the United States' first invasion of a foreign country.

101. Foner and Garraty, *Reader's Companion*, p. 723.

102. Herman Melville, *Moby Dick* (Modern Library, New York: 2000; orig. 1851), p. 576.

103. Robert W. Johannsen, *To the Halls of the Montezumas: The Mexican War in the American Imagination* (Oxford University Press, New York: 1985), p. 304.

104. Ibid., p. 157.

105. The full title of the work is *Memoir of an Eventful Expedition in Central America; Resulting in the Discovery of the Idolatrous City of Iximaya, in an unexplored region; and the possession of two Remarkable Aztec Children, Descendants and Specimens of the Sacerdotal Caste (now nearly extinct) of the Ancient Aztec Founders of the Ruined Temples of that Country; Described by John L. Stevens [sic], Esq., and other Travellers. Translated from the Spanish by Pedro Velasquez, of San Salvador.* The Library of Congress lists Velasquez as the pamphlet's author, adding the caveat that the work is "apocryphal." Although Barnum fails to provide the name of a publisher, real or imagined, he presumably produced the work in New York sometime in early 1850. For Van Hagen's treatment of this hoax, see *Maya Explorer*, pp. 140–141.

106. *New York Republic* 3 (February 1852), cited in Catherine Hoover Voorsanger and John K. Howat, eds., *Art and the Empire City: New York, 1825–1861* (Yale University Press, New Haven, Conn.: 2000), p. 26.

107. Philip Kunhardt, Jr., *P. T. Barnum: America's Greatest Showman* (Alfred A. Knopf, New York: 1995), p. 150.

108. Ibid.

109. *American Quarterly Review* 10 (April 1849), p. 334.

CHAPTER 3

1. Stephens, *Central America*, 1:96–97.

2. Joseph Smith, trans., *The Book of Mormon: An Account Written by the Hand of Mormon upon Plates Taken from the Plates of Nephi and Translated by Joseph Smith, Jr.* (E. B. Grandin, New York: 1838), p. iii. Aside from references to this introductory section of the Book of Mormon, I will use the book-chapter-verse citation format commonly applied to biblical citations. Furthermore, in accordance with the Mormon Church's practice, references to the Book of Mormon will not be italicized.

3. Ibid., p. ii.

4. Discovered in August 1799, the so-called Rosetta stone had provided Champollion and his three rivals, Antoine Silvestre de Sacy, Thomas Young, and Johann David Akerblad, with the means to decipher the Egyptian pictographic system. Working throughout the 1810s and 1820s, Champollion and a team of assistants deciphered the Ptolemaic decree that had been written on the stone in three languages—hieroglyphic Egyptian, a form of Arabic, and Greek. Given the popular interest in Champollion's work, it is reasonable to assume Mormons' familiarity with this parallel-text translation aid. Jean Vercoutter, *The Search for Ancient Egypt* (Harry N. Abrams, New York: 1992), pp. 88–91.

5. Smith, Book of Mormon, 1 Nephi 8:10–18.

6. The description of these boats' "curious workmanship" (1 Nephi 18:1) directly recalls the witnesses' account of the plates themselves; the ships' compasses, which represent one of the Book of Mormon's greatest anachronisms, are mentioned in 1 Nephi 18:12. Frederick Williams, cited in John Sorenson, *An Ancient American Setting for the Book of Mormon* (Deseret Book Co., Salt Lake City: 1985), p. 1.

7. Parley Pratt, *A Key to the Science of Theology* (F. D. Richards, Liverpool: 1855), p. 23.

8. The account of the Tower of Babel appears in Genesis 11:1–8.

9. This discovery is related in the eighth chapter of the Book of Mosiah, as well as the twenty-first chapter of the Book of Alma.

10. Robert Wauchope, *Lost Tribes and Sunken Continents: Myth and Method in the Study of American Indians* (University of Chicago Press, Chicago: 1975), p. 57.

11. Before his departure, Lehi had in fact predicted the imminent fall of Jerusalem, a factor that led to his expulsion from the city and subsequent emigration. Smith, Book of Mormon, 1 Nephi 20.

12. Jan Ships, *Mormonism: The Story of a New Religious Tradition* (University of Chicago Press, Chicago: 1985), p. 7.

13. Robert L. Millet, ed., *Joseph Smith: Selected Sermons and Writings* (Paulist Press, Mahwah, N.J.: 1989), p. 9.

14. Ships, *Mormonism*, p. 7.

15. The Mormon Articles of Faith were first articulated by Smith in a letter to John Wentworth, the editor of the *Chicago Democrat,* who had asked the Mormon leader in 1842 for a history of the church. The text of the letter, later considered a sacred scripture, first appeared in the Mormon's official newspaper, *Times and Seasons,* on March 1, 1842. See Millet, *Joseph Smith,* pp. 107–108.

16. Smith, Book of Mormon, 3 Nephi 11:24–28 and 12:11–30.

17. The Mormon Church has denied permission to reproduce Friberg's images here, but they are easily found within any contemporary copy of the Book of Mormon.

18. Jacques Lafaye provides the fullest treatment of this enduring colonial-era belief in *Quetzalcóatl and Guadalupe: The Formation of Mexican National Consciousness, 1531–1813,* trans. Benjamin Keen (University of Chicago Press, Chicago: 1976).

19. Ibid., 262–266, and Benjamin Keen, *The Aztec Image in Western Thought* (Rutgers University Press, New Brunswick, N.J.: 1971), p. 304.

20. Smith, Book of Mormon, Mosiah 8:8 and Alma 50:1–5.

21. *Battleboro Messenger* (Vermont), October 30, 1830; cited in Dan Vogel, *Indian Origins and the Book of Mormon: Religious Solutions from Columbus to Joseph Smith* (Signature Books, New York: 1986), p. 30.

22. Fawn Brodie, *No Man Knows My History: The Life of Joseph Smith* (Alfred A. Knopf, New York: 1976), p. 19.

23. Ephraim G. Squier, *Antiquities of the State of New York: Being the Results of Extensive Original Surveys and Explorations* (George H. Derby and Co., New York: 1851), p. 55. Although many of Squier's surveys were original, most of his explorations were not; mounds such as the one at Canandaigua and others had been known for decades.

24. DeWitt Clinton, "A Memoir on the Antiquities of the Western Parts of the State of New York," *Transactions of the Literary and Philosophical Society of New York* 2 (Albany, N.Y.: 1815–1825), p. 82.

25. John Yates and Joseph Moulton, *History of the State of New-York* (Hoffman and White, Albany, N.Y.: 1824), pp. 19–20. Although these branches of Lehi's family were related by blood, the Lamanites were characterized as darker-skinned—leading to the Mormons' insistence that this group formed the ethnic foundation of all native North American tribes.

26. Smith, Book of Mormon, Helaman 3:4.

27. Vogel, *Indian Origins*, p. 26.

28. Although the ancient setting of the Book of Mormon is clearly centered in Mesoamerica, rather than South America, church leaders hypothesized a South American landing point for Lehi's family. See introduction, n. 4.

29. Smith, Book of Mormon, 2 Nephi 5:16, Helaman 3:7, and Alma 50:13.

30. Ibid., 2 Nephi 5:16–17.

31. Ibid., Mosiah 2:5.

32. "Moroni did employ his men in preparing for war, yea, and in making fortifications to guard against the Lamanites"; ibid., Alma 53:7.

33. Ibid., Mormon 5:1 and Alma 22:28.

34. Given the Lamanites' ancestry, it is clear that their preference for tents is linked to the established, nomadic traditions of Semitic peoples (rather than representing a new development). It is this connection, in fact, that strengthens the Mormon belief in Native Americans' Hebrew origins.

35. Vogel, *Indian Origins*, pp. 30–31.

36. One of the great inconsistencies in Smith's doctrines is that, whereas he claimed his followers' genealogical descent from the Nephites, the Book of Mormon asserts that the group was entirely destroyed at the Battle of Cumorah.

37. Smith, Book of Mormon, 2 Nephi 1:8–9 and 1:11.

38. Ibid., 2 Nephi 12:8 and 15:19.

39. Ibid., 2 Nephi 10:11.

40. Charles Blancher Thompson, *Evidence in Proof of the Book of Mormon* (C. B. Thompson, Batavia, N.Y.: 1841), p. 101.

41. *Times and Seasons,* October 1, 1842, p. 927.

42. Orson Pratt, in *Latter-day Saints' Millennial Star,* no. 10 (November 1848), p. 347. In this passage Pratt writes that "the Nephites inhabited Yucatan at the time they were driven from the land southward."

43. John Taylor, "The Discovery of Ruins," *Latter-day Saints' Millennial Star,* no. 13 (March 1851), pp. 93–94.

44. Ibid., p. 93.

45. One of the Mormon Church's tenets of faith is its belief in the gift of continual revelation; this power is extended not only to church leaders but also to members of the laity.

46. Parley Pratt, "Address to the Red Man," *Latter-day Saints' Millennial Star,* no. 14 (September 1852), p. 469.

47. The full title of Jones' work echoes that of Catlin's 1844 publication: *Forty Years among the Indians: A True yet Thrilling Narrative of the Author's Experience among the Natives* (Juvenile Instruction Office, Salt Lake City: 1890; repr. Westernlore Press, Los Angeles: 1960). The Mormons' thwarted efforts to convert Native American tribes are noted in F. LaMond Tullis, *Mormons in Mexico: The Dynamics of Faith and Culture* (Utah University Press, Logan: 1987), p. 6.

48. Tullis, *Mormons in Mexico*, p. 13.

49. Jones, *Forty Years among the Indians*, p. 211.

50. Tullis, *Mormons in Mexico*, p. 25.

51. Ibid., p. 41.

52. Jones, *Forty Years among the Indians*, p. 239.

53. Brigham Young, *Journal of Discourses* 18, pp. 355–356; cited in Tullis, *Mormons in Mexico*, p. 32.

54. Foner and Garraty, *Reader's Companion*, p. 748.

55. Although the Mormons perceived indigenous groups as the descendants of the Lamanites, they did not recognize the mestizos, or Spanish-derived inhabitants of Latin America, as members of the original Israelite family.

56. Examples of the twentieth-century Mormon Church's interest in Latin American archaeology include Brigham Young University's *Archaeology Bulletin* and the Mormon-supported New World Archaeological Foundation; both founded in 1953, the *Bulletin* and the foundation maintain the Nephite basis of Mesoamerican culture.

CHAPTER 4

1. Désiré Charnay, *Cités et ruines américaines: Mitla, Palenqué, Izamal, Chichen-Itza, Uxmal, receuillés et photographiés par Désiré Charnay avec un texte par M. Viollet-le-Duc* (Gide, Paris: 1862–1863).

2. Although the work was originally published in French in 1885, the English translation represents the primary source for Charnay's American readership—for this reason, this and subsequent citations will refer to the English translation.

3. Charnay's early career in New Orleans is discussed in Leo Deuel's *Conquistadors without Swords: Archaeologists in the Americas* (Schocken Books, New York: 1974), p. 178.

4. Désiré Charnay, *The Ancient Cities of the New World: Being Voyages and Explorations in Mexico and Central America from 1857–1882*, trans. J. Gonino and Helen S. Conant (Harper and Brothers, New York: 1887), p. 1.

5. Ibid., p. xi.

6. Helmut Gernsheim, *The History of Photography* (McGraw-Hill, New York: 1969), p. 26.

7. Keith Davis, *Désiré Charnay: Expeditionary Photographer* (University of New Mexico Press, Albuquerque: 1981), p. 6.

8. Charnay's inventory at Veracruz is noted in Baudez, *Lost Cities*, p. 86.

9. Davis, *Désiré Charnay*, p. 16.

10. Ibid., p. 166.

11. In the 1850s, Charnay would have had to transport all of the plaster necessary to make these casts; his new paper-molding technique was not used until the second expedition.

12. Charnay, *Ancient Cities*, p. 1.

13. Davis, *Désiré Charnay*, p. 22.

14. Despite his support for the war, Stephens never acknowledged his political position in his archaeological writings. Johannsen, *To the Halls of the Montezumas*, p. 304.

15. Charnay, *Cités et ruines*, p. 202–203; Keith Davis' translation, in Davis, *Désiré Charnay*, p. 21.

16. Although Charnay returned to Mexico briefly in 1864, accompanying troops sent to support Maximilian, he performed no fieldwork on that trip.

17. Davis, *Désiré Charnay,* p. 2.

18. Walter Benjamin, "The Work of Art in the Age of Mechanical Reproduction" (1936), in Stephen Bayley, ed., *Commerce and Culture: From Pre-Industrial Art to Post-Industrial Value* (Design Museum, London: 1989), p. 35.

19. My translation. In full, Viollet-le-Duc's passage reads: *"Mais à quelle râce appartenaient ces peuples qui jetèrent un si vif éclat vers le VIIe siècle de notre ère? Appartenaient-elles aux râces blanches pures, ou aux râces melangées de blanc?"* Viollet-le-Duc in Charnay, *Cités et ruines américaines,* p. 4.

20. My translation. In the original French, Viollet-le-Duc speaks of *"un peuple dont la caractère ethnique rapelle les plus beaux types blancs, quoique très étrangers à la râce celtibérienne ou espagnole."* Viollet-le-Duc in Charnay, *Cités et ruines américaines,* p. 9.

21. My translation. *"Il serait difficile de nier aujourd'hui l'éxistence des relations Scandinaves avec l'Amérique dès le IXe siècle de notre ère,"* he writes, adding that this is a group *"dont l'origine apparâit sur les hauts plateaux septentrionaux de l'Inde."* Viollet-le-Duc in Charnay, *Cités et ruines américaines,* pp. 10 and 9, respectively.

22. My translation. *"En admettant à priori que les Amériques aient été occupées par des peuplades venues de nord ... toujours en cherchant un ciel plus doux, descendre vers l'États de l'Ohio, occuper le littoral de la Caroline, s'étendre jusque dans la péninsule des Florides, reconnaître l'île de Cuba, et bientôt l'Yucatan."* Viollet-le-Duc in Charnay, *Cités et ruines américaines,* p. 7.

23. Because Viollet-le-Duc's 1876 work appeared in English almost immediately following its publication, and reached its U.S. audience in translated form, I will refer to the American version of this work: Viollet-le-Duc, *Habitations of Man in All Ages,* trans. Benjamin Bucknall (James R. Osgood, Boston: 1876).

24. Viollet-le-Duc, *Habitations of Man,* chap. 5.

25. Ibid., pp. 297 and 308-309.

26. Ibid., p. 306.

27. Mary Miller, *The Art of Mesoamerica from Olmec to Aztec* (Thames and Hudson, London: 1986), p. 171.

28. Although it was long believed lost, Landa's manuscript resurfaced in the Academy of History in Madrid in 1864. Representing one of Brasseur de Bourbourg's greatest discoveries, this colonial document provided invaluable information concerning Maya language patterns.

29. Landa, *Yucatan before and after Conquest,* p. 83.

30. Brasseur de Bourbourg, *Quatre lettres sur le Méxique: une exposition absolue du système hieroglyphique mexicain à la fin de l'âge de pierre* (Maisonneuve et Cie., Paris: 1868), p. iii.

31. Brasseur de Bourbourg's Atlantis theories are given their fullest treatment in Brunhouse, *In Search of the Maya,* pp. 110-131.

32. Brasseur de Bourbourg's connection between the Toltecs and Scandinavia first appeared in Henry Bancroft's five-volume work, *The Native Races of the Pacific Coast* (San Francisco: 1883), 5:112.

33. Although distancing himself from Brasseur de Bourbourg's scholarship in his preface to *Ancient Cities,* Charnay concedes that "science in recent times has gone to show that a vast extent of dry land formerly existed between America and Europe." Charnay, *Ancient Cities,* p. xiv.

34. Ibid., p. xxvii.

35. Allen Thorndike Rice, "Ruined Cities of Central America," *North American Review* 285 (August 1880), pp. 90–91.

36. Ibid., p. 90.

37. A French immigrant, Lorillard had established the enormously successful Continental Tobacco Company in the 1850s; by the 1880s, the Lorillard family home at 36th Street and Fifth Avenue had become "one of the centers of fashionable life of the city"—seconded by their home in Tuxedo Park, New York, a community founded by Lorillard. Cited in the obituary of Lorillard's son, Pierre Lorillard, Jr., *New York Times*, August 7, 1940, p. 19.

38. Charnay, *Ancient Cities*, p. x.

39. Ibid., preface.

40. Miller writes that "the skill of the builders at Tula, Hidalgo, was not exceptional, and in fact, much of the workmanship there can be considered shoddy." Miller, *Art of Mesoamerica*, p. 171.

41. Charnay, *Ancient Cities*, p. 108.

42. Ibid., p. 91.

43. Ibid., p. 121.

44. Ibid., p. 97.

45. Ibid., p. 132.

46. Ibid., pp. 144–145.

47. Ibid., p. 181.

48. Peter Tompkins, *Mysteries of the Mexican Pyramids* (Thames and Hudson, London: 1976), p. 150.

49. Charnay, *Ancient Cities*, p. 178.

50. Ibid., p. 98.

51. Ibid., p. 60.

52. Enrique Florescano, "The Creation of the Museo Nacional de Antropología of Mexico and Its Scientific, Educational, and Political Purposes," in Elizabeth Hill Boone, ed., *Collecting the Pre-Columbian Past* (Dumbarton Oaks, Washington, D.C.: 1993), pp. 88–89.

53. Charnay, *Ancient Cities*, p. 55.

54. Ibid., p. 150.

55. Ibid., p. 245.

56. Ibid., p. 249.

57. Ibid., p. 208.

58. Ibid., p. 504.

59. Ibid., p. 278.

60. Ibid., p. 247.

61. Ibid., p. 253.

62. Charnay credits a Frenchman by the name of Lotin de Laval with the invention of this process. Ibid., p. 254.

63. Ibid.

64. Ibid.

65. Ibid., p. 337.

66. Ibid., p. 254.

67. Ibid.

68. Stephens, *Central America*, 2:470.

69. Charnay, *Cités et ruines américaines*, p. 347.

70. Charnay, *Ancient Cities*, p. xxiii.

71. Charnay had heard of the city from the mayor of Yaxchilán's neighboring town, Tenosique; the mayor, who claimed to have visited the site in 1869, described the city's towers in terms that recalled (to Charnay's mind, at least) Stephens' descriptions of the "lost city." David Grant Adamson, *The Ruins of Time: Four and a Half Centuries of Conquest and Discovery among the Maya* (Praeger Publishers, New York: 1975), p. 193.

72. Charnay's scholarly claim to the site of Yaxchilán derived from Maudslay's extraordinary sense of generosity. "You need have no fear on my account," Maudslay assured Charnay, "for I am only an amateur . . . and as for the ruins, I make them over to you. You can name the town, claim to have discovered it, in fact do what you please." Charnay, *Ancient Cities*, p. 436.

73. Adamson notes that the name "Villa Lorillard" retained currency among scholars until as late as 1928. Adamson, *Ruins of Time*, p. 200.

74. Charnay, *Ancient Cities*, p. 436.

75. Charnay's band of soldiers is cited in Rice, "Ruined Cities," p. 90.

76. Davis, *Désiré Charnay*, p. 162.

77. Charnay, *Ancient Cities*, p. 91.

CHAPTER 5

1. Rice, "Ruined Cities," p. 96.

2. Ibid.

3. The most useful source on the Le Plongeons' career, to date, is Lawrence Gustave Desmond and Phyllis Mauch Messenger's *A Dream of Maya: Augustus and Alice Le Plongeon in Nineteenth-Century Yucatan* (University of New Mexico Press, Albuquerque: 1988). Le Plongeon's connection to Squier is mentioned on pp. 8–10.

4. Ibid., p. 10.

5. Brunhouse explores this lecture at length in *In Search of the Maya*, pp. 141–146.

6. Augustus Le Plongeon, *Vestiges of the Mayas* (John Polhemus, New York: 1881), p. 15.

7. Le Plongeon recognizes this sponsorship in his *Sacred Mysteries among the Mayas* (Robert Macoy, New York: 1886), p. vii.

8. Desmond and Messenger, *A Dream of Maya*, p. 18.

9. Ibid., p. 38.

10. Le Plongeon mentions his armed patrol in *Vestiges of the Mayas*, p. 57. Desmond and Messenger confirm the presence of this armed guard in *A Dream of Maya*, p. 27.

11. His "telegraph" discovery is now a staple of Le Plongeon scholarship; Desmond and Messenger include the story on p. 26 of *A Dream of Maya*, as does Tompkins in *Mysteries of the Mexican Pyramids*, p. 167.

12. Augustus Le Plongeon, *Sacred Mysteries among the Mayas*, p. 152.

13. Augustus Le Plongeon, *Vestiges of the Mayas*, p. 55.

14. Edward H. Thompson, "A Maya Legend in the Making," *Proceedings of the American Antiquarian Society* 61 (1931), pp. 340–343.

15. Stephen Salisbury, "Dr. Le Plongeon in Yucatan. The Discovery of a Statue Called Chac-Mool, and the Communications of Dr. Le Plongeon concerning Exploration in the Yucatan Peninsula," *Proceedings of the American Antiquarian Society* 69 (1877), p. 93; referenced by Miller, "A Re-examination," p. 7.

16. Alice Le Plongeon, *Here and There in Yucatan: Miscellanies* (J. W. Bouton, New York: 1886).

17. Blavatsky's work, *The Secret Doctrine*, first appeared in 1888. I owe Desmond and Messenger, *A Dream of Maya*, p. 106, for this reference.

18. Augustus Le Plongeon, *Vestiges of the Mayas*, p. 55.

19. The best treatment of this type and its history can be found in Mary Ellen Miller's "A Re-examination of the Mesoamerican Chacmool," *Art Bulletin* 67:1 (March 1985), pp. 7–17.

20. Karl Ruppert, *Chichen Itza* (Carnegie Institution of Washington: 1952), p. 166; cited in Miller, "A Re-examination," p. 7.

21. Miller, "A Re-examination," p. 7.

22. Salisbury, "Dr. Le Plongeon in Yucatan."

23. Augustus Le Plongeon, *Vestiges of the Mayas*, p. 55.

24. The current spelling of the term "chacmool," a label now applied to all similar works, is the result of a transcription error by Stephen Salisbury in reporting Le Plongeon's find. Because this is the current usage, I will refer to Le Plongeon's "Chaac Mool" as "chacmool."

25. Miller, "A Re-examination," p. 12.

26. Salisbury, "Dr. Le Plongeon in Yucatan," p. 97.

27. Desmond and Messenger, *A Dream of Maya*, p. 42

28. Augustus Le Plongeon, letter to Stephen Salisbury, *Proceedings of the American Antiquarian Society* 59 (1877), p. 88.

29. Desmond and Messenger, *A Dream of Maya*, p. 49.

30. Salisbury, "Dr. Le Plongeon in Yucatan," p. 95.

31. Miller, *Maya Art and Architecture* (Thames and Hudson, London: 1999), p. 186.

32. This fictional drama, as related in the following paragraphs, is told most succinctly in Le Plongeon's *Sacred Mysteries among the Mayas*, pp. 78–82. The narrative resurfaces in a variety of forms, however, in his other works — including *Vestiges of the Mayas* and especially *Queen Móo and the Egyptian Sphinx* (Augustus Le Plongeon, New York: 1896).

33. Augustus Le Plongeon, *Vestiges of the Mayas*, pp. 63–67.

34. Móo means "macaw" in Yucatec Maya. Desmond and Messenger, *A Dream of Maya*, p. 30.

35. Ibid., p. 36.

36. Augustus Le Plongeon, *Vestiges of the Mayas*, pp. 67–68.

37. Augustus Le Plongeon, *Queen Móo and the Egyptian Sphinx*, p. 166.

38. According to the subtitle of his second work, *Sacred Mysteries among the Mayas* (1886), Le Plongeon believed these events to have occurred 11,500 years ago.

39. Alice Dixon Le Plongeon, *Queen Móo's Talisman: The Fall of the Maya Empire* (Peter Eckler, New York: 1902).

40. Augustus Le Plongeon, *Sacred Mysteries among the Mayas*, p. xi.

41. Alice Le Plongeon to Phoebe Hearst, n.d., Bancroft Library, University of California, Berkeley.

42. Desmond and Messenger, *A Dream of Maya*, pp. 71–80.

43. During his first period of work at Chichen Itza, for example, Le Plongeon amassed more than

five hundred stereoptic images of the site—far more images than Charnay had produced, in the 1860s, at half a dozen sites.

44. Desmond and Messenger, *A Dream of Maya*, p. 80.

45. Ibid., p. 77.

46. Augustus Le Plongeon, *Sacred Mysteries among the Mayas*, p. 11.

47. Albert Gallatin Mackey, *The History of Freemasonry: Its Legendary Origins* (Gramercy Books, New York: 1996), p. 178.

48. Augustus Le Plongeon, "An Interesting Discovery: A Temple with Masonic Symbols in the Ruined City of Uxmal," *Harper's Weekly* (December 17, 1881), pp. 851–852.

49. Augustus Le Plongeon, "An Interesting Discovery," p. 852.

50. In 1847, Mason Thomas Pryer publicly confirmed that the ceremonies of Freemasonry were modern inventions; any attempts to link them historically—rather than symbolically—with ancient Egypt were, he said, "absurdities and purely imaginary." Pryer, "On the Study of Masonic Antiquities," *Freemason's Quarterly Review* (1947), p. 262.

51. Lynn Dumenil, *Freemasonry and American Culture: 1880-1930* (Princeton University Press, Princeton, N.J.: 1984), pp. xi-7.

52. Herbert Singer and Ossian Lang, *New York Freemasonry: A Bicentennial History, 1781-1981* (Grand Lodge of Free and Accepted Masons of the State of New York: 1981), pp. 235–241.

53. Dumenil, *Freemasonry and American Culture*, p. 4.

54. Patterson, *Toward a Social History of Archaeology*, p. 10.

55. See chap. 3 n. 11.

56. Augustus Le Plongeon, *Sacred Mysteries among the Mayas*, p. 19.

57. Anonymous, "Our American Obelisk," *Daily Graphic* (New York), August 28, 1880, p. 433. Le Plongeon's probable authorship of this article discussed in the text, below.

58. Soon after Macpherson's death in 1796, these two poems were found to be primarily by his own hand. "James Macpherson," *Columbia Encyclopedia*, 6th ed. (Columbia University Press, New York: 2001).

59. David A. Traill, *Schliemann of Troy: Treasure and Deceit* (St. Martin's Press, New York: 1995), p. 176.

60. Roland and Françoise Etienne, *The Search for Ancient Greece* (Harry N. Abrams, New York: 1992), p. 110.

61. Augustus Le Plongeon, *Sacred Mysteries among the Mayas*, p. viii.

62. Ibid., p. ix.

63. Martina D'Alton, "The New York Obelisk or How Cleopatra's Needle Came to New York and What Happened When it Got Here," *Metropolitan Museum of Art Bulletin* (Spring 1993); repr. Harry N. Abrams (New York: 1993).

64. Ibid., p. 2.

65. Ibid., p. 15.

66. Ibid., p. 42.

67. Augustus Le Plongeon, *Sacred Mysteries among the Mayas*, p. 17.

68. Anonymous, "Our American Obelisk," p. 433.

69. Ibid.

70. Ibid.

71. Desmond and Messenger, *A Dream of Maya*, p. 58.

72. Augustus Le Plongeon, *Sacred Mysteries among the Mayas*, p. ix.

73. Desmond and Messenger, *A Dream of Maya*, p. 112.

74. Augustus Le Plongeon, *Vestiges of the Mayas*, p. 84.

75. Augustus Le Plongeon, *Sacred Mysteries among the Mayas*, p. 153.

EPILOGUE

1. Brian Fagan, *Elusive Treasure: The Story of Early Archaeologists in the Americas* (Charles Scribner's Sons, New York: 1977), p. 270.

2. Trumbull White, *World's Columbian Exposition: A Complete History* (P. W. Ziegler and Co., Philadelphia: 1893), pp. 429-430.

3. Maudslay's photographs were later included in his four-volume 1889-1902 work, *Biologia Centrali-Americana* (R. H. Porter: London). The original set of Maudslay's prints from the fair have recently been identified in the Brooklyn Museum's collection (cited by Rebecca Stone Miller in "The Influence of Mayan Architecture on Frank Lloyd Wright," unpublished, 1982). Maler, an Austrian photographer who traveled throughout Mexico and Central America recording the ruins, primarily augmented Maudslay's documentation of Maya-area sites; see Barbara Braun, *Pre-Columbian Art and the Post-Columbian World* (Harry N. Abrams, New York: 1993), p. 33.

4. L. G. Moses, *Wild West Shows and the Images of Native Americans, 1883-1933* (University of New Mexico Press, Albuquerque: 1996), p. 132.

5. The re-creation of the ancient Anasazi cliff dwellings at the fair was not arranged by Putnam but was an independent, for-profit concession, granted to the H. Jay Smith Exploring Company of Minneapolis. Diane Dillon, personal communication, April 28, 1998.

6. Lewis Henry Morgan, "Montezuma's Dinner," *North American Review* 122 (April 1876), pp. 265-308.

7. Keen, *The Aztec Image in Western Thought*, p. 388.

8. In Mauricio Tenorio-Trillo's otherwise excellent study, *Mexico at the World's Fairs: Crafting a Modern Nation* (University of California, Berkeley: 1996), p. 185, he erroneously locates these temple reproductions along the Midway; however, it is their *separation* from Putnam's exhibits on the Midway that link them to the nonexotic historical narrative of White City.

9. Diane Dillon (personal communication, April 28, 1998) has pointed out that although the location of the Palace of Fine Arts was carefully conceived, the Anthropology Building's placement at the opposite end of the fair was merely a planning afterthought. Even in the absence of a planned, programmatic symbolism here, however, the fact remains that fairgoers experienced the two sites as physically opposed poles.

10. Neil Harris, Wim de Wit, James Gilbert, and Robert Rydell, *Grand Illusions: Chicago's World's Fair of 1893* (Chicago Historical Society, Chicago: 1993), frontispiece map.

11. It is not clear whether Putnam's suggestion ever made its way to the drafting table. His original proposal is cited in Bruce Hatton Boyer, *The Natural History of the Field Museum: Exploring the Earth and Its People* (Field Museum, Chicago: 1993), p. 12.

12. Miller and Schele, *The Blood of Kings*, p. 21.

13. Although Goodman's system was not immediately recognized by all Maya scholars, including

the early twentieth-century Mesoamericanist Herbert Spinden, Goodman's chronology gained full acceptance by midcentury.

14. James Oles, *South of the Border: Mexico in the American Imagination, 1914-1947* (Smithsonian Institution Press, Washington, D.C.: 1993), p. 3.

15. This fair is not to be confused with the Panama-Pacific Exposition in San Francisco of the same year. As Tenorio-Trillo has shown, postrevolutionary Mexico had been eager to participate in the fairs, yet the assassination of Francisco Madero—and the political instability that followed in its wake—made Mexico's presence in San Francisco impossible (Tenorio-Trillo, *Mexico at the World's Fairs*, pp. 196-197). Consequently, exhibits related to ancient Mesoamerican architecture were restricted to the San Diego fair and, as explained above, were placed within the California Building.

16. Edgar L. Hewett, "America's Archaeological Heritage," *Art and Archaeology* 4:6 (December 1916), p. 260.

17. Ibid., p. 259.

18. Wright had visited the San Diego fair in January 1915 as the guest of Alfonso Ianelli, a sculptor who had worked with Wright in the 1910s. At the fair, Ianelli introduced Wright to the Southwest painter Alice Klauber, who presented him with a collection of photographs of the Maya exhibits (Anthony Alofsin, *Frank Lloyd Wright: The Lost Years, 1910-1922* [University of Chicago Press, Chicago: 1993], p. 225). Although Wright's first exposure to Maya architecture dates to the earlier World's Columbian Exposition (where he oversaw the construction of the fair's Transportation Building), the Mesoamerican exhibits at the San Diego fair appear to have made a stronger visual impact on the architect. In his written response to Dmitri Tselos' 1953 article, "Exotic Influences in the Architecture of Frank Lloyd Wright" (*Magazine of Art* 47 [April 1953], pp. 160-184), Wright asserted that pre-Columbian forms represented "the primitive basis of world architecture" (Alofsin, *Frank Lloyd Wright*, p. 225).

19. Edgar L. Hewett, "Ancient America at the Panama-California Exposition," *Art and Archaeology* 2:3 (November 1915), pp. 99-101.

20. Hewett, "America's Archaeological Heritage," p. 257. For the fullest treatment of this phenomenon, see Marjorie Ingle, *The Mayan Revival Style* (Peregrine Books, Salt Lake City: 1984).

21. This next phase of Mexico-U.S. relations is deftly handled in Oles' *South of the Border.*

22. George G. Crawford, *A Tourist's Guide to Points in and Near the City of Mexico* (G. G. Crawford, New York: 1890), p. 3.

BIBLIOGRAPHY

Alexander, Michael, ed. *Discovering the New World: Based on the Works of Théodore De Bry*. Harper and Row, New York: 1976.

Alofsin, Anthony. *Frank Lloyd Wright: The Lost Years, 1910–1922*. University of Chicago Press, Chicago: 1993.

American Antiquarian Society. *An Account of the American Antiquarian Society, 1812–1854*. Worcester, Mass.: 1854.

_____. *Archaeologica Americana: Transactions and Collections of the American Antiquarian Society*. Worcester, Mass.: 1820.

_____. *Proceedings of the American Antiquarian Society*. Worcester, Mass.: 1877.

American Quarterly Review. Vol. 2 (Sept./Dec. 1827); vol. 10 (April 1849).

Anonymous. "Our American Obelisk." *Daily Graphic* (New York), August 28, 1880, p. 433.

Bancroft, Henry. *The Native Races of the Pacific Coast*. 5 vols. San Francisco: 1883.

Bancroft, Walter. *The Book of the Fair*. Vol. 7. Chicago: 1893.

Baradère, Henri, ed. *Antiquités Mexicaines: Relation des trois expéditions du Colonel Dupaix, ordonnés en 1805, 1806, et 1807, par le Roi Charles IV. . . .* 2 vols. Firmin Didot frères, Paris: 1834.

Barnum, Phineas T. (under pseudonym Pedro Velasquez). *Memoir of an Eventful Expedition in Central America; Resulting in the Discovery of the Idolatrous City of Iximaya, in an unexplored region; and the possession of two Remarkable Aztec Children, Descendants and Specimens of the Sacerdotal Caste (now nearly extinct) of the Ancient Aztec Founders of the Ruined Temples of that Country; Described by John L. Stevens [sic], Esq., and other Travellers; Translated from the Spanish by Pedro Velasquez, of San Salvador*. New York: 1850.

Baudez, Claude. *Lost Cities of the Maya*. Harry N. Abrams, New York: 1992.

Benjamin, Walter. "The Work of Art in the Age of Mechanical Reproduction" (1936). In Stephen Bayley, ed., *Commerce and Culture: From Pre-Industrial Art to Post-Industrial Value*, p. 35. Design Museum, London: 1989.

Boone, Elizabeth Hill, ed. *Collecting the Pre-Columbian Past*. Dumbarton Oaks, Washington, D.C.: 1993.

_____. *Falsifications and Misreconstructions of Pre-Columbian Art*. Dumbarton Oaks, Washington, D. C.: 1978.

Boyer, Bruce Hatton. *The Natural History of the Field Museum: Exploring the Earth and Its People*. Field Museum, Chicago: 1993.

Brasseur de Bourbourg, Charles-Étienne. *Histoire des nations civilisées du Méxique et de l'Amerique centrale*. 4 vols. Paris: 1859.

_____. *Quatre lettres sur le Méxique: une exposition absolue du système hieroglyphique mexicain à la fin de l'âge de pierre*. Maisonneuve et Cie., Paris: 1868.

Braun, Barbara. *Pre-Columbian Art and the Post-Columbian World*. Harry N. Abrams, New York: 1993.

Brodie, Fawn. *No Man Knows My History: The Life of Joseph Smith*. Alfred A. Knopf, New York: 1976.

Brunhouse, Robert L. *In Search of the Maya: The First Archaeologists*. Ballantine Books, New York: 1990.

Bullock, William. *Six Months' Residence and Travels in Mexico*. Vol. 2. John Murray, London: 1824.

Catherwood, Frederick. *Views of Ancient Monuments in Central America, Chiapas, and Yucatan*. F. Catherwood, London: 1844.

Catlin, George. *Letters and Notes on the Manners, Customs, and Conditions of the North American Indians: Written during Eight Years of Travel amongst the Wildest Tribes of Indians of North America in 1832, '33, '34, '35, '36, '37, '38, and '39*. David Bogue, London: 1841.

Charnay, Désiré. *The Ancient Cities of the New World: Being Voyages and Explorations in Mexico and Central America from 1857–1882*. Trans. J. Gonino and Helen S. Conant. Harper and Brothers, New York: 1887.

_____. *Cités et ruines américaines: Mitla, Palenque, Izamal, Chichen-Itza, Uxmal*. With introduction by Eugène-Emmanuel Viollet-le-Duc. A. Morel et Cie., Paris: 1862.

Church of Jesus Christ of Latter-Day Saints. *Times and Seasons*. Nauvoo, Ill.: March 1842, October 1842.

Cline, H. F. "The Apocryphal Early Career of J. F. Waldeck Pioneer Americanist." *Acta Americana* 5 (Inter-American Society of Anthropology and Geography, Los Angeles: 1947), pp. 278–299.

Clinton, DeWitt. "A Memoir on the Antiquities of the Western Parts of the State of New York." *Transactions of the Literary and Philosophical Society of New York* 2 (Albany, N.Y.: 1815–1825).

Coe, Michael D. *Breaking the Maya Code*. Thames and Hudson, London: 1992.

Cortés, Hernando. *Five Letters of Cortés to the Emperor*. Trans. J. Bayard Morris. W. W. Norton, New York: 1928.

Crawford, George G. *A Tourist's Guide to Points in and Near the City of Mexico*. G. G. Crawford, New York: 1890.

de Acosta, José. *Historia natural y moral de las Indias*. 1590.

D'Alton, Martina. "The New York Obelisk or How Cleopatra's Needle Came to New York and What Happened When it Got Here." *Metropolitan Museum of Art Bulletin* (Spring 1993); repr. Harry N. Abrams, New York: 1993.

Daniel, Glyn. *The Idea of Prehistory*. C. A. Watts and Co., London: 1962.

Davis, John. *The Landscape of Belief: Encountering the Holy Land in Nineteenth-Century American Art and Culture*. Princeton University Press, Princeton, N.J.: 1996.

Davis, Keith. *Désiré Charnay, Expeditionary Photographer.* University of New Mexico Press, Albuquerque: 1981.

De Bry, Théodore, and J. I. De Bry. *Grands Voyages.* Vol. 9, *De novi orbis natura.* . . . Francof., Apud M. Beckerum, Amsterdam: 1601.

Del Río, Antonio. *Description of the Ruins of an Ancient City Discovered near Palenque in the Kingdom of Guatemala in Spanish America, Translated from the Original Manuscript Report of Captain Antonio Del Río, Followed by Teatro Critico Americano, or, A Critical Investigation and Research into the History of the Americans, by Dr. Felix Cabrera.* Ed. and trans. Henry Berthoud. Henry Berthoud, London: 1822.

Desmond, Lawrence Gustave, and Phyllis Mauch Messenger. *A Dream of Maya: Augustus and Alice Le Plongeon in Nineteenth-Century Yucatan.* University of New Mexico Press, Albuquerque: 1988.

Deuel, Leo. *Conquistadors without Swords: Archaeologists and the Americas.* Schocken Books, New York: 1974.

Díaz del Castillo, Bernal. *The Discovery and Conquest of Mexico.* Trans. Alfred P. Maudslay. Noonday Press, New York: 1956.

_____. *Historia Verdadera de la Conquista de la Nueva España.* 2 vols. Editorial Porrua, Mexico: 1968.

Dumenil, Lynn. *Freemasonry and American Culture, 1880–1930.* Princeton University Press, Princeton, N.J.: 1984.

Etienne, Roland and Françoise. *The Search for Ancient Greece.* Harry N. Abrams, New York: 1992.

Fagan, Brian. *Elusive Treasure: The Story of Early Archaeologists in the Americas.* Charles Scribner's Sons, New York: 1977.

Fehrenbach, T. R. *Fire and Blood: A History of Mexico.* Da Capo Press, New York: 1995.

"Fire at Catherwood's." *New York Herald* (August 1, 1842), p. 2.

Florescano, Enrique. "The Creation of the Museo Nacional de Antropología of Mexico and Its Scientific, Educational, and Political Purposes." In Elizabeth Hill Boone, ed., *Collecting the Pre-Columbian Past,* pp. 88–89. Dumbarton Oaks, Washington, D.C.: 1993.

Foner, Eric, and John Garraty, eds. *The Reader's Companion to American History.* Houghton Mifflin Co., Boston: 1991.

Foucault, Michel. *The Order of Things: An Archaeology of the Human Sciences.* Vintage Press/Random House, New York: 1994.

Franch, José Alcina. "Los viajes de exploracíon arqueológico por Mexico de Guillermo Dupaix." *Anuario de Estudios Americanos* 12 (Seville: 1965).

Gage, Thomas. *Le Voyage de Thomas Gage.* Paul Marret, Amsterdam: 1720.

Gernsheim, Helmut. *The History of Photography.* McGraw-Hill, New York: 1969.

Gerbi, Antonello. *The Dispute of the New World: The History of a Polemic, 1750–1900.* University of Pittsburgh Press, Pittsburgh: 1973.

Hamilton, John D. *Material Culture of the American Freemasons.* University Press of New England, Lebanon, N.H.: 1994.

Harris, Neil, Wim de Wit, James Gilbert, and Robert Rydell. *Grand Illusions: Chicago's World's Fair of 1893.* Chicago Historical Society, Chicago: 1993.

Hearn, M. F., ed. *The Architectural Theory of Viollet-le-Duc: Readings and Commentary.* MIT Press, Cambridge: 1990.

Hewett, Edgar L. "America's Archaeological Heritage." *Art and Archaeology* 4:6 (December 1916), pp. 36–79.

_____. "Ancient America at the Panama-California Exposition." *Art and Archaeology* 2:3 (November 1915), pp. 64–102.

Hight, Kathryn S. "'Doomed to Perish': George Catlin's Depictions of the Mandan." *Art Journal* 49 (summer 1990), pp. 30–45.

Ingle, Marjorie. *The Mayan Revival Style.* Peregrine Books, Salt Lake City: 1984.

Johannsen, Robert W. *To the Halls of the Montezumas: The Mexican War in the American Imagination.* Oxford University Press, New York: 1985.

Jones, Daniel. *Forty Years among the Indians: A True yet Thrilling Narrative of the Author's Experience among the Natives.* Westernlore Press, Los Angeles: 1960; orig. Juvenile Instruction Office, Salt Lake City: 1890.

Kant, Immanuel. "What Is Enlightenment?" Trans. Peter Gay. In *Introduction to Contemporary Civilization in the West,* 1:1071. Columbia University Press, New York: 1954.

Keen, Benjamin. *The Aztec Image in Western Thought.* Rutgers University Press, New Brunswick, N.J.: 1971.

King, Edward, Lord Kingsborough, ed. *Antiquities of Mexico.* 9 vols. Robert Havell, London: 1831–1848.

Kubler, George. *Esthetic Recognition of Ancient Amerindian Art.* Yale University Press, New Haven, Conn.: 1991.

Kunhardt, Philip. P. T. *Barnum: America's Greatest Showman.* Alfred A. Knopf, New York: 1995.

LaBastida, Jaime L., ed. *Alejandro de Humboldt: Aportaciones a la Antropología Mexicana.* Editorial Katún, Mexico: 1986.

Lafaye, Jacques. *Quetzalcóatl and Guadalupe: The Formation of Mexican National Consciousness, 1513–1813.* Trans. Benjamin Keen. University of Chicago Press, Chicago: 1974.

Landa, Diego. *Yucatan before and after Conquest.* Trans. William Gates. Dover Publications, New York: 1978.

Lears, T. Jackson. *No Place of Grace: Antimodernism and the Transformation of American Culture, 1880–1920.* University of Chicago Press, Chicago: 1981.

Le Plongeon, Alice Dixon. *Here and There in Yucatan: Miscellanies.* J. W. Bouton, New York: 1886.

_____. Miscellaneous letters and pamphlets, 1899–1905 (many undated). Phoebe Hearst archive, Bancroft Library, University of California, Berkeley.

_____. *Queen Móo's Talisman: The Fall of the Maya Empire.* Peter Eckler, New York: 1902.

Le Plongeon, Augustus. "An Interesting Discovery: A Temple with Masonic Symbols in the Ruined City of Uxmal." *Harper's Weekly* (New York: December 17, 1881), pp. 851–852.

_____. Letter to Stephen Salisbury. *Proceedings of the American Antiquarian Society* 59 (1877), p. 88.

_____. *Queen Móo and the Egyptian Sphinx.* Augustus Le Plongeon, New York: 1896.

_____. *Sacred Mysteries among the Mayas and the Quichés 11,500 Years Ago: Their Relations to the Sacred Mysteries of Egypt, Greece, Chaldea, and India; or, Free Masonry in Times Anterior to the Temple of Solomon.* Robert Macoy, New York: 1886.

_____. *Vestiges of the Mayas, or, Facts Tending to Prove that Communications and Intimate Relations Must Have Existed, in Very Remote Times, between the Inhabitants of Mayab [sic] and Those of Asia and Africa.* John Polhemus, New York: 1881.

Mackey, Albert Gallatin. *The History of Freemasonry: Its Legendary Origins.* Gramercy Books, New York: 1996.

Maudslay, Alfred P. *Biologia Centrali-Americana.* 4 vols. R. H. Porter, London: 1889–1902.

McCulloh, James H., Jr. *Researches, Philosophical and Antiquarian, concerning the Aboriginal History of America.* Fielding Lucas, Jr., Baltimore: 1829.

Miller, Mary Ellen. *The Art of Mesoamerica from Olmec to Aztec.* Thames and Hudson, London: 1986.

———. *Maya Art and Architecture.* Thames and Hudson, London: 1999.

———. "A Re-examination of the Mesoamerican Chacmool." *Art Bulletin* 67:1 (March 1985), pp. 7–17.

Miller, Mary, and Linda Schele. *The Blood of Kings: Dynasty and Ritual in Maya Art.* George Braziller, New York: 1986.

Miller, Rebecca Stone. "The Influence of Mayan Architecture on Frank Lloyd Wright." Unpublished manuscript, 1982.

Millet, Robert, ed. *Joseph Smith: Sermons and Writings.* Paulist Press, Mahwah, N.J.: 1989.

Molina-Montes, Augusto. "Archaeological Buildings: Restoration or Misrepresentation." In Elizabeth H. Boone, ed., *Falsifications and Misreconstructions of Pre-Columbian Art,* p. 136. Dumbarton Oaks, Washington, D.C.: 1982.

Morgan, Lewis Henry. "Montezuma's Dinner." *North American Review* 122 (April 1876), pp. 265–308.

Moses, L. G. *Wild West Shows and the Images of Native Americans, 1883–1933.* University of New Mexico Press, Albuquerque: 1996.

Oles, James. *South of the Border: Mexico in the American Imagination, 1914–1947.* Smithsonian Institution Press, Washington, D.C.: 1993.

Patterson, Thomas C. *Toward a Social History of Archaeology in the United States.* Harcourt, Brace College Publishers, New York: 1995.

Peabody Museum of Archaeology and Ethnology. *The Art of Hieroglyphic Writing.* Peabody Museum, Cambridge, Massachusetts: 1971.

Pike, Fredrick B. *The United States and Latin America: Myths and Stereotypes of Civilization and Nature.* University of Texas Press, Austin: 1992.

Pratt, Mary Louise. *Imperial Eyes: Travel Writing and Transculturation.* Routledge, New York: 1992.

Pratt, Orson. In *Latter-day Saints' Millennial Star* (Salt Lake City), November 1848.

Pratt, Parley. "Address to the Red Man." *Latter-day Saints' Millennial Star* (Salt Lake City), no. 14 (September 1852), p. 469.

———. *A Key to the Science of Theology.* F. D. Richards, Liverpool: 1855.

Prescott, William H. *History of the Conquest of Mexico.* Modern Library, New York: 1936; orig. 1843.

Priest, Josiah. *American Antiquities and Discoveries in the West, Being an Exhibition of the Evidence that an Ancient Population of Partially Civilized Nations, Differing Entirely from Those of the Present Indians, Peopled America, Many Centuries before Its Discovery by Columbus.* Packard, Hoffman, and White, Albany: 1833.

Pryer, Mason Thomas. "On the Study of Masonic Antiquities." *Freemason's Quarterly Review* (1947), p. 262.

Rice, Allen Thorndike. "Ruined Cities of Central America." *North American Review* 285 (August 1880), pp. 89–96.

Robertson, William. *The History of America.* Francfort O. M., London: 1828; orig. 1788.

Rydell, Robert. *All the World's a Fair: Visions of Empire at American International Expositions, 1876–1916*. University of Chicago Press, Chicago: 1984.

Salisbury, Stephen. "Dr. Le Plongeon in Yucatan. The Discovery of a Statue Called Chac-Mool, and the Communications of Dr. Le Plongeon concerning Exploration in the Yucatan Peninsula." *Proceedings of the American Antiquarian Society* 69 (1877), pp. 70–119. Referenced by Miller, "A Re-examination of the Mesoamerican Chacmool."

Ships, Jan. *Mormonism: The Story of a New Religious Tradition*. University of Chicago Press, Chicago: 1985.

Singer, Herbert, and Ossian Lang. *New York Freemasonry: A Bicentennial History, 1781–1981*. Grand Lodge of Free and Accepted Masons of the State of New York: 1981.

Smith, G. Eliot. *Elephants and Ethnologists*. E. P. Dutton and Co., New York: 1924.

Smith, Joseph, Jr. *The Book of Mormon: An Account Written by the Hand of Mormon upon Plates Taken from the Plates of Nephi and Translated by Joseph Smith, Jr.* E. B. Grandin, New York: 1830.

Sorenson, John L. *An Ancient American Setting for the Book of Mormon*. Deseret Book Co., Salt Lake City: 1985.

Squier, Ephraim G. *Antiquities of the State of New York: Being the Results of Extensive Original Surveys and Explorations*. George H. Derby and Co., New York: 1851.

Stephens, John Lloyd. *Incidents of Travel in Central America, Chiapas, and Yucatan*. 2 vols. Harper and Brothers, New York: 1841.

_____. *Incidents of Travel in Egypt, Arabia Petraea, and the Holy Land*. Harper and Brothers, New York: 1837.

_____. *Incidents of Travel in Yucatan*. 2 vols. Harper and Brothers, New York: 1843.

Stuart, George E. "Quest for Decipherment: A Historical and Biographical Survey of Maya Hieroglyphic Investigation," in Elin C. Danien and Robert J. Sharer, eds., *New Theories on the Ancient Maya*, pp. 1–63. University Museum, University of Pennsylvania, Philadelphia: 1992.

Stewart, Susan. *On Longing: Narratives of the Miniature, the Gigantic, the Souvenir, and the Collection*. Duke University Press, Durham, N.C.: 1993.

Taylor, John. "The Discovery of Ruins," *Latter-day Saints' Millennial Star* (Salt Lake City), no. 13 (March 1851), pp. 93–117.

Tenorio-Trillo, Mauricio. *Mexico at the World's Fairs: Crafting a Modern Nation*. University of California Press, Berkeley: 1996.

Thompson, Charles Blancher. *Evidence in Proof of the Book of Mormon*. C. B. Thompson, Batavia, N.Y.: 1841.

Thompson, Edward H. "The Home of a Forgotten Race: Mysterious Chichen Itza in Yucatan, Mexico." *National Geographic* 25:6 (June, 1914), pp. 16–40.

_____. "A Maya Legend in the Making." *Proceedings of the American Antiquarian Society* 61 (1931), pp. 340–343.

Tompkins, Peter. *Mysteries of the Mexican Pyramids*. Thames and Hudson, London: 1976.

Traill, David A. *Schliemann of Troy: Treasure and Deceit*. St. Martin's Press, New York: 1995.

Tselos, Dmitri. "Exotic Influences in the Architecture of Frank Lloyd Wright." *Magazine of Art* 47 (April 1953), pp. 160–184.

Tullis, F. LaMond. *Mormons in Mexico: The Dynamics of Faith and Culture*. Utah University Press, Logan: 1987.

Van Hagen, Victor. *Frederick Catherwood, Architect.* Oxford University Press, New York: 1950.

_____. *Maya Explorer: John Lloyd Stephens and the Lost Cities of Central America and Yucatan.* University of Oklahoma Press, Norman: 1947.

Vercoutter, Jean. *The Search for Ancient Egypt.* Harry N. Abrams, New York: 1992.

Viollet-le-Duc, Eugène-Emmanuel. *The Habitations of Man in All Ages.* Trans. Benjamin Bucknall. James R. Osgood and Co., Boston: 1876.

Vogel, Dan. *Indian Origins and the Book of Mormon: Religious Solutions from Columbus to Joseph Smith.* Signature Books, New York: 1986.

von Humboldt, Alexander. *Views of the Cordilleras and Monuments of the Indigenous Peoples of America.* . . . Trans. Helen Maria Williams. 2 vols. Longman et al., London: 1814.

Voorsanger, Catherine Hoover, and John K. Howat, eds. *Art and the Empire City: New York, 1825–1861.* Yale University Press, New Haven, Conn.: 2000.

Wauchope, Robert. *Lost Tribes and Sunken Continents: Myth and Method in the Study of American Indians.* University of Chicago Press, Chicago: 1975.

_____. *They Found the Buried Cities.* University of Chicago Press, Chicago: 1965.

Waldeck, Jean-Frédéric. "Extrait d'un lettre . . . à M. Jomard." *Foreign Quarterly Review* 18 (October 1836), pp. 243–251.

_____. *Voyage pittoresque et archéologique dans la province d'Yucatan pendant les années 1834 et 1836.* Bellizard Dufour et cie., Paris: 1838.

Waldeck, Jean-Frédéric, and Charles-Étienne Brasseur de Bourbourg. *Monuments anciens du Méxique: Palenque et autres ruines d'ancienne civilisation du Méxique.* Arthus Betrand, Paris: 1866.

White, Trumbull. *World's Columbian Exposition: A Complete History.* P. W. Ziegler and Co., Philadelphia: 1893.

Wilford, John Noble. "Splendid Maya Palace Is Found Hidden in Jungle." *New York Times,* September 8, 2000, pp. A1 ff.

Williams, Stephen. *Fantastic Archaeology: The Wild Side of North American Prehistory.* University of Pennsylvania Press, Philadelphia: 1991.

Yates, John, and Joseph Moulton. *History of the State of New-York.* Hoffman and White, Albany, N.Y.: 1824.

INDEX

Adair, James, 35
Adams-Onis, Treaty of, 55
Aegean civilization, ancient, 29
age of ruins. *See* dating of ruins
Albert, Prince, 136
Allende, Ignacio, 32
Almendáriz, Ricardo, *18, 21,* 19–22, 165n.18, 166n.47
American Antiquarian Society, 44, 46–48, *47,* 57, 129, 134. *See also* Salisbury, Stephen
American Geographical Society, 128, 150
Anasazi, 156, 161, 181n.5
Ancient Cities of the New World (Charnay: 1887), 105, 109, 111, 115, 124–125
Antiquités Mexicaines (Baradère: 1834), 10, 35
Antiquities of Mexico (King: 1830–1848), 35
Antiquities of the State of New York (Squier: 1851), 96
arch of Constantine, 64, *65,* 66
archaeology, Egyptian. *See* Egypt
archaeology, Latin American
   authorship of ruins, 2–3, 11, 18, 23–24, 34, 42–43, 57, 62–64, 127, 165n.26
   in colonial era, 8, 10–36
   dating of ruins, 5, 9, 34, 43, 67–68, 99–100, 115, 127, 128, 130, 136, 151, 160, 181–182n.13
   professionalization of, 4, 8, 152, 163n.6
   Spanish attitude toward, 11–12, 14, 16–17, 22–23

in twentieth-century, 6–7
archaeology, Near Eastern, 145–148, *146, 147*
archaeology, psychic, 131, 145
archaeology and nationalism. *See* nationalism and Mesoamerican archaeology
Art Institute of Chicago, 158
Assyria, ancient, 93
Atlantis, 2, 113–114, 176nn.31,33
authorship of ruins. *See* Archaeology, Latin American; Stephens, John Lloyd
Aztec civilization
   and the ancient Maya, 67, 160
   "Aztec Children" hoax, 85–87, *86,* 172n.105
   Huitzilopochtli, war god of, 14, *15,* 116
   and human sacrifice, *12, 13,* 35
   and the Iroquois, 157
   and the Mormon Church, 102
   origin of, 42, 163n.5, 167n.70
   in popular imagination, *86,* 85–87, 170n.47, 172n.105
   sacred architecture/sites of, 13, *15,* 101
   sculpture of, 13, 119, 120, *120,* 164n.12, 165n.25
   Tenochtitlan, capital city of, 11–13, 67, 113
   and the Toltecs, 8, 112–113

Baradère, Henri, ed., *Antiquités Mexicaines* (1834), 10, 35–36, 45, 70, 76, 107
Barnum, Phineas T., 85–87, 172n.105
Barrientos, Tomas, 163n.2

Belize, 48
Bering Strait, 117, 121, 128, 150
Bernasconi, Antonio, 17, 17–18, 29, 165n.17
Berthoud, Henry, 32, 34, 36
Bible, 11, 34, 43, 89–90, 91, 92, 94, 164n.1
Blavatsky, Helena, 131
Bonpland, Aimée, 22
Book of Mormon
    architectural typologies included within, 94,
        95–98
    authorship/narrative of, 4, 6, 88–92, 94;
        96–98, 98
    chronology of, 89, 91–93, 98–100, 173n.6
    Cumorah, final battle in, 90, 92, 96, 98,
        174n.36
    discovery/appearance of, 88–89, 90–91
    and Jaredite peoples, 92, 95–99
    Jesus Christ, appearances within, 90, 94
    and Lamanite peoples, 92, 94, 96–98, 100, 102,
        145, 174nn.25,34, 175n.55
    Lehi, protagonist of, 89, 91–93, 97–98,
        100–101, 173n.11, 174nn.25,28
    Moroni, custodian of, 90, 92
    and Nephite peoples, 92, 94–99, 102, 145,
        174nn.36,42, 175n.56
    and race, 97, 174n.25
    similarities to Bible, 89, 90, 92, 94
    use by Mormon Church, 99, 139, 144–145,
        173nn.15,17
    verification of original source, 88, 90, 91
    See also Latter-day Saints, Church of Jesus
        Christ of; Smith, Joseph
Boullée, Étienne-Louis, 40–42, 42
Brasseur de Bourbourg, Charles-Étienne
    archival discoveries of, 164n.10, 176n.28
    belief in Atlantis, 113–114, 176nn.31,33
    diffusion theory of, 5, 113–114, 127–128, 130
    Histoire des nations civiliseés du Mexique
        (1857–1863), 113
    Quatre Lettres sur le Mexique (1868), 113, 127
British Empire. See England
British Museum, 56
Bullock, William, 165n.18, 166n.47

Cabrera, Félix, 34
Calderón, Frances "Fanny" de la Barca, 85
Calderón, José Antonio, 16, 17, 18

Calendar Stone, Aztec. See Aztec civilization,
    sculpture
Calleja, Félix, 32
camera lucida, 53, 64
Cancuen, 1–2, 9
Carlos III, 17, 32
Carlos IV, 22–23
Carrera, Rafael, 62, 169n.41
Casas Grandes, 101
Cass, Lewis, 67
Casteñada, José Luciano, 2, 23–32, 24–25, 28, 29,
    30–31, 33, 62
Caste War, 124–125, 127, 128–129. See also Santa
    Cruz Maya
casts. See plaster casting of monuments
Catherwood, Frederick
    Broken Idol at Copan, 76
    collaboration with Stephens, 48–53, 56–62,
        69–70, 75, 76, 87
    early career of, 2–3, 44–45, 50–53
    and engravings, 5, 45, 51, 52, 59, 60, 61, 64–66,
        64, 65, 70, 74, 76, 77, 79, 156
    independent work of, 50, 76–83
    and lithographs, 76, 77, 78, 78, 81, 82, 84
    and panoramas, 52–53, 72–73, 78, 169nn.15,16,
        171n.99
    and photography, 53, 105
    and plaster casting, 169n.30
    style of, 3, 45, 49, 50, 53–54, 56–57, 58–59,
        64–66, 70, 75–83
    View of Mt. Aetna from Tauramania, 49
    Views of Ancient Monuments (1844), 76–83,
        77, 78, 81, 82, 84
    work at Chichen Itza, 107, 108
    work at Copan, 52, 53–54, 76–80, 77, 78, 79
    work at Kabah, 64–66, 73, 74, 75
    work at Palenque, 16, 60, 64, 170n.49
    work at Uxmal, 80, 81, 82, 107, 109
Catholic Church, 14, 93, 98, 101
Catlin, George, 71–73, 100, 169n.16, 171n.80,
    174n.47
Centennial Exposition, Philadelphia (1876), 134,
    153
Central American Federation, 49
Central Park, 148–149
Chaacmol, Chaac mool. See chacmool
Chablé, Mariano, 130
Chac (Maya deity), 39, 94

chacmool, 132–135, *132, 133, 143*, 146, 179nn.19,24
Champollion, Jean-François, 91, 172n.4
Charles V, Emperor, 12
Charnay, Desiré
  Ancient Cities of the New World (1887), 105,
    109–111, 124–125, 128, 139
  belief in Toltec diffusion, 4, 104, 111, 113–115,
    118–121, 125, 176n.33
  Cités et ruines américaines (1862), 104,
    107–109, 111, 115, 117, 126, 139, 156
  early career of, 105, 175n.3
  nationalist agenda of, 114
  patronage of, 6, 103, 105, 124, 125, 129
  and photographic engraving, 116, *117, 118, 120,*
    123, 125
  and photography, 103–107, *108, 109,* 110, 114,
    121–123, 125, 127, 139
  and plaster casting, 103–105, 106, 119, 122–125,
    127, 139, 151, 155, 156, 175n.11, 177n.62
  racial theories of, 103, 105, 117, 118, 121
  work at Chichen Itza, 106, 107, *108,* 121, 122
  work at Mitla, 106
  work at Palenque, 106, 120–122
  work at Uxmal, 106, 121, 122
  work at Yaxchilán, 115, 124, 129, 178nn.71,72
Chiapas, 14, 16, 48, 68, 116, 124, 129, 156, 168n.9
Chicago. *See* World's Columbian Exposition,
  Chicago
Chichen Itza
  Akab Dzib structure, 130
  and Caste War, 124
  in Catherwood's work, 107, *108*
  in Charnay's work, 106, 107, *108,* 121, 122,
    130–136
  colonial accounts of, 14
  discovery of chacmool figure at, 132–135, *132,*
    133
  El Castillo pyramid, 130–131, 162
  Great Ball Court, 135
  Iglesia structure, 107, 108
  in Le Plongeon's work, 130–136, 140–141, 145
  Nunnery complex (also, Casa de las Monjas),
    157
  occupation by Toltecs, 121, 132
  Platform of the Eagles, 132, 136
  Platform of Venus, 141, *143*
  Sacred Cenote, 163n.7

Temple of the Jaguars, 135, *137*
  in Thompson's work, *154,* 155
Chicomoztoc, 42, 167n.70
Children of Mu, The (Churchward: 1931), 151
Chile, 91, 92, 163n.4
Cholula, 14, 22, 165n.26
Chongo, Señor. *See* Flessa, Joseph
Churchward, James, 151–152
Cités et ruines américaines (Charnay: 1862), 104,
  107–111, 117, 126
Civil War, American, 110, 127
classicizing of Mesoamerican ruins
  in Charnay's work, 116–117
  in colonial accounts, 2, 13–14, 19–20, 22–24,
    26–29, 34, 43, 166nn.36,37,48
  in Stephens and Catherwood's work, 62–63,
    64–66, 170n.47
  at World's Columbian Exposition, Chicago,
    158
Cleopatra's Needle, 148–150
cliffdwellers. *See* Anasazi
Cline, Howard, 37, 165n.24, 166n.45
Clinton, DeWitt, 96
Clytemnestra, Tomb of, 146, *147*
Coe, Michael, 7, 48
Coh, Prince, 130–136, *137,* 141, 145. *See also*
  chacmool; Le Plongeon, identity as Prince
  Coh
colonial period
  archaeology, 2, 5, 8, 9, 10–36, 43,
    166nn.36,37,48
  and indigenous groups, 14
  in Latin America, 22–23, 68–69, 99
  in Mexico, 10–12; 22–23, 47, 68–69
  and Palenque, 16–22, 32, 34, 166n.31, 168n.3
  and Uxmal, 14
Columbus, Christopher, 69, 153
Continental Tobacco Company, 115, 177n.37
Contreras, Juan Péon, 131
Copan
  Stele C, 76–78, *77*
  Stele F, *52,* 53, *78, 79,* 80
  in Stephens' work, 48, 53–54, 56, 57, 63, 69, 72,
    124
Cordilleras mountains, 22, 68
Cortés, Hernando, 12, 68–69, 85
Cosmic Forces of Mu, The (Churchward: 1936),
  151

Costa Rica, 48–49
Cret, Paul, 162
Cruger, John Church, 62, 171–172n.99

daguerreotypes. *See* photography
dating of ruins
  in colonial era, 2, 5, 9, 11, 18
  correlation with Christian calendar, 5, 9, 160,
    181–182n.13
  in Le Plongeon's work, 127, 128, 130, 136, 151
  in Stephens' work, 67–68, 69, 76, 87, 115
David, Jacques-Louis, 37
de Acosta, José, 13, 164n.6
De Bry, Théodore, *12*, 13, 22, 164n.6
de Iturbide, Agustín, 32
de Laval, Lotin, 139, 177n.62
Del Río, Antonio, 2, 19–22, 34, 36, 45, 48, 62,
    165n.17, 165n.24, 166n.45, 168nn.3,11
Demarest, Arthur, 2, 9, 163n.2
Description of the Ruins of an Ancient City (Del
    Rio: 1822), 34, 36
Desmond, Lawrence, 128, 136
De Solís, Antonio, 16
Díaz, Colonel (Le Plongeon's guard), 130,
    178n.10
Díaz, Porfirio, 135
Díaz del Castillo, Bernal, 12–13, 14, 164n.5
di Cesnola, Luigi Palma, 151
Diderot, Denis, 23, 37
Diego, Juan, 95
diffusion theory, 4, 5, 87, 104, 111, 113–115, 118–121,
    125, 126–128, 130, 152, 176n.33
Dixon, Alice. *See* Le Plongeon, Alice (née
    Dixon)
Dos Pilas, 2
Dresden Codex, 35
Druids, the, 141
Dumenil, Lynn, 144
Dupaix, Guillermo, 23–32, 34, 35, 36, 45, 48,
    165n.27, 166nn.31,37, 168n.11
Durán, Diego, 164n.2

Egypt
  Alexandria, 148
  in Castañeda's work, *24*, 24–26
  Colossus of Memnon, 50, *51*
  correspondence to ancient Mesoamerica in
    Baradère's work, 35

denial of, in Stephens' work, 63
  in Le Plongeon's work, 128, 136–137, 139, 141,
    144, 149–150
  in Mormon belief, 100, 172n.4
  in Waldeck's work, 37–42, *38*, *39*, *40*, *41*
  deities of: Hathor, 38; Isis/Osiris, 136, 141;
    Typhon, 141
  and Freemasonry, 141, 143–144, 148–149,
    180n.50
  hieroglyphs of, 50, 63, 90–91, 150, *150*, 172n.4
  Luxor, 56
  Napoleon's expedition to, 10, 23, 37, 42, 47, 141
  obelisks in, 141, 148–150, *150*
  Sphinx, the, 136, 139
  in travel literature, 49–50
Elephants and Ethnologists (Smith: 1924), 40
elephants in ancient Mesoamerica, 38–40, 42,
    167n.63, 170n.49
El Salvador, 48–49, 87
El Tajín. *See* Tajín
Encyclopédie, 3, 23, 37
England
  cultural acquisition/imperialism, 10, 52, 56,
    136
  and Freemasonry, 141, 144
  Royal Academy, London, 49, 50, 64, 170n.50
Enlightenment, 17, 23, 37, 41, 43
Espita, 130
Estachería, Joseph, 16–17, 18, 165n.17
Etruscan civilization, 29
Evidence in Proof of the Book of Mormon
    (Thompson: 1841), 99
evil eye, practice of, 131
export laws, Mexican, 60, 134–135, 169n.31

*Fall of Maya, The: A Tragic Drama of Ancient
    America* (Alice Le Plongeon: 1908), 136
Farcy, Charles, 29
Field, Marshall, 160
Field Museum of Natural History, Chicago, 160,
    181n.11
Fingal (Macpherson: 1761), 145
Finney, Charles Grandison, 93
Flessa, Joseph, xii
Florentine Codex, 35
Florida. *See* Adams-Onis Treaty
Forsyth, John, 49, 62

Fox Talbot, William Henry, 105
France
  and the Enlightenment, 3, 37
  and Freemasonry, 141
  literary traditions of, 145
  occupation of Mexico, 101, 105, 110, 176n.16
  patronage of archaeology, 56, 103, 105, 114–115
  Trocadéro Museum, Paris, 115, 119, 120
  See also Napoleon; Napoleon III; Egypt,
    Napoleon's expedition to
Freemasonry
  and ancient Egypt, 141, 143–144, 148–149,
    180n.50
  in Le Plongeon's work, 5, 127, 139, 141, 143–145,
    152
  as practiced in Europe, 140, 141
  as practiced in United States, 144, 148–149,
    180n.50
  protoreligious qualities of, 93, 144–145
Friberg, Arnold, 94, 173n.17
Fuseli, Henry, 49

Gage, Thomas, 13–14, 15
Galindo, Juan, 53, 168n.3
Garrido, Jacito, 20
glyphs, Maya
  decipherment of, 7, 9, 32, 91, 113, 127, 151
  at Dos Pilas, 2
  at Palenque, 32, 170n.49
  in Stephens and Catherwood's work, 63–64,
    68, 73
  in Waldeck's work, 39–40, 40, 170n.49
Gobineau, Arthur, 111
Goodman, J.T., 5, 9, 160, 181–182n.13
Goodwin, Isaac, 46
Great Lakes region, 48, 95, 96–97
Greco-Roman architecture. See classicizing of
  Mesoamerican ruins
Guadalupana. See Virgin of Guadalupe
Guadalupe-Hidalgo, Treaty of, 83
Guatemala, 1, 9, 14, 16, 17, 22, 34, 48–49, 62, 156,
  166nn.45, 46
Guerrero, Vicente, 32

Habitations of Man in All Ages (Viollet-le-Duc:
  1876), 111–112, 117
hacienda system, 129
Harper and Brothers, 49, 125

Harvard University, 155, 163n.7
Hathor. See Egypt, deities of
Hearst, Phoebe (Mrs. William Randolph
  Hearst), 139
Hearst, William Randolph, 139
Helen of Troy, 146
Herculaneum, 47
Here and There in Yucatan (Alice Le Plongeon:
  1886), 131
Hewett, Edgar, 161
Hidalgo, Mexico, 113, 116
Hidalgo, Miguel, 32
hieroglyphs. See Egypt, hieroglyphs; glyphs,
  Maya
Hissarlik, Turkey, 145
Histoire des nations civiliseés du Mexique
  (Brasseur de Bourbourg: 1857–1863), 113
History of the Conquest of Mexico (Prescott:
  1843), 75–76
Honduras, 48–49, 53, 59, 156. See also Copan;
  Quirigua
Huitzilopochtli. See Aztec civilization
human sacrifice, 12, 13, 35, 80, 164n.12
Humboldt, Alexander von. See von Humboldt,
  Alexander

Iliad, the, 145
Incidents of Travel in Central America, Chiapas
  and Yucatan (Stephens: 1841)
  economy/format of, 3, 44–45, 70, 75–76, 107,
    109
  lack of theoretical rigor in, 45
  and Mormon Church, 99
  popularity of, 70, 75, 109, 125, 139
Incidents of Travel in Egypt, Arabia Petraea, and
  the Holy Land (Stephens: 1837), 49
Incidents of Travel in Greece, Turkey, Russia and
  Poland (Stephens: 1838), 49
Incidents of Travel in Yucatan (Stephens: 1843)
  economy/format of, 3, 44–45
  and indigenous Maya, 67
Indian Removal Act of 1830, 67
Irish/Gaelic literary tradition, 145
Iroquois nation, 157
Isis. See Egypt, deities of
Israelites, ancient. See lost tribes of Israel
Iximaya (Barnum's "Aztec" city), 85, 87, 172n.105
Izamal, 106

Japanese architecture, 121, *123*
Jaredites. *See* Book of Mormon
Jerusalem, 49, 52, 89, 92, 93, 94, 100, 173n.11
Jesus Christ, 90, 91, 94, 100, 141. *See also* Latter-
    day Saints, Church of Jesus Christ of
John the Baptist, 94
Jomard, Edme François, 37
Jones, Daniel, 100, 174n.47

Kabah
    in Stephens and Catherwood's work, 62,
        64–66, 65, 71–75, 74, 80–83, 84, 171–172n.99
    in Thompson's work, 155
Kansal, Desiderio, 131
Kearney, Stephen, 85
King, Edward, Lord Kingsborough
    Antiquities of Mexico (1830–1848), ed., 35–36,
        45, 70, 76, 107
    financial ruin of, 45
    lost tribes of Israel, theories concerning, 35,
        42, 166–167n.51
    Waldeck, patronage of, 40–42
Kingdom of Móo. *See* Móo, Kingdom of
Kingsborough, Lord. *See* King, Edward

Labná, *154*, 155, 156
Laguna, 55, 57
Lamanites. *See* Book of Mormon
Landa, Diego, 14, 113, 164n.10, 176n.28
Latin America
    colonial period in, 22–23, 68–69, 99
    contemporary indigenous populations of, 4,
        11, 14–15, 26–27, 58, 67, 100–102, 113,
        128–129. *See also* Maya, contemporary
    and custodianship of ruins, 2, 58–59, 78,
        134–135
    and expulsion of Spain, 2, 8, 32, 55
    nineteenth-century politics of, 2–3, 7, 43, 49,
        62, 101, 105, 124, 127, 128–129, 135, 168nn.9,13
    and the United States, 9, 49, 58, 83, 127, 155,
        160–161
    See also archaeology, Latin American;
        Mexico
Latour-Allard, François, 35, 166n.50
Latter-day Saints, Church of Jesus Christ of
    belief in Israelite colonization of Americas,
        97, 100–101, 127, 163n.4, 174n.34, 175n.55

conflation of Moundbuilder/Meso-
    american cultures, 36, 88–89, 96–97
foundation and mission of, 4, 88–89, 103,
    144–145, 173n.15
and proselytization, 100–102, 174n.47
See also Book of Mormon; Smith, Joseph
Leggett, William, 49
Lehi. *See* Book of Mormon
Lenoir, Alexandre, 35
Le Plongeon, Alice (née Dixon)
    collaboration with Augustus Le Plongeon, 4,
        127, 128, 139, 145, 146, *147*, 151–152
    Fall of Maya, The: A Tragic Drama of Ancient
        America (1908), 136
    Here and There in Yucatan (1886), 131, *138*
    and identity as Queen Móo, 136, *138*, 146
    and the occult, 131
    Queen Móo's Talisman: The Fall of the Maya
        Empire (1902), 126, 136, 145
    and Theosophy, 131, 139
Le Plongeon, Augustus
    amateur status of, 8, 151
    and chacmool statue, 132–135, 146
    and Cleopatra's Needle, 148–150
    and contemporary Maya, 129–134, *133*, 146,
        147
    and dating of ruins, 127, 128, 130, 136, 151
    and diffusion theory, 4, 127–128, 130, 152
    early career of, 128, 150
    and Freemasonry, 5, 127, 139, 141, 143–145,
        148–150, 152
    and Heinrich Schliemann, 145–148
    and identity as Prince Coh, 130–131, 132–134,
        132, *133*, 135–136, *137*, 146
    and Kingdom of Móo narrative, 130–139, 141,
        145, 150, 179n.32
    and Maya language (ancient and modern),
        129, 132, 145
    nationalist objectives of, 134–135, 141, 144–145,
        148, 150
    patronage of, 6, 129, 134, 139
    and photography, 4–5, 127, 128, *132*, *133*, 134,
        139–141, *142*, *143*, *147*, 179–180n.43
    and plaster casting, 105, 127, 139–140, 143, 148,
        150–151, 155
    and psychic archaeology, 131, 145
    Queen Móo and the Egyptian Sphinx (1896),
        139

Sacred Mysteries among the Maya and the Quichés 11,500 Years Ago (1886), 139, 148, 149

scholarly discrediting of, 129, 130, 135, 139, 144, 149, 151–152

unorthodox theories of, 127, 130–139, 149–150, 151–152

Vestiges of the Mayas (1881), 137

work at Chichen Itza, 130–136, 140–141, 145

work at Uxmal, 136, 140–141, *142, 143, 147*, 150

writing style of, 130, 137, 139, 149

Letters and Notes on the Manners, Customs and Conditions of the North American Indians (Catlin: 1841), 71–72

Life in Mexico (Calderon: 1843), 85

Loffreda, Beth, xii

Lord Chaacmool, Lord Chaac Mool. *See* chacmool

Lord Kingsborough. *See* King, Edward

Lorillard, Pierre, 115, 124, 129, 177n.37

Lost Continent of Mu, The (Churchward: 1926), 151

lost tribes of Israel
and ancient Maya architecture, 2, 4, 35, 42, 126, 166nn.48,51
in colonial American thought, 92
in Mormon belief, 88–95, 97, 100–101, 127, 163n.4, 174n.34, 175n.55

Louisiana Purchase, 55

Macpherson, James
Fingal (1761), 145
poetry of, 145, 180n.58
Temora (1763), 145

Madero, Francisco, 182n.15

Maler, Teobart, 181n.3

Mandan peoples, 71, 171n.80

manifest destiny, 3, 44, 87, 101–102

Maria, José, 54

"Marine Hymn," 85

Martin, John, 49

Masons, Masonic culture. *See* Freemasonry

Mather, Cotton and Increase, 92

Maudslay, Alfred, 124, 156, *157*, 178n.72, 181n.3

Maxcanú cave, 72

Maximilian, Emperor, 110, 176n.16

Maya, ancient
art and architecture: collapse of Classic

cities, 11, 66–68, 76, 112; colonial accounts of, 14; construction techniques of, 18, 19, 20, 39, 68, 94, 141, 161–162; presentation at world's fairs, 5–6; recent discoveries of, 1, 9; sculpture/murals (Toltec-Maya), 130–131, 132–135, *132*, 135–136, *137*; vases, 120, 134; *See also* archaeology, Latin American; *and individual site names*

calendar of, 5, 9, 160, 181–182n.13

links to contemporary Maya, 5, 11, 26–27, 58, 66–68, 69, 116, *117*

Maya, contemporary
and the ancient Maya (*see* Maya, ancient)
and Caste War, 124–125, 128–129
in Catherwood's work, 49, 65, 66, 76–83, *78, 79, 81, 82, 84*
in colonial period, 14
knowledge and use of ancient sites, 14–15, 58–59, 67–68, 129, 131, 164–165n.12, 167n.70
language of, 113, 129, 132, 170n.57 (for ancient Maya language, *see* glyphs)
in Le Plongeon's work, 129–134, *133*, 146, *147*
and native North American tribes, 72–73
sacred texts/religion of, 113, 131
in Stephens' work, 66–69
See also Latin America, contemporary indigenous populations

Mayapan, 167n.69

Maya Revival style, The, 7, 160–162, 181nn.3,11, 182nn.18,20

Medici Venus, 27

Melville, Herman, 83

Mendoza Codex, 35

Mérida, 68, 124, 129, 131, 134–135

Messenger, Phyllis, 128, 136

Metropolitan Museum of Art, 148–151

Mexican-American War. *See* Mexican War

Mexican Revolution, 8, 160–161

Mexican War, 7–8, 83–85, 87, 100, 103, 110, 172n.100, 175n.14

Mexico
archaeology, governmental support for, 35, 57, 59–60, 119, 134–135, 166n.46, 169n.31
colonial period in, 10–12, 22–23, 47, 68–69
criollo groups of, 32, 47–48
expulsion of Spain from, 2, 8, 32
first decades of independence in, 2–3, 5, 7–9, 10–11, 44, 47–48, 49

and Mormon Church, 100–102
occupation by France, 101, 110
Reforma period in, 101, 105, 127
tourism in, 125, 162
See also Caste War; Latin America; Mexican
Revolution; Mexican War; Mexico City;
Yucatan
Mexico City, xii, 11, 23, 34, 36, 83, 101, 114, 118,
164n.11. *See also* National Museum, Mexico
City
Michoacán, 36
Miller, Mary Ellen, xi, 113, 134, 170n.47, 177n.40,
179n.19
Mississippi Valley archaeology. *See*
Moundbuilder cultures
Mitla
in Castañeda's work, 24–25, 25, 26, 29
in Charnay's work, 106
in von Humboldt's work, 22
Moby Dick (Melville: 1851), 83
molds. *See* plaster casting of monuments
Monroe, James, 55
Monroe Doctrine, 3, 44, 55–56
Monte Alban, 27–28, 29
"Montezuma's Dinner," (Morgan: 1876), 157
Monuments anciens du Méxique (Waldeck:
1866), 36
Móo, Kingdom of (also, Mu)
and ancient Mesoamerica, 127, 130–139, 151,
179n.32
Children of Mu, The (Churchward: 1931), 151
Cosmic Forces of Mu, The (Churchward:
1936), 151
derivation of name, 179n.34
legacy of Móo scholarship, 151–152
Lost Continent of Mu, The (Churchward:
1926), 151
monarchs of, 5, 136
See also Móo, Queen; Coh, Prince
Móo, Queen
in Alice Le Plongeon's work, 126, 136, 145
in Augustus Le Plongeon's work, 136, 139, 141,
142, 145, 150, 151
Queen Móo and the Egyptian Sphinx
(Augustus Le Plongeon: 1896), 139
Queen Móo's talisman, 136, 138, 146
*Queen Móo's Talisman: The Fall of the Maya
Empire* (Alice Le Plongeon: 1902), 126, 136,
145

See also Le Plongeon, Alice, identity as
Queen Móo
Morazán, Francisco, 62
Morgan, Lewis Henry, 157–158
Mormons, Mormon Church. *See* Book of
Mormon; Latter-day Saints, Church of
Jesus Christ of; Smith, Joseph
Moundbuilder cultures, North America, 29,
35–36, 44, 46, 48, 57, 88, 91, 95–96, 104, 125,
161
Mu. *See* Móo, Kingdom of
Muñoz, Juan Bautista, 16–18
Museo Yucateco, Mérida, 131
Museum of Natural History, New York City, 151
museums
in Europe, 56, 105, 115, 148, 151. *See also*
panoramas
in Mexico, 36, 119–120, 120, 131, 135, 167n.55
in United States, 4, 54, 56, 71–73, 76, 105, 115,
124, 148–151, 155, 158, 160, 163n.7, 181n.11
See also Centennial Exposition, Philadelphia;
Panama-California Exposition, San Diego;
panoramas; World's Columbian
Exposition, Chicago

Nahua-speaking peoples, 14, 112, 163n.5
Napoleon, 23, 32, 37, 42, 47, 141. *See also* Egypt,
Napoleon's expedition to
Napoleon III, 111
nationalism and Mesoamerican archaeology
in Charnay's work, 114
in colonial Mexico, 32, 47–48
English, 10, 52, 56, 136
French, 56, 103, 105, 114–115
in Le Plongeon's work, 134–135, 141, 144–145,
148, 150
in Mormon belief, 89, 144–145
in Stephens' work, 43, 44, 54, 55, 56–57, 58, 60,
72–73, 76, 107, 124, 125, 153, 175n.14
U.S. claims to Mesoamerican past, 1–3, 5–6,
8–9, 43, 44–45, 47–48, 55, 58–59, 69, 76, 89,
96, 127, 135, 153, 162
at World's Columbian Exposition, Chicago
(1893), 153, 155–160
See also world's fairs/expositions
National Museum, Mexico City, 36, 119–120, 120,
135, 167n.55
native North American tribes (contemporary),

4, 35, 67, 71–73, 97, 100–101, 153, 157–158, 161; 174nn.25,34,47
Near Eastern archaeology. *See* archaeology, Near Eastern
Nephites. *See* Book of Mormon
New Spain. *See* Mexico
New York (city), 4, 53, 54, 55, 71, 72, 87, 131, 143, 148–151
New York (state), 44, 49, 88, 90–91, 92, 93, 96, 98, 115, 128, 144, 173n.23
New York Times, 1–2, 9
Nicaragua, 48–49

obelisks. *See* Egypt, obelisks
Ohio Valley archaeology. *See* Moundbuilder cultures
Ordóñez, Ramón, 16, 34
Osiris. *See* Egypt, deities of
Ossian (ersatz Gaelic literary hero), 145
"Ozymandias," 78

Palenque
    in Charnay's work, 106, 120–121, 122
    and Chiapas rebellion, 129
    Cross Group temples, 16, *17*, 17, 18, 20, 29, 32, *33*, 121, *123*
    Palace complex, *18–19*, 20, *21*, 26, *27*
    rediscovery in colonial era, 16–22, 32, 34, 166n.31, 168n.3
    in Stephens' work, 48, 54, 55, 57, 59, 63, 68, 169n.31
    Temple of the Inscriptions, *17*, 17–18, 32, 60, *60*, *61*, 64, *64*, 170n.49
    village of Palenque, 57, 60, 123
    in Waldeck's work, 37–39, *39*
Panama-California Exposition, San Diego (1915), 5, 153, 160–162, 182nn.15,18
Panama-Pacific Exposition, San Francisco (1915), 182n.15
panoramas, 52, 53, 72–73, 169nn.15,16, 171–172n.99
Peabody Museum, Harvard, 155, 163n.7
Penn, William, 92
Penney, J.C., 144
Peru, 128
Phidias, 14, 116
Philadelphia. *See* Centennial Exposition, Philadelphia

Phoenician contact in Mesoamerica, presumed, 20
photography
    in Charnay's work, 103–107, 110, 114, 121–123, 125, 127, 139, 140
    daguerreotypes, 53, 105
    developments in, 105–106, 140
    in Le Plongeon's work, 4–5, 127, 128, 139–141, 179–180n.43
    in Maudslay's work, 156
    in Stephens' work, 53, 105
    stereoptic images, 140, 179–180n.43
    use in field archaeology, 4, 106, 140
    at World's Columbian Exposition, Chicago, 155–156, *157*, 181n.3
    See also camera lucida
Piedras Negras, 135
Piranesi, Giovanni Battista, 64–66, *65*, 170n.50
plaster casting of monuments
    in Charnay's work, 103–105, 114, 119, 122–125, 143, 151, 156, 175n.11, 177n.62
    in Le Plongeon's work, 105, 127, 139–140, 148, 150–151
    in Stephens and Catherwood's work, 56, 57, 169n.30
    at the World's Columbian Exposition, 5, *154*, 155–158, 161
Polk, James, 83
Pompeii, 47
Popocatépetl, Mount, 101
Popol Vuh, 113
Pratt, Parley, 100
Prescott, William, 75–76, 85
Priam, King, 145
Prince Coh. *See* Coh, Prince; Le Plongeon, as Prince Coh
psychic archaeology. *See* archaeology, psychic
Putnam, Frederick, 148, 151, 155–157, 160, 181n.11
Puuc region (Post-Classic Maya), 39, 94, 129, 156

Quatre Lettres sur le Mexique (Brasseur de Bourbourg: 1868), 113, 127
Queen Móo. *See* Móo, Queen
Queen Móo and the Egyptian Sphinx (Augustus Le Plongeon: 1896), 139
Queen Móo's Talisman (Alice Le Plongeon: 1902), 126, 136, 145
Queen Victoria. *See* Victoria, Queen

Quetzaltenango, 49
Quirigua, 7, 48, 54, 56, 99

race
    in the Book of Mormon, 97, 174n.25
    in Charnay's work, 103, 105, 118, 121
    in Dupaix's work, 166n.31
    Essai sur l'inegalité des races humaines
        (Gobineau: 1855), 111
    in King's work, 35, 166-167n.51
    nineteenth-century theories of racial
        hierarchy, 29, 111
    in Stephens' work, 58, 66-67
    in Viollet-le-Duc's work, 111-112, 117, 118, 121
    in Waldeck's work, 42
    at world's fairs, 104, 153, 157, 161
Reforma period, 101, 105
reincarnation, 5, 130, 131, 133, 134, 136, 152
Rice, Allen Thorndike, 114-115, 126-127
Rosetta stone, 91, 172n.4
Royal Academy, London, 49, 50, 64, 170n.50
Russell, Charles, 55

Sacred Mysteries. *See* Freemasonry
*Sacred Mysteries among the Maya and the
    Quichés 11,500 Years Ago* (Augustus Le
    Plongeon: 1886), 139, 148, 149
Sahagún, Bernardino de, 35, 164n.2
Salisbury, Stephen, 129, 134, 179n.24
San Pablo del Monte, 27, *28*
Santa Cruz Maya, 124, 129-130
Sayil, 71
Scandinavians and ancient America, 111, 113, 114,
    176n.32
Schliemann, Heinrich, 145-148, *146, 147*
Schliemann, Sophie, *146, 146, 147*
Scott, Winfield, 83, 85
Second Great Awakening, 93
Shelley, Percy, 78
Smith, G. Elliot, 40
Smith, Joseph
    assassination of, 102
    authorship of Book of Mormon, 88-92, 144
    foundation of Mormon Church, 88-89
    and Mesoamerican ruins, 4, 144-145
    nationalist goals of, 89, 144-145
    See also Book of Mormon; Latter-day Saints,
        Church of Jesus Christ of

Smithsonian Institution, 115, 119, 151, 158,
    171-172n.99
Soane, Sir John, 49, 170n.50
Song of Roland, 145
Spain
    Bourbon monarchy of, 16-17
    conquest of Mexico, 12-13, 43, 67, 68-69, 75,
        76, 98
    expulsion from Latin America, 2, 7, 10-11, 32,
        47
    and Florida, 55
    and pre-Columbian past, 11-12, 14, 16-17,
        22-23, 43, 59
Spinden, Herbert, 181-182n.13
Squier, Ephraim, 96, 128, 173n.23
Stacy-Judd, Robert, 162
Stephens, John Lloyd
    amateur status of, 8
    and *American Antiquities*, 76
    archaeological narratives of, 1-2, 6, 44-45,
        48-75, 76, 128, 139
    collaboration with Catherwood, 44-45,
        49-53, 56-60, 70, 75, 76, 87
    and dating of ruins, 67-68, 69, 76, 87, 115
    death of, 103, 105
    diplomatic career of, 2-3, 49, 54-55, 62, 105,
        124
    early career of, 2-3, 44, 49, 62, 70
    and glyphs, 63-64, 68, 127
    identification with Columbus, 69
    *Incidents of Travel in Central America,
        Chiapas and Yucatan* (1841), 3, 44-45, 58,
        69, 70, 75-76, 99, 125
    *Incidents of Travel in Egypt, Arabia Petraea,
        and the Holy Land* (1837), 49
    *Incidents of Travel in Greece, Turkey, Russia
        and Poland* (1838), 49
    Incidents of Travel in Yucatan (1843), 3, 44-45,
        67, 69, 76
    and indigenous authorship of ruins, 22, 43,
        62-64, 66-68, 76, 78, 87, 127
    itineraries in Latin America, 48, 70-71
    knowledge of colonial sources, 45-46, 168n.11
    and "lost city," 68, 85, 124, 178n.71 (*see also*
        Iximaya)
    museum plans of, 4, 54, 71-73, 76, 105, 148
    nationalist objectives of, 43, 44, 54, 55, 56-57,
        58, 60, 72-73, 76, 107, 124, 125, 153, 175n.14

and photography, 53, 105
and plaster casting, 56, 57, 169n.30
and "salvation archaeology," 59, 71–73
work at Copan, 48, 53–54, 56, 57, 63, 69, 72, 124
work at Kabah, 62, 64–66, 65, 71–75, 74, 80–83, 84, 171–172n.99
work at Palenque, 54, 55, 56, 57, 68, 169n.31
work at Quirigua, 48, 54, 56
work at Uxmal, 54, 55, 68, 71, 73, 80, 82, 164–165n.12
writing style of, 43, 45, 49, 53–54, 70, 104
Stewart, Susan, 73
Stiles, Ezra, 92
St. Thomas (the apostle). See Thomas, Saint

Tajín, 23, 165n.27
Talud-tablero system, 116
Taylor, John, 99
Tejado, President, 134–135
Telleriano-Remensis Codex, 35
Temora (Macpherson: 1763), 145
Temple of Solomon, 97
Temple of Zeus at Olympia, 116
Tenenepanco, 119
Tenochtitlan. See Aztec civilization, Tenochtitlan
Teotihuacan, 94, 118–119, 118, 120–121
Tepeyacan, 27, 28
Teresa de Mier, Servando, 95
Texas, 44, 48, 57, 83, 168n.9
Theosophy, 131, 139
Thomas, Saint (the apostle), 95, 173n.18
Thompson, Charles Blancher, 99
Thompson, Edward, 131, 154, 155–157, 163n.7
Tikal, 68
Tlaxcala, 29
Toltec civilization
    and the ancient Maya, 112, 116, 160
    and the Aztecs, 8, 112–113
    in Charnay's work, 4, 104, 111, 113–121, 125, 176n.33
    collapse of, 112–113, 119
    construction techniques of, 116
    invasion of Yucatan, 112, 121, 132
    and Scandinavia, 114, 118, 176n.32
    in Viollet-le-Duc's work, 112
    in von Humboldt's work, 22, 165n.26
    See also Tula

tourism, 49–50, 125, 162
Trocadéro Museum, 115, 119, 120, 151
Troy, 145–146
Tula
    and the Aztecs, 113
    capital of Toltecs, 112–113, 116, 118
    in Casteñada's work, 24
    in Charnay's work, 114, 116, 119–121
    collapse of, 119
    quality of construction at, 116, 177n.40
    See also Toltec civilization
Tulum, 67, 129
tumuli, Etruscan, 29
Turkey, 145
Turner, J. M. W., 49
Tyler, John, 83

United States
    and the Book of Mormon, 98–99
    Civil War, U.S., 110, 127
    claims to Mesoamerican past, 1–3, 5–6, 8–9, 43, 44–45, 47–48, 55, 58–59, 69, 76, 89, 96, 127, 135, 153, 155–160, 162
    domestic archaeology of. See Moundbuilder cultures
    domestic and foreign policy of, 3, 44, 49, 55, 83, 100–101, 127, 160–161, 172n.100
    economy of, 127, 144, 153
    and native North Americans, 67, 97, 101
    perceived archaeological inferiority of, 46–48, 87, 115, 126, 134, 148, 162
U.S.-Mexican War. See Mexican War
Usumacinta River, 124
Utah Wars, 100, 102
Uxmal
    in Charnay's work, 106, 107, 109, 121, 122
    colonial accounts of, 14
    House of the Governor (also, Governor's Palace, Palace of the Governor), 80, 81, 140, 142, 147, 154, 156, 162
    in Le Plongeon's work, 136, 140–141, 142, 143, 147, 150
    Nunnery complex, 94, 107, 109, 140, 154
    at Panama-Pacific Exposition, San Diego, 162
    Pyramid of the Magician (also, Pyramid of the Dwarf), 37, 38, 40–42, 41, 80, 82, 107, 140, 167n.67
    in Stephens' work, 48, 49, 63, 68, 71, 73, 80

in Waldeck's work, 37–38, *38*, 40–42, *41*, 143
at World's Columbian Exposition, Chicago,
154, 155, 156

Valladolid, 124
Vanderbilt, William H., 144, 148
Vanderbilt, William K., 144
Van Hagan, Victor, 48
Veracruz, 23, 106
Vestiges of the Mayas (Augustus Le Plongeon:
1881), 137
Victoria, Queen, 136
Vien, Joseph, 37
Views of Ancient Monuments (Catherwood:
1844), 76–83, *77*, *78*, *81*, *82*, 84
*Views of the Cordilleras and Monuments of the
Indigenous Peoples of America* (von
Humboldt: 1810–1813), 22
Vikings and ancient America. *See*
Scandinavians and ancient America
Villa Lorillard. *See* Yaxchilán
Viollet-le-Duc, Eugène-Emmanuel, 109, 111–114,
117, 121
Virgin of Guadalupe, 95
Voltaire, 37
von Humboldt, Alexander, 22–23, 45, 48, 76, 85,
165n.25–27, 168n.11
*Voyage pittoresque et archéologique dans la
province d'Yucatan* (Waldeck: 1838), 36, 37,
40, 43, 46, 168n.11

Waldeck, Jean-Frederic
and ancient Egypt, 37–42
early career of, 34, 36, 37
and "elephant thesis," 38–40, 42, 167n.63,
170n.49
patronage of, 40–41
travel writing of, 2, 36–43, *38*, *39*, *40*, *41*, 45–46,
48, 62, 127, 128, 139, 166n.47, 167n.56,
168n.11, 170n.49
work at Uxmal, 37–38, *38*, 40–42, *41*, 143,
167n.67
Wanamaker, John, 144
Warden, David Bailie, 35–36
Wilford, John, 1
Williams, Frederick, 91
Williams, Roger, 92

World's Columbian Exposition, Chicago (1893),
159
archaeological exhibits at, 5, 104, 148, 153, *154*,
157, *159*, 161, 181nn.5,8, 182n.18
Midway Plaisance, 157–158, 181n.8
and nationalism, 153, 155–160
Palace of Fine Arts, 158, 160, 181n.9
and photography, 155–156, *157*, 181n.3
and race, 104, 153, 155, 157, 161
White City, 155, 156–158, 160, 181n.8
world's fairs/expositions, 5–6, 104, 134, 148, 153,
155–158, 160–162, 181nn.3,5,8,9,11,
182nn.15,18
Wright, Frank Lloyd, 161–162, 181n.3, 182n.18

Xochicalco, 22

Yale University, xi, 92
Yaxchilán, 115, 124, 129, 178nn.71,72
Yucatan
and Caste War, 124–125, 128–129
in Charnay's work, 116, 121, 122
colonial accounts, *14*
Here and There in Yucatan (Alice Le
Plongeon: 1886), 131
legal protection of ruins, 60, 134–135
in Le Plongeon's work, 128–129, 136, 139, 143,
145
in Maudslay's work, 156
in Mormon belief, 89, 97, 99, 174n.42
Museo Yucateco, 131
practice of evil eye in, 131
relations with Mexico, 7, 48, 135, 168n.9
in Stephens' work, 48, 53, 67, 69, 71, 72
Toltec invasion of, 112, 121, 132
in Viollet-le-Duc's work, 112
in Waldeck's work, 36, 37, 40, 42
at World's Columbian Exposition, Chicago,
154, 155–156
See also *Incidents of Travel in Central
America, Chiapas and Yucatan* (Stephens:
1841); *Incidents of Travel in Yucatan*
(Stephens: 1843); and individual sites
within Yucatan

CPSIA information can be obtained
at www.ICGtesting.com
Printed in the USA
FFOW01n1413240714
6461FF